AGILE ENGAGEMENT

How to Drive Lasting Results
by Cultivating a
Flexible, Responsive, and
Collaborative Culture

SANTIAGO JARAMILLO
TODD RICHARDSON

WILEY

Published by John Wiley & Sons, Inc., Hoboken, New Jersey
Published simultaneously in Canada

Library of Congress Cataloging-in-Publication Data is available:

ISBN 9781119286912 (Hardcover)
ISBN 9781119286929 (ePDF)
ISBN 9781119286936 (ePub)

Cover Design: Wiley

Printed in the United States of America
10 9 8 7 6 5 4 3 2 1

To our loving parents, who prepared us to face life's challenges with humility, energy, and appreciation for all the blessings bestowed upon us.

To all employees who desire true engagement in their work lives. May this book help enlighten organizations around the world and make our dream of full engagement for all workers a reality.

To all bosses, coworkers, and partners who demonstrate the power of engagement and the amazing results that are possible when hearts, minds, and hands align at work.

Thank you.

Contents

Chapter 22

Unique Organizational Characteristics

Engagement Canvas Box 5

Chapter 23

Communication Channels

Engagement Canvas Box 6

Chapter 24

Culture Statements

Engagement Canvas Box 7

Chapter 25

Culture Aspirations

Engagement Canvas Box 7

Chapter 26

Resources Applied

Engagement Canvas Box 8

Chapter 27

Emplify Score

Engagement Canvas Box 9

Chapter 28

Three Key Employee Needs

Engagement Canvas Box 10

Chapter 29

Engagement Canvas FAQs

Chapter 37

Chapter 38

Chapter 39

Preface

Behind every worker—including you—is a unique combination of motivations. It gets you up in the morning when you would rather stay in bed. It keeps you coming back to work when you would rather quit. It makes you want to do better than you did yesterday, to *be* better.

For some people, they work in order to provide for their families, to send their kids to colleges, to care for aging parents, or to put food on the table while their spouses pursue educational ambitions. For others, they appreciate the mental or physical challenge, the opportunity to travel, or are personally passionate about the subject matter. Or, perhaps, they genuinely enjoy their colleagues and their managers, and that's enough to keep them coming back day after day.

Though the *why* behind each worker differs, the desire for professional engagement is universal.

Given the individuality of motivation, however, how are companies supposed to engage their workforces at large? How can they build and develop cultures that advance both organizational goals and the individual goals of every worker? It's not easy, but it is possible. And this book shows you how.

The topic of employee engagement and workplace cultures is not new. In fact, in recent years, it seems like every corporate blogger, speaker, and consultant touts the importance of culture and employee engagement. Theoretical discussions abound, but few people have put forth concrete strategies that help get you from point A (unengaged) to point B (fully engaged). The workplace is evolving so rapidly, in fact, that employees are feeling less and less engaged with their work. Collectively, we are in the midst of an engagement crisis. The only way out is to focus on people over processes, real engagement over cookie-cutter programs, consistent intentionality over passive manipulation, and healthy change over rigid planning. For those already familiar with technology management philosophies, what we are suggesting is the application of agile principles to the world of employee engagement.

People, and consequently employees, are extremely complex. There is not a single set of engagement rules that can be outlined during your company launch party that are guaranteed to still work at by the time you reach your 10-year anniversary. People change. Companies change. Your approach must change alongside them. And you must involve employees in the process.

Enter *Agile Engagement*, which provides practical advice and counsel to demystify engagement and culture. We wrote this book to dramatically impact the way the world works and the way we all work within it. We wrote this book as a way to apply the proven principles of agile software development to the world of employee engagement. Most of all, we wrote this book to help heighten the level of engagement for *all* workers—not only managers, not only white-collar, and not only high-tech workers. *All* workers.

For engagement is, at its core, the great equalizer.

True engagement can be attained (and sustained) by *anyone, anywhere,* doing *anything.* However, engagement doesn't just happen. It requires intentionality, strategic workplace culture building, an employee engagement plan that is unique to your organization and your workers, and a commitment to continuous measure and improvement.

In the following pages, we will help you understand the importance of engagement and workplace culture. Moreover, we will give you a proven framework within which to create, build, and execute your engagement strategy over the long haul. We call this framework the Engagement Canvas and it leverages the powerful Emplify Score tool.

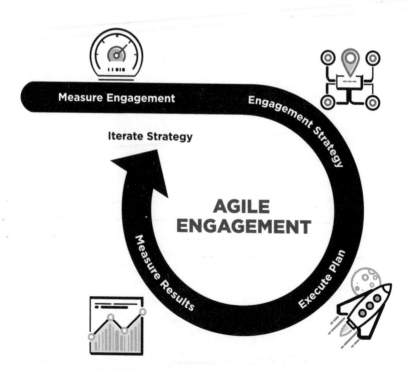

Agile Engagement Framework

The framework we utilize infuses agile principles throughout the employee engagement process. Consistent and frequent measurement of employee engagement reveals real insights that then guide engagement strategies and action plans. This process repeats itself, because the opportunity to drive engagement should be an unending pursuit.

The Engagement Canvas is our answer to a troubling trend we noticed in the course of our work. We talked with many executives and HR leaders who told us that culture was a key aspect of their companies' future successes. They painstakingly explained how seriously they took employee engagement. Then, when we asked those same business leaders to describe their cultures (current and desired) . . . crickets. More troubling, when we asked how they were cultivating their workplace culture and driving employee engagement, we received blank stares.

Mind you, these business leaders are highly successful businessmen and businesswomen in their respective fields. They have mastered complex supply chain issues, cross-market campaign difficulties, technical security challenges, and more. But when it came to culture and engagement, they were comparatively dumbfounded. Try as they might, they did not understand how to construct an engagement strategy or measure success.

Engagement is too important for such widespread confusion. We are on a mission to provide the clarity organizations so desperately need. Alongside us on this journey are our guest contributors, both operational and strategic leaders, who provide their insights, commitment to, and appreciation for workplace culture and employee engagement. Spanning a variety of industries, company sizes, and geographies, these culture gurus prove that powerful engagement is not only achievable but well worth the effort.

We also provide our own insights gained from professional careers spent launching, forming, and perpetuating powerful company cultures. We originally met at ExactTarget, a fast-paced Midwest-based, technology company. ExactTarget epitomized a thriving culture with highly engaged employees. The culture was branded "Orange" after the company's primary brand color (Pantone 144). We experienced firsthand the importance of making culture a priority and saw the business impact of truly engaged employees. An exceptional culture was the driving force behind the company's successful initial public offering, listing on the New York Stock Exchange, and ultimate $2.5 billion sale to tech juggernaut Salesforce.com.

ExactTarget veteran and now Yext chief marketing officer Jeff Rohrs explained the experience this way:

> I was involved in the initial conception of "Be Orange" at Exact-Target, an effort to give our culture, passion, commitment, talent, and energy a name. Having that effort tie into our core brand

color—and having that color represent the best of who we wanted to be—helped everyone understand what culture meant within our organization.

Another key was not having Marketing or HR solely own culture. It was owned by our people, and they added so many great ideas and activities to the expression of our culture that every engaged employee felt a sense of ownership. Having the shorthand of what "Being Orange" meant even helped accelerate our hiring efforts by making it easier to evaluate people for key skills that were needed to work in an organization where change was a constant. (Rohrs, 2016).

Former ExactTarget vice president of global total rewards, talent, and HR operations and current Appirio senior vice president, human resources, Ellen Humphrey remembers the Orange culture with similar fondness:

We had an engaging and exciting culture at ExactTarget because (a) we were transparent about the business and its goals; (b) we empowered everyone to live out our culture; (c) our employees believed that our senior leaders lived out the culture; and (d) we were winning in our space. I think winning makes a big difference. Our employees were proud to be part of a company that was growing, landing the big customers, and opening new offices. The collective momentum attracted high-caliber talent, which led to more winning, which continued to engage employees, which kept the culture amped, which attracted more talent. Rinse and repeat. (Humphrey, 2016)

What we experienced at ExactTarget was so special that we wanted to help more organizations experience the power of culture and engagement to drive business results. So we joined forces and created a mobile-first employee engagement app software-as-a-service platform called Emplify. We help companies develop and implement engagement strategies through the use of native, branded, mobile apps. With our employee engagement platform, employers can finally foster a deeper level of employee engagement and measure their success in real time.

As you continue reading, remember that culture and employee engagement are components of—not replacements for—good ol' business results. Terri Kelly, president and chief executive officer of W. L. Gore & Associates, explains that "If you're not careful, the culture can become the outcome and become disconnected from achieving the desired business result. The culture needs to be the 'how' you achieve results, and you must continue to monitor and evolve your practices and values to ensure there is strong alignment to achieving the business outcomes" (Kelly, 2016).

Cheers to the start (or continuation) of your workplace culture and employee engagement journey. We are here to serve as your guides, and we look forward to helping you unlock the potential that comes from having truly engaged employees and a winning culture.

Part

The Engagement Engine

Engagement and Culture Redefined

(Or, Why Culture Belongs in the Boardroom)

Culture is the engine behind engagement. It is the power and the driving force, plain and simple. Employee engagement and culture get plenty of lip service in the business world, and plenty of books have been written on the subjects. We are not here to add hot air to the existing conversation. We are here to change the conversation completely.

This book is for those who are already convinced of and believe in the power of workplace culture. This book is for those who want to take action and transform culture and engagement in their organizations. This book is for those who believe culture should not be relegated to a back office, but rather invited with open arms (and a fistful of confetti) into the boardroom.

Supporting evidence abounds. It's widely accepted that positive cultures lead to more engaged employees, and more engaged employees sustain positive cultures. But it has also been proven that positive cultures and high levels of employee engagement drive tangible bottom-line benefits. An engaged workforce helps boost profits, increase employee loyalty and tenure, and heighten customer satisfaction.

Yet despite all the culture talk and widespread alarm around the engagement crisis in business, engagement levels remain stubbornly low. Why? Because most leaders are at an utter loss of how to affect real change in their organizations.

Before we dive too deep in the culture and engagement trenches, however, we should briefly define culture and engagement. Many books, articles, blogs, vlogs, podcasts, and academic pieces have been written about these topics, each with differing definitions. How many smart people does it take to define a pervasively common topic? A dizzying amount, apparently, for there is no public consensus.

For the purposes of this book, we studied hundreds of definitions and arrived at the following.

Defining Employee Engagement

We define employee engagement as an employee's emotional and intellectual connection with an employer, as demonstrated by his or her motivation and commitment to positively impact the company's vision and goals.

Not surprisingly, countless elements can impact positive or negative employee engagement, but we consider the most potent to be the following:

- *Strategic Alignment.* Employees can both verbalize and actualize the core business strategies.

- *Understanding of Success.* Employees understand their organizational, departmental, and personal success metrics and tangibly grasp their contribution to the company's overall success.

- *Clear Communication.* Employees trust the company because of coherent and frequent contact, timely feedback, and clear expectations.

- *Workplace Vibe.* The overall environment fosters effective work in everything from the physical workspace to interactions between employees.

- *Growth Paths.* Employees have the opportunity to grow their skills through new work challenges and positions over time, in both managerial and independent contributor roles.

Employers directly influence employee engagement, but workers remain independent, unique humans. What drives engagement for one person may be different from what engages the person sitting next to him or her. Furthermore, what drives an employee's engagement today may not be the same thing that drove his or her engagement two years ago (or two months ago). One of the unending challenges as an employee or as a leader is the need to remain agile, constantly reevaluating what engages you, your team members, and your constituents.

Defining Workplace Culture

We define workplace culture as the customs, social expectations, and attitudes formed around work and personal interactions in the work environment.

The nature of our business exposes us to a wide variety of companies with all shapes, sizes, and cultural maturities. One of the first questions we always ask when we sit down with a new company is, "How would you describe your culture?" We quickly follow with a second question: "How would your employees describe your culture?" Child's play, right? Wrong. We are flabbergasted by how frequently and dramatically those two answers differ.

What's going on? Why would leadership ever tolerate such stark contrasts in how employees work alongside each other at the same company, in the same office, toward the same goals? More times than not, it boils down to a classic lack of intentionality. It is the responsibility of leadership to clearly acknowledge the workplace culture, facilitate discussions on its positive and negative aspects, and strategize and improve it over time.

Engagement in Action

Employee engagement looks different to everyone. Here are some examples from business leaders who understand the importance of culture and engagement to business success.

What do engaged employees look like?
Here is what prominent business leaders had to say.

- "Energized, aggressive, and creative. Culture means having a passion for our customers, colleagues, and company (3 Cs)."—Brad Morehead, CEO, LiveWatch Security
- "People who, when they get in the cars in the morning to go to work, look forward to getting there four out of five days. When they leave their jobs, they also feel like they have accomplished

something four out of five days."—Hank Orme, Former President, Lincoln Industries

- "People who want to come do work they love with people they enjoy. Engaged employees like working with other employees who challenge them to grow, learn, and build excellence as a team." —Nicole Bickett, Chief Administrative Officer, Mainstreet

- "One who routinely gives discretionary effort."—Chuck Hyde, Soderquist Leadership

- "An engaged employee participates in and contributes to the culture of the company."—Rob Edwards, Director of Engineering & Race Operations, Andretti Motorsports

- "An individual who clearly shows through his or her emotions and communications that he or she enjoys coming to work every day and feels empowered to make important decisions that impact the company."—Wil Boren, Former Vice President and General Manager, Zimmer Biomet

- "An engaged employee is, first and foremost, aligned to the vision and mission of the company and aware of and energized by how his or her role fits into it. These qualities drive employees to achieve outstanding results for the organization, as well as his or her career aspirations."—Blair West, Director of Corporate Communications at Cummins, Inc.

- "Someone who takes pride in her work, cares about what she's doing, engages in customer communication, and is present in her conversations and work."—Laura Angotti, Owner of Rowdy Sprout

- "An engaged employee is intrinsically motivated to go above and beyond on behalf of her employer. She is enthusiastic about the work she does and is an evangelist for her employer. She gets satisfaction from her work and takes pride in her contribution to the greater organization."—Ellen Humphrey, Senior Vice President, Human Resources, Appirio

- "Someone who shows up with a great attitude ready to do whatever it takes to get the job done."—Clay Robinson, Co-Founder and Owner, Sun King Brewing

- "An individual who goes beyond his job description to help others, seek out additional opportunities for growth, and contribute to the culture both through active participation and interest in fellow coworkers."—Jeff Rohrs, Chief Marketing Officer, Yext

- "Someone who is excited to come to work every day, believes deeply in our vision and mission, acts like a team player, has incredibly high expectations for himself and his colleagues, prioritizes what is best for our collective movement above individual goals or motivations, and operates with integrity at all times."—Rebecca Thompson Boyle, Former Executive Director, Teach for America

- "Interested and enthusiastic about work, has meaningful relationships with colleagues and participates in the life of the organization, and willing to go above and beyond."—Tom Froehle, Chair and Managing Partner, Faegre Baker Daniels, LLP

- "Engaged employees accept empowerment and drive innovation independently and as a fluid organization."—Scott Kraege, Co-Founder and CEO, MOBI

- "Engaged employees are passionate about their work and feel they are making a meaningful impact on the organization. They have a strong sense of personal ownership and responsibility for the success of the organization. They feel connected to the mission and vision, and they go beyond their core commitments to help others and support the broader goals of the company."—Terri Kelly, President and CEO, W. L. Gore & Associates

Chapter

Happiness Versus Engagement
(Or, Why Free Snacks Fall Short)

Meaningful engagement cannot simply be bought. No amount of holiday bonuses, Starbucks gift cards, or frequent flyer miles will guarantee employees' loyalty and engagement. Frankly, workers are too smart for that. They know better than to base their loyalty on fleeting rewards or accolades. They require a deeper connection to their company, leaders, and coworkers. They want to understand their place in the bigger picture and know that what they do matters and is appreciated.

Most people spend around a whopping one third of their adult lives working. The idea of spending that much time working in a negative workplace culture is insufferable. But the remedy for unhappiness at work is not happiness. It is engagement.

Netflix, Patagonia, and Zappos attract a lot of public attention because of their free massages, surf breaks, and unlimited vacation policies. Those practices are easy to pinpoint, weird enough to make good news stories, and fun to talk about around the watercooler. At first glance, it may appear that these fun fringe benefits make their employees happy. But the truth is, happy employees are not the same as engaged employees, and those perks are not the driving force behind these companies' culture successes. They are only the tip of the iceberg—the proverbial icing on top of powerful, optimized organizational cultures.

When Gallup released their alarming <u>State of the Global Workplace study revealing that only one-third of U.S. employees are "engaged" at work,</u> many organizations scrambled to remedy this unengagement plight, looking for quick fixes and easy ways to increase happiness in the workplace (Crabtree, 2013). Gallup followed up to the frenzy, saying that "Indulging employees is no substitute for engaging them" (Sorenson, 2013). Or as Jim Clifton, CEO of Gallup, succinctly put it, "The idea of trying to make people happy at work is terrible" (Crowley, 2014).

Let's face it: <u>Free lunches and snacks have little direct impact on long-term human performance</u> (Sorenson, 2013). I can be happy at work without acting in the best interest of the organization. Scanning Facebook and catching up with an old friend on work time make me happy, as does saving money by refilling my personal stock of home office goods from the supply cabinet. Happy, but not engaged. We do not need more cool perks, we need more meaningful investment in growing our people. Focusing on short-term pleasures over long-term engagement is not sustainable and may even disillusion people over time.

Any office can buy a quick-fix pinball machine and sit perplexed as nothing changes. Those perks are well intentioned but are not change agents. We can admire the companies who work this way, but we admire them for how thoroughly and intentionally they foster a positive workplace culture, not for a day-to-day focus on fun. These hailed companies don't just brighten employees' Fridays, they engage them constantly. Moral of the story? Focus on strong culture, not free candy.

<u>Ultimately, engagement is about knowing the organization's purpose and our purpose within it, having the tools to perform at our best, and having passion to contribute to our full potential.</u> It is about maximizing strengths, making meaningful contributions, and feeling valued. Even the best office perks will not change a boss who is a jerk, a job with no potential for growth, or mind-numbingly boring work. <u>Highly engaged employees can even seem like a handful at times.</u> They <u>care too much</u>, they <u>have wild ideas</u>, they <u>push the envelope</u>, and they <u>get frustrated</u> when things fall through. At Netflix, they recognize it as the "person who picks up trash lying on the floor" (Hastings, 2009). At Basecamp, they call it "giving a damn" and list it as one of their core values (We the Basecamp). It can't all be sugarplums. <u>A little dissatisfaction is natural and can fuel drive, productivity, and improvements.</u>

Martin Seligman, former president of the American Psychological Association and founder of the field of positive psychology, breaks down happiness into these three elements (Seligman, 2008):

- *The Pleasant Life:* The rosy glow of ebullience and good cheer, with as much positive emotion as possible. Unfortunately, this is about 50 percent heritable, only 15 to 20 percent modifiable, and loses luster rapidly.
- *The Engaged Life:* The sense of flow, being drawn into and absorbed by the present moment, when time seems to stop. It arises from knowing your highest strengths and using them as much as possible.
- *The Meaningful Life:* The purpose, fulfillment, and belonging that come from using your highest strengths in the service of something beyond yourself.

Together, these three parts comprise happiness, but not in equal measure. Pleasure has almost no contribution to overall life satisfaction (Seligman, 2008). Long-term happiness stems foremost from meaning, closely followed by engagement. Once both of those are in line, pleasure serves as the cherry on top. Employees at a place like Google, where meaning and engagement already abound, can properly savor a massage day because their other happiness needs are met. What drives talent to the organization is not the perks but getting to do cool things that matter.

Luckily for employers, both meaning and engagement are surprisingly malleable through our habits, interactions with coworkers, and overall perspective (Achor, 2012). Each of these five simple, quick hacks, every day for 21 days, is enough to elicit statistically significant changes.

- Write down three things for which you are grateful.
- Write a positive message to someone in your social support network.
- Meditate at your desk for 2 minutes.
- Exercise for 10 minutes.
- Take 2 minutes to reflect on the most meaningful experience of the past 24 hours.

That's it. Simple reframing and small new habits are enough to significantly boost our levels of meaning and engagement. In fact, high levels of social support may be the greatest predictor of life satisfaction, particularly when we *provide* them, rather than receive (Achor, 2012). Employees who initiate social interactions, pick up slack, invite people to lunch, and organize office activities are 10 times more likely to be engaged at work than those who keep to themselves. That is the kind of culture we should be striving to develop.

Beyond increased levels of employee satisfaction, companies with high engagement perform better financially. Parnassus exemplifies this well. They invest based on both performance and principles, almost exclusively in firms proven to have outstanding workplaces, many of which are included in the 100 best companies to work for list (Parnassus). From 2005 to 2013, Parnassus had a 9.63 percent annual return, compared with the Standard & Poor's (S&P) annual return of 5.58 percent during that time (Crowley, 2013). From 2008 to 2013 (during the recent recession), their annual return was 10.81 percent, compared with the S&P of 3.97 percent (Crowley, 2013). The founder says, "The performance of the fund confirms what I've always believed: treating people well and authentically respecting them does lead to far better business performance. We proved it works" (Crowley, 2013).

Strong engagement is essential for ultimate success, and too often we see organizations trying to increase happiness in all the wrong ways. Employees appreciate perks, but those don't serve to engage workers or even boost happiness beyond temporary pleasure. What people truly want is an intrinsic connection to their work and their company. They want to *want* to keep coming back, to be inspired to move forward. And as Gallup CEO Clifton says, "There aren't enough foosball tables in the world to provoke that kind of commitment" (Crowley, 2014).

Chapter

Common Misconceptions

(Or, Why Culture Isn't Just HR's Problem)

N ow that we have dispelled the magical powers of foosball tables and gift cards, you may find yourself wondering what other preconceived notions about culture are untrue. Here are the most common misconceptions we hear during our culture conversations.

Misconception #1: Culture Is Just HR's Problem

We may lose it if we hear another executive say their culture sucks because their HR department is not getting it right. The bottom line is, culture affects the bottom line. It's everyone's responsibility, not just the folks sitting in HR. Culture is a top issue for all business leaders. Eighty-seven percent of organizations now cite it as a top challenge because the ones who are getting it right are getting ahead (Dupress, 2015).

- Employee engagement programs can increase profits by $2,400 per employee per year (Wang, 2015).

- Ninety-one percent of highly engaged employees always or almost always try their hardest at work (Wang, 2015).
- Half of workers would rather "go to the DMV" or "watch paint dry" than attend a status update meeting (Mateo, 2015).

If you are in HR or executive leadership, it is not your job to single-handedly create the culture. Align and strategize, but remember that it is about *we* not *me*. Just like it can't all happen at once, it can't come all from one place. Ask the question, "Who do we want to be when we grow up?" Ask employees to define driving forces, and take time to make them collectively yours.

Wil Boren, former vice president and general manager of Biomet Zimmer, explains, "Team members know when an organization is truly being genuine about the importance of culture. You cannot outsource assistance in this area. You must truly seek to engage your employees in shaping what will ultimately be your company's legacy, its enduring culture," (Boren, 2016). How do you impose culture? You don't impose it. Although you may tailor input discussions to various groups (leaders, influencers, or employees) differently, involve everyone. You're all part of this. Figure out what's working and what's not working, and move forward accordingly.

Misconception #2: Cultures Are Static

Culture is dynamic because human beings are dynamic. We as individuals are constantly evolving, and we are evolving in relation to one another also. Even just 10 years ago students turned in homework on paper instead of online and YouTube was just making its debut. Culture, as the aggregate of human behavior, is never static.

If left to themselves, cultures can quickly go down the tube. Tony Hsieh gives an excellent example with his pre-Zappos experience at LinkExchange (Hsieh, 2010, 47–48). They ran out of like-minded friends to hire, so they started hiring other people en masse, looking for competence, forgoing culture. Soon enough, going to work in the morning felt like "death by a thousand papercuts" because what had once been obvious and easy was lost. When it comes to creating and nurturing a culture, you are never done.

According to Clay Robinson, owner of award-winning Sun King Brewing Company, "I always knew that culture was important, and we needed to lead by example in order to plant the seed of a winning culture and allow it to grow. Over the years, we have worked to continually steer our culture in the right direction as it evolves. Our staff comes to work happy, knowing that they are respected, and our company has grown and blossomed because of it," (Robinson, 2016).

Nicole Bickett, chief administrative officer at Mainstreet, describes the need to remain vigilant when curating culture:

> Focus, commit, and invest in your people and their engagement. The only way you will create a strong culture is by desiring and creating it. If you do not, a culture will be created by default and it may not be the one you want. Engage anyone and everyone in its creation and cultivation, and make sure leadership is driving it every single day. Don't create it and then relegate it to others. Focus on it, talk about it, and continue to innovate on it. If you do this, you will be able to advance your culture and create the business success that comes with it. (Nicole Bickett, 2016)

Similar to civic culture, inhabitants of one company may decide that some behaviors they see in another culture appeal to them, so they incorporate those new behaviors and voilà, dynamic culture. The beauty is, if you're cognizant of it, you can decide what to accept and what to reject from other styles and alternatives. Everything is borrowed, synthesized from other ideas, and pieced together in creative ways. Retain the significant aspects of your own culture that you value, and actively tend to what you want to develop.

A culture is bound to emerge, so you might as well make sure it's a great one. Clay Robinson of Sun King Brewing agrees. "You have to continually and actively engage people," says Robinson. "Culture needs to be curated in order to continue to grow and evolve,"

Tom Froehle, Chair and Managing Partner for Faegre Baker Daniels law firm, understands how critical it is to intentionally nurture a positive culture. He played an important role in the combining of two nationally recognized legal giants, Baker & Daniels and Faegre & Benson.

> As it relates to the combination of Baker & Daniels and Faegre & Benson, culture was critically important. In identifying potential prospects for a combination, we researched firm culture by reviewing websites, searching publications, and talking with people who had firsthand experiences. Through that process, we discovered that like Baker & Daniels, Faegre & Benson shared our cultural values.

They had a rich history of community involvement and commitment to pro bono service, high expectations for quality, and strong reputations, not only as great lawyers, but as good people, as well. (Froehle, 2016)

At the outset, both firms recognized that any strategic opportunities could not be realized without a strong cultural fit. We started with the leadership teams and spent significant time getting to know each other and developing trust and confidence between the teams.

We also recognized that lawyers are naturally skeptical, and thus included them in the process at an early stage. We were intentional about sharing the possibility of a combination early on with all of our people and providing a significant due diligence period in which lawyers from the two firms could meet each other and decide for themselves whether there was a good cultural fit.

After approval of the merger, but before it took effect, we began investing heavily in making sure that lawyers could continue to find ways to interact and get to know each other. That included substantial travel but also a very substantial investment in video-conferencing capabilities so internal meetings could be held virtually face-to-face, rather than by telephone. We recognized that the best way to integrate was to encourage people to collaborate on client work. We measured the amount of "cross-firm" work and celebrated successes that included cross-office teams, and we continue to do so today.

Every step of the way, we focused on one of our guiding principles, "One Firm," which reflects both our desire to assemble the best teams regardless of location and our focus on firm success over individual or group success. We still have plenty of work to do, but we are off to a good start.

Misconception #3: One Size Fits All

We share 99.9 percent of our genetic makeup with all other humans, but that 0.1 percent manifests itself in many different expressions, values, and lifestyles ("National Human Genome Research Institute," 2016). <u>Do culture in the way that makes sense for you, so people are engaged with and living out the core values</u>. At Kayak, that looks like every employee picking up the phone to handle service calls, decision-making meetings requiring only three people, and hiring managers boasting that working for them is "the most fun job a person will ever have" (Daisyme, 2015). At Edward Jones, that looks like deep community roots, generous associate ownership opportunities, and firm-sponsored European trips for employees and their families (Mucciolo, 2009). Very different approaches, but both companies are financially successful and recognized as great places to work.

Remember, this is your culture we are talking about. It comes from a combination of your leadership team, the people of your organization, and the unique aspects that make your company what it is today and what it will be in the future. The outcomes of engagement, profit, and retention are defined, but the methods can be different. The very nature of many successful company cultures is that they're quirky. Steve Jobs, in his famous Stanford address, advised to "Stay hungry, stay foolish" (You've Got to Find What You Love, 2005). Even the best advice may be irrelevant to you and your people. You cannot do anyone else's version of this work. You have to find your own way for what is uniquely effective in your organization. Emulate others where it makes sense, but do not lose sight of the fact that "<u>one size fits one</u>" when <u>it comes to culture</u>.

Chapter 4

Cross-Industry Engagement

(Or, Why You Don't Have to Sell Software to Be Cool)

Though we now understand the tech industry's infamous perks, like free massages, hoodies, and fancy parties, are not silver bullets, it's still easy to think tech companies get all the culture fun and all the fame. But you don't have to sell software to attract, engage, and retain top talent. Your company may sell farm equipment, educate children, or make duck whistles. The culture gods do not care what you do; they will bless your culture intentionality and thoughtfulness all the same. Allow us to shine the spotlight on some other types of companies that are making huge cultural strides and seeing real results.

Case in Point: Teach for America—Education

Many of us are familiar with the work of Teach for America, an education innovator that enlists, develops, and mobilizes some of our nation's most promising leaders in the push to overcome education inequality. But we are perhaps less familiar with their impressive work internally as well.

Long story short, their HR team is doing some things right. Their benefits rival those of corporate behemoths, including perks like eight weeks of paid parental leave, childcare reimbursement during business travel, and 150 hours per year of training.

And get this: <u>94 percent of their employees report that they feel they carry a lot of responsibility in the organization</u>, and <u>80 percent say their leaders allow them autonomy to meet challenges without always peering over their shoulders</u> (Barnes, 2014). It is especially remarkable given the industry: ever-elusive and exhausting education reform.

In fact, Rebecca Thompson Boyle, former executive director of Teach for America, acknowledges, "Keeping culture exceptionally strong is challenging when your work is centered around issues of social justice. While staff passion and motivation are unarguable, the work is physically and emotionally exhausting and never fully done."

She explains, "Culture is at the core of everything we do. If we do not have a strong, aligned, and passionate team that holds each other accountable to high expectations and commitment to integrity, we will be unable to best serve our teachers, students, and communities."

Case in Point: Reynolds Farm Equipment—Agriculture

Owner and president Gary Reynolds inherited Reynolds Farm Equipment from his father, the original founder, and it epitomizes the sort of homegrown investment we esteem. In the community, they are widely recognized for their philanthropic contributions, alongside job growth and agricultural support.

In 2015, Reynolds received the Lifetime Achievement Award from his town (Annual Business Excellence Awards in Carmel, 2015). And as a company, they strive to maintain high benchmarks of progress, growth, and honesty, saying, "Anything less would be inconsistent with our mission to our customers and to each other." In a volatile, high-turnover industry, Reynolds stands out by cultivating a strong culture and reaps the resulting personnel stability, which, as Gary says, "has had a huge impact on the profitability of our company, even in tough economic environments" (Annual Business Excellence Awards, 2015).

Case in Point: Mainstreet—Real Estate / Health Care

CEO and founder Zeke Turner left a job as a Wall Street investment banker at the age of 25 to return home to his native Indiana (Mainstreet). He founded Mainstreet in 2002 with a bold mission and initial capital of just $10,000, and now he has propelled the company into becoming the nation's largest developer of transitional care properties.

Skill, savvy, innovation, luck—all sure secrets to their success. But unique among their competitors, they also boast a remarkably flexible, family-friendly culture. And they are not just saying it; bringing children to work is actually encouraged. Turner happens to have seven of his own. They offer unlimited paid time off to all employees, under the rationale that employees can manage their own lives and should be able to see their family members stress- and guilt-free.

Turner says, "Most companies get the employee relationship backward. They fear you'll leave at any moment, so they end up making you feel trapped. I try to create an environment where they can thrive and feel they belong, that they're not just a replaceable cog" (Smith, 2016). All of this culminated in Mainstreet being named Best Place to Work, among a host of other workplace accolades (Smith, 2016).

Case in Point: Everlane—Fashion

Taken from Everlane's career page, this call exemplifies Everlane's unique cultural style as a new apparel company: "Dear rule breakers, questioners, straight-A students who skipped class: We want you" (Factories). Everlane is a new apparel company that is rocking the fashion industry with an emphasis on radical transparency, top-tier strategy, and innovative processes. They sell quality pieces that on their own would be appreciated, but they also feature each of their factories on their website, where consumers can learn about the employees and production (Factories).

Over the 2015 holidays, they had a pay-what-you-choose sale, in which customers could choose a price point ranging from covering pure cost of production to supporting long-term growth (Kahn, 2015). They tout the merits of knowing your factories, knowing your costs, and always asking why, and they tap into the transparency, sustainability, and responsibility ethic deeply ingrained in younger generations. After studying computer engineering and economics, their CEO left a job in venture capital to found the company at age 25. They attract employees from Google, Goldman Sachs, J. Crew, American Apparel, Yelp, and the like. Everlane is a quintessential example of talented people taking proven models and disrupting an industry. From 2013 to 2014, their sales grew 200 percent (Ransom, 2014).

Dig Deeper

In the end, culture is not about having the coolest gadgets or the best free snacks, nor is it solely a HR problem. It is about engaging your employees and creating the optimal conditions for them to thrive. It may look different at each organization, but done right, engagement renders tremendous business results.

Part

The Workplace of Now

Workplaces without Borders

(Or, Why the War for Talent Has Gone Global)

There is a good reason why culture and engagement are part of our everyday vocabulary, but our grandparents' generation probably never spoke of them during their careers. They talked of things like loyalty, dependability, and opportunity, all of which are still part of the culture equation, but in varying degrees than in the past. The workplace of now differs greatly from the workplace of just 20 years ago. It was a different time and place. Society valued different things. People behaved in different ways.

For one thing, our increasingly globalized and freelance economy means that talent is now borderless. Consider the movement of people.

- In 1990, the world had 154 million international migrants (generally defined as people who reside in a country in which they were not born) (Engaging and Integration a Global Workforce, 2015, 13).
- In 2000, we had 173 million international migrants (244 Million International Migrants Living Abroad Worldwide, 2016).
- As of 2015, that number had grown to 244 million (244 Million International Migrants, 2016).

And about *half* of those international migrants reside in only *10* countries. The United States alone houses 20 percent of international migrants, followed by Russia, Germany, Saudi Arabia, the United Arab Emirates, and the United Kingdom.

Let's frame it another way. In 1990, all of us in the world put together took 400 million trips abroad annually, including all business, touring, studying, and everything else (Exploding Digital Flows in a Deeply Connected World, 2016). In 2016, we have nearly tripled that to more than 1.1 billion.

Or consider the growth of emerging economies. In 2015, Brazil, Russia, India, China, and South Africa (the BRICS countries) claimed 30 percent of global gross domestic product (BRICS, 2015). Toss in the other developing economies, and together they accounted for 42 percent of world merchandise trade and for 35 percent of trade in world commercial services (Engaging and Integration a Global Workforce, 2015, 8).

What's more, the World Economic Forum's latest 2016 survey on "The Future of Jobs" projects that by 2030, Asia alone will account for 66 percent of the global middle class and for 59 percent of middle-class consumption (World Economic Forum, 2016). We are seeing the world's economic center of gravity shift away from North America, away from Europe, and toward emerging economies that are emerging as hubs of talent, entrepreneurship, and consumption.

So what does this mean for us? It means the workplace of the future looks unmistakably different than the workplace we know today. We need to expand our thinking of where and when work gets done and who does it.

But before we get too far ahead of ourselves, take another trip back in the culture time machine. Picture this: you step into a fresh morning and determine what the day will hold. You commit yourself to useful and collaborative work. You achieve the mighty and intoxicating realm of flow. This is a professional dream, right? Welcome to the surprisingly alluring workplace world of 12,000 years ago, when people mostly foraged wild food for sustenance. According to renowned psychologist Mihaly Csikszentmihalyi (who coined the notion of "flow"), our hunter-gatherer ancestors may not have had it too bad, professionally speaking (Kawamura, 2014). People used their skills to collaborate with others in service of clear goals, and they received immediate, actionable feedback.

Then along came agriculture, which, for all its merits, brought a surplus of resources and newfound notions of ownership, property, and wealth. And consequently, it brought the ability to hire others and the need for a hierarchical society. With hierarchy came competition, increased efficiency, envy, vulnerability, and so on. Flash forward several millennia, and our workplace has expanded to this messy conglomerate we see now, rampant with surplus, wealth, hierarchy, and exploitation. Technology, though, might have something to say about that.

The research and academic literature around global political economics is rich and diverse and worth reading, and we are not here to offer sound or comprehensive novelty to that space (though we can recommend some fascinating places to start: *Poor Economics, Post-American World, Collapse, The World Is Flat*). But as businesspeople, as mobile app people specifically, we cannot help but see firsthand how technology is seismically shifting the game. Here are a few key ways technology has enabled a workplace without borders.

Access

This one is really key, because it is more recent, unprecedented, and honestly thrilling. Technology levels the playing field. Companies gain greater access to talent, talent gains access to resources and opportunities, consumers can access products from nearly anywhere, and companies can advertise and sell to anyone. The McKinsey Global Institute (MGI) dubs this phenomenon a "massive democratization of the global economy" (Exploding Digital Flows in a Deeply Connected World, 2016).

In the past, globalization was driven predominantly by large, multinational, Western companies like Coca-Cola, Nestle, and Monsanto. In today's shifting landscape, however, technology and digital platforms enable small businesses around the world to participate directly in globalization. As MGI notes, today there are 50 million small businesses on Facebook, twice as many as only two years ago (Exploding Digital Flows, 2016). From this kind of digital platform, these companies can reach out to, connect with, cater to, and study customers from all over the world. Of the people who have liked these small business pages on Facebook, 30 percent are from different countries than the business.

The same goes for platforms like Alibaba (which facilitates 10 million small businesses connecting to customers) and Amazon (2 million). In fact, MGI conducted a survey and found that 86 percent of technology startups around the world today initially create their business models and strategies oriented to a global market (Exploding Digital Flows, 2016). The old hindrances to global expansion like resources, talent, customers, and communication are falling by the wayside.

So what does this mean for us? The main takeaway is that technology, with its resulting speed, interconnectedness, and access, gives us the ability to source the best talent and the best input the world has to offer. It drives efficiency, innovation, and economic growth. And it connects us with exceptional communication, heightening our ability to work seamlessly across these dissolving borders. Between videoconferencing, voice messaging, online collaboration, in many ways it's not too much more difficult for us to have an employee halfway around the world as it is to have an employee one state over (McGregor, 2016).

Legal Tools

Yes, it's true, employing foreign-born workers entails some additional steps. But the steps are not onerous, they do not add exorbitant material costs, and they are well worth it. Talent reigns supreme, and the need for competent people far outweighs the cost associated with pursuing foreign-born employees.

With the help of immigration resources and experts, you can hire people for positions ranging from accountants to software engineers, help desk administrators to salespeople, mechanical engineers to attorneys, nurses, scientists, teachers, and everything in between. No matter what business you are in, you are in the talent business. In a world with rapidly dissolving borders, hiring foreign workers is a viable option for almost every employer. Hire a trusted practitioner, leverage legal tools and processes to streamline the extra paperwork, embrace the workplace landscape of the future, and make the most of the unique talent that can be found around the globe.

Michael L. Kim, immigration attorney at Hall Render, adds the following:

I was fortunate to have commenced my employment-based immigration practice during the great dot-com bubble of 1997 to 2000. I personally had friends who were creating business-to-business Internet startup companies, and it was during those years that I began to imagine a business community that was no longer constrained by national borders or the expanse of the Atlantic or Pacific Oceans.

Instead, I witnessed firsthand the previously burdensome and inflexible hurdles of jurisdictional and geographical lines begin to crumble. Indeed, I had the opportunity to work with an Internet startup company founded by a U.S. expat living in Tokyo during the dot-com bubble. The founder formed her company in Japan, secured funding from a European venture capital firm, and then established a U.S. subsidiary that just happened to require a foreign-born professional worker, using the H-1B Specialty Occupation classification. The confluence of these elements opened my eyes to how quickly and thoroughly our business community was becoming borderless.

I took a calculated risk and focused my practice exclusively on employment-based immigration law. Fast forward 17 years, and I now assist billion dollar enterprises, national health care systems, and cutting edge technology companies, as well as local businesses, in securing foreign-born talent to fill critical roles in their U.S. operations. We interact with these foreign-born workers every day, largely relying on the services or products they produce. They are our physicians, our aerospace engineers, our information technology experts, our teachers, our neighbors, and even our favorite professional athletes.

The world's most sophisticated employers leverage international workforces to gain a strategic advantage over their competitors. Partnering with expert immigration counsel, who can quickly and efficiently navigate the immigration regulatory framework, today's employers can fearlessly wade into the world of employment-sponsored visa workers. It should be noted that all employers can take advantage of the opportunities provided through hiring foreign-born talent. Those businesses that do not take the time to learn and understand what hiring options exist, immigration-related or otherwise, will be at a disadvantage in the increasing war for global talent.

The conversations of today's workers sound different because the work landscape has evolved. We no longer simply work in an office, in a town, in a state, or in a country. We work in a global world, and there's a good chance your next manager could live thousands of miles away and still never miss a beat.

Chapter

Working Across Generations

(Or, Why Variety Is the Spice of Work)

In addition to drawing from a borderless talent base, we are also expanding our workforce across generations. An increasingly competitive global marketplace demands talent from workers of all ages. Leading and successfully engaging a multigenerational workforce is a business imperative that few organizations can ignore.

That does not mean it will be easy, though. Nearly 60 percent of HR managers at large companies say they have seen office conflicts rise from generational friction (The Multi-Generational Workforce, 2–3). Inexperienced youngsters. Out-of-touch elders. We have seen this movie many times, haven't we?

Several years ago, business media was in a tizzy about the unprecedented phenomenon of four generations in the workplace. Buckle up, HR nerds and managers everywhere, because the fifth generation is already on its way. And thanks to medical advancements and economic downturn, it will not be uncommon for older Americans to stay in the workforce into their 70s.

We are overridden with information and caveats about the workplace generational divide, much of it dangerously polarizing and unproductive. Although it is true we should acknowledge different generational workplace needs, it is also true that the divide is not as vast, and certainly not as insurmountable, as we are often led to believe.

Let's look at each generation at a glance (Leading a Multigenerational Workforce, 8–13).

Traditionalists

Born before 1946. Growing up in the wake of the Great Depression and World War II, they developed a strong commitment to family and country, and they see work as a privilege. Their values and work ethic built the infrastructure of modern American business and politics. They are disciplined, stable, and very experienced.

Boomers

Born 1946 to 1964. They were born into the relative ease and global recovery of the post–World War II economy, and they grew up in an era of liberations: the civil rights movement, women's rights, landing on the moon. They are optimistic visionaries who want to make things different, have a voice, prove their worth, and do whatever it takes. They are team oriented, good communicators, and emotionally mature.

Generation X

Born 1964 to 1979. They grew up in an era of uncertainty and distrust with the Cold War, AIDS, Nixon's Watergate scandal, Chernobyl, Exxon Valdez, Tiananmen Square, corporate layoffs, and a huge spike in divorcing parents. They learned to thrive in chaos and change. They saw the rise of computers and entrepreneurship, and came to value autonomy, work-life balance, and self-reliance. They are skeptical, pragmatic, authentic, and cautious with loyalty.

Millennials

Born 1980 to 1997. The first digital natives, they grew up in a connected, 24/7 world, shaped by the rise of the Internet and social media, the end of apartheid, Columbine, 9/11, corporate scandals, war in the Middle East, and natural disasters (the Pacific tsunami, Hurricane Katrina, climate change). They are achievement oriented, innovative, and extremely socially aware. They feel the weight of national and global issues and seek input, meaning, and collaboration with smart, committed people. As of 2015, millennials are the largest generation in the workforce, currently representing more than one in three workers (Fry, 2015).

Generation Z

Born after 1997. They are hyperconnected, having been born into a global digital world operating in real time. They were raised in the post–9/11 era when the world became more complicated and scary, where climate change, terrorism, a shrinking middle class, and school shootings are accepted reality. They are ambitious, socially aware, and reaching unprecedented levels of technological savvy. Some may never have sent an email when they enter the workforce, which is baffling even to the millennials!

Variety Is Invaluable

As with all generalizations, these can be helpful but are not universally prescriptive. We are told not to judge a book by its cover, and the same can be said for a worker's age. Take time to assess the individual and move beyond his or her generational label. It's important to educate, understand, and nourish the unique strengths each generation brings to the workplace, but stay focused on how to most effectively work together, not on unearthing every last nuance. Do your internal market research to learn what motivates and irks your employees. Maybe it has to do with their generations, or maybe simply the place they live, their interests, or their family dynamics.

A seven-year Center for Creative Leadership study of 3,000 corporate leaders (Deal, 2007), and a similarly extensive study by Deloitte, concluded that essentially all the generations have similar values (Smith, 2008). The number one priority is family, followed by a workplace of respect with trustworthy leaders who coach people.

Where we differ is *how* we view work, demonstrate respect, and prefer to communicate and learn. For example, many traditionalists probably had one career, even one employer, their whole lives. Millennials, on the other hand, will job and career hop. They may be freelance writers, take three-month breaks to go hiking, then become software engineers, and that seems completely reasonable to them. Both value work, but they express it differently.

Many of us in HR leadership have seen too many walls go up between generations. There are quick assumptions, mistrust, unease, and misunderstanding. Who suffers the most from this? The organization. Your goal is to help your team move beyond the labels. You have to determine and uphold the *company* culture above a particular individual's or generation's culture.

Managing Across Generations

How do we bring different generations together and lead authentically? Here are six tips to engage a multigenerational workforce.

- *Acknowledge shared needs.* Everyone wants to be respected, included, and invested in. Everyone values face-to-face communication for important issues and a sincere "thank you." Everyone could use more flexibility—millennials seeking balance, boomers caring for aging parents, and Xers in dual-income families who want to be involved in their kids' lives.

- *Respect and draw on unique talents.* Great ideas and innovation come from all ages. Be careful to not equate skill with being a computer whiz. A multigenerational workforce offers a wellspring of talent—the work ethic of traditionalists, optimism of boomers, self-reliance of Gen X, enthusiasm and collaboration of millennials, and technological fluency of Gen Z.

- *Set the tone.* Be adaptive. Be open. Show respect. Coworkers all unconsciously spread and pick up on others' emotions (Leadership and Emotional Cognition, 2011). Especially as leaders, because subordinates pay such close attention, it is crucial to demonstrate the desired culture for the group.

- *Overcome stereotypes through outcome interdependence* (Halvorson, 2015). First impressions are particularly stubborn, but one of the most effective methods to overcome them in the workplace is by making people work together in ways where their outcomes depend on each other. If your success hinges on someone else, you become (unconsciously) much more invested in understanding that person, and your brain reexamines evidence. Dan Gilbert calls this our psychological immune system kicking in (Halvorson, 2015). We try to see things in a way that makes life less painful for us. It's easier to like the people we have to work with.

- *Build collaborative relationships.* Take it one step further by developing mentoring programs to build relationships across generations. Colleagues are more apt to learn from each other than from formal training. Younger workers can demystify technology and share innovations that drive business results. Older workers can lend their extensive industry expertise, and especially now, in the widespread anticipation that boomers retiring will be the biggest brain drain in U.S. history.

- *Recognize the tremendous value of disagreeableness* (Heffernan, 2012). Exposure to unfamiliar perspectives fosters creativity because the obvious answer stops being our only answer (Lehrer, 2012). Dissent is difficult but mentally invigorating. We have to reassess assumptions and try out new ways of thinking. In creative groups, shoot for quantity of ideas over quality, limit the time allotted for coming up with ideas (10–30 minutes is often plenty), and try "brain writing," where individuals first anonymously write ideas, then come together to vote—a meritocracy of ideas (Thompson, 2013). Debate ideas fiercely, but do not attack intentions or personality. The most creative spaces are often those that hurl varied opinions together.

Managing Millennials

We also want to highlight the nuances of leveraging millennials, especially because they typically (and unfairly) bear the brunt of generational scorn. Todd worked with and managed many millennials at ExactTarget, and Santiago happens to be one himself (he started his first company, Bluebridge Digital, at age 21).

By 2025, they are estimated to comprise roughly 75 percent of the workforce (Dews, 2014). There are a lot of them, and we should know how to get along effectively. Yet, unfortunately, Google "millennials at work" or talk to any embittered older manager, and you'll see millennials get a lot of grief for being lazy, self-serving, and flaky.

You will find an array of articles about how to manage them, how to get them to step up, and how to react when they don't take ownership of their work. You will find studies demonstrating how, increasingly, young Americans "believe their lives are controlled by outside forces rather than their own efforts" (Twenge, 2004).

Given that millennials are the largest generation represented, the workplace is slowly adapting to meet their expectations. Millennials bring to the workplace several new expectations, including the following:

- *Innovation.* It's news to no one that these digital natives expect to use technology to help them work, and many of them know no other way.

- *Meaning.* Millennials crave an exciting, innovative environment with meaningful work. More than any other generation, they happily exchange cash rewards in favor of perks like career progression, flexibility, strong positive culture, and leaders who value and listen to them (Challenges for Human Resource Management and Global Business Strategy).

- *Social entrepreneurship.* Distinct from other generations, millennials disavow the traditional notion that profit and good are necessarily at odds. Growing up in a global, connected world, they are incredibly socially aware and tout those views publicly, in how they broadcast on social media, how they shop, and where they choose to loan their talent.

Case in Point: THINX

Quintessential millennial Miki Agrawal worked in investment banking, played professional soccer, started two companies, and wrote a book—basically cycling through five minicareers—all before age 34. Her latest endeavor, THINX, has earned a slew of awards for disruptive innovation, social entrepreneurship, and *TIME* magazine's best new inventions of 2015. The stroke of brilliance? Period underwear.

We realize it's a little usual for us, as two men, to talk about this topic. But that is exactly what THINX seeks to shift and exactly the kind of dauntless, purposeful doggedness that millennials exude.

In Agrawal's words, "I think millennials are more comfortable with the idea of breaking taboos and discussing the uncomfortable." When you think about all of the world's past innovations and advancements, you realize just how many uncomfortable conversations were required along the way (Wachob).

But millennials are not interested in uncomfortable topics for the sake of argument. They are willing to have difficult conversations in pursuit of something greater. Agrawal says, "I think the future of entrepreneurship is social entrepreneurship. People won't care about business if it's purely for profit anymore. A spirit of giving back should be interwoven in all companies, not just an afterthought, but a key measurement of the company's success" (Wachob).

Her entire company revolves around the millennial hot button issue of social entrepreneurship. Listen to the THINX mission statement: "We see a world where no woman is held back by her body. We will work proudly and tirelessly until every single girl has an equal opportunity for the brighter future she deserves. By reimagining feminine hygiene products to provide support, comfort, confidence, and peace of mind, we aim to eliminate shame, empowering women and girls around the world," (Hinde, 2016).

Does this really make a difference? Absolutely. Take Uganda, for example, where 50 percent of girls do not go to school for an entire week every month once they reach puberty. Their education falls behind, they get discouraged, and they drop out. THINX sees this crucial need, and for every pair of underwear they sell, they fund a pack of reusable pads to go to girls in the developing world, through their partners Afripads.

Whether as entrepreneurs in their own right, like Agrawal, or as members of your team, millennials bring vigor and vision to the workplace that is unmatched. If we can collectively learn to harness that power, it will have huge implications on the overall business landscape and the world at large.

Free Agents on the Rise
(Or, Why We're Finally Free to Be You and Me)

As if five generations in a global workforce were not enough to tip the business world on its axis, the rise of the freelance economy (or the gig economy) forces us to rethink the entire way we work. In his book *Free Agent Nation* (2001), Dan Pink details his transition from chief speechwriter for vice president Al Gore to freelance work:

> A few months ago I was working in the White House. Now I tell people I'm working in the Pink House, since my office is on the third floor of our compact home in Washington, D.C. For many years, I held down a job, often one that people considered a "good job." But I'd grown tired—tired of politics in general and of office politics in particular, tired of doing assignments I didn't enjoy on a schedule I couldn't control, tired of wingtips that felt like vises and neckties that seemed like nooses, and most of all, tired of seeing my stunningly cute daughter only when she was asleep and her very attractive mom only when I was complaining. So I left. On Independence Day.
>
> When asked, "Would you go back?" he replies, "I can't imagine why" (Pink, 1997).

38

Pink's sentiments hit home for a growing portion of the workforce, and business leaders must address how to cultivate diverse and dispersed talent. Currently, there are 53 million Americans, or 34 percent of the U.S. workforce, working as freelancers (defined by the Freelancers Union as "individuals who have engaged in supplemental, temporary, or project- or contract-based work in the past 12 months"). These freelancers add $715 billion annually to the U.S. economy through their work (Freelancing in America, 3).

The most familiar and common type of freelancer is the independent contractor, who has no employer and works on a project-to-project basis. They comprise 40 percent of the freelance sector. But the term also applies to moonlighters (27 percent) who do additional work outside of their primary jobs, temporary workers (10 percent), diversified workers (18 percent) who combine traditional and freelance work, and freelance business owners (5 percent) who have one to five employees while maintaining their freelance status (Freelancers in America, 3).

In the 1990s, the freelance sector amounted to just less than 10 percent of the workforce (DiNatale, 2001, 28). But in the past two decades, the way we work has undergone a significant shift, and it has major implications for how we organize. Bye-bye 9 to 5. Now work transcends our traditional constructs of where work gets done and who does it, and we need to break free from the assumption that traditional employment agreements are the best method for sourcing top talent.

People take the freelance route for a number of reasons. Some reasons are voluntary, such as extra money, flexibility, or autonomy, and some are compulsory, like restructuring or economic downturns. They come in all demographics, including millennials seeking more flexibility, stay-at-home parents seeking additional income or professional fulfillment, and retirees wanting to dabble in the workplace with special knowledge. Whatever the reason, these freelancers are doing work that was previously reserved for full-time employees. We are moving beyond drivers, custodians, and caterers, and we are now also outsourcing roles like software engineers, accountants, and graphic designers.

In an economy that runs on brainpower, talent is in high demand, and 83 percent of organizations believe they are losing the battle (Forman, 2014, 2). We all know that the most important talent is the toughest to get and very well may not want to work where you need them. That's why the burgeoning free agent talent base offers such thrilling new opportunities for business leaders. It really is a win-win: Freelance workers get to pursue more meaningfully independent lives, and businesses get access to precise skills at the exact time they need them, even if the best candidate lives in another state or country.

Why Freelance Works

Leveraging freelance and contingent workers is in your best interest for three primary reasons.

- *The best talent.* It's no secret that leading companies relentlessly follow, recruit, and optimize top talent. So when that talent decides they prefer to work on a temporary, project-by-project basis, organizations find ways to make that work. As Dan Pink writes, "Corporate leaders need to recognize that in many cases the very, very best talent is in this piece of the population. It isn't a bunch of people who are flaky. It isn't a bunch of people who couldn't get a job anywhere. Now it's the people who have the power in the talent market who are going that way" (Pink, 2012).

- *The best model.* Companies often need intermittent access to specific skills, and they often make the mistake of hiring people with those skills permanently. For small businesses especially, this remains a feeble and exorbitant solution. We need a model better suited to both the quandary and the current landscape, a way to meet skills gaps as they arise. Looking at the spike in high-end contract work (e.g., consultancy), Peter Drucker (2002) wrote in *Managing in the Next Society*, "This is the future of outsourcing," and he called it "intellectual capital on demand."

- *Your best interests.* Tapping into this extended workforce affords organizations some of the most coveted, advantageous capabilities: agility, lean growth, and access to high-performing talent, all with decreased friction and greater economic value. The open-source, collaborative economy fuses high quality with economic efficiency.

In his 2005 TED talk, Clay Shirky, prominent thinker on the social and economic effects of Internet technology, identifies the shift from classic institutional frameworks to cooperative infrastructure models (Shirky, 2005). The Internet has brought what he dubs "mass amateurization," breaching the walls between professional and amateurs. For example, thanks to Flickr (or more recently, Instagram), "people with cameras" can now join the professional ranks of "photographers" without belonging to an institution. Likewise, bloggers disseminate information to mass audiences apart from the formal class of "journalists."

Similarly, Chris Anderson expands on this idea in his book *The Long Tail*. What we now take somewhat for granted, Anderson fleshed out way back in 2006, and indeed his theories underscore successes like Google AdWords and

Amazon. He points out that although bloggers might not be associated with any professional entity, they may have more knowledge, better access to information, equal talent, and faster turnaround on their specific areas of expertise. Plus they often work for free. How can our traditional, printed, subscription newspapers compete with on-demand information, free distribution, and no advertising? They can't, and they know it. Many professional publications work closely with and depend heavily on freelancers (Anderson, 2006).

These unprecedented developments in technology and collaboration bring seismic changes and challenges to our traditional institutional models, and HR needs to snatch this opportunity. Shirky illustrates it well: Take, for example, someone who comes in, has one really good idea, and then eats your snacks and hangs out for three years. According to our traditional notions, this person would land squarely into the "bad hire" category. But within the cooperative infrastructure model, the question becomes not "Is this person a good employee?" but "Do you want that contribution?"

Traditional institutions cannot take those people on because the overall return on investment is too costly. But what if we no longer have to think like that? What if the investment plummeted to face value? According to the cooperative infrastructure model, we can reengineer the system so that anyone can contribute any amount. This has profound implications in an economy constantly casting its net in a scarce resource of talent.

In 1995, Netscape introduced the first bug bounty program, to reward users for finding and reporting bugs in their software, a form of "self-help through collaboration." Netscape recognized that they needed an extensive, open review process in order to create products of the highest caliber—that it takes a village to raise a software (Netscape Announces 'Netscape Bugs Bounty,' 1997).

Since then, an entire online community of bug bounty hunters has sprouted, dedicated to tracking and eliminating corporate glitches. Hundreds, if not thousands, of companies participate by posting bounties, establishing programs for reporting bugs, and honoring the bug hunters in Halls of Fame. Large, established companies like Google (Google Application Security) and Facebook (Information, 2016) will happily dish out thousands of dollars to these brilliant sleuths under the rationale that people will hack software anyway, so we might as well get them on our side first and pay them tempting sums to disclose bugs responsibly. It saves the companies millions of dollars in security breaches and rewards the hackers with more fame and money than they would probably get otherwise.

In October 2013, Microsoft paid $100,000 to a bug hunter who submitted a security exploit technique affecting Windows 8.1, reasoning, "It's better to pay third-party talent than attempt to fight against it" (Adhikari, 2013).

And in March 2016, a 10-year-old Finnish schoolboy became the youngest programmer ever to receive such a bounty (Woolf, 2016). Facebook doled out $10,000 to him for disclosing a bug that had allowed Instagram comments to be deleted. Instagram gets to improve its code while the 10 year old gets to stay in school, earn lifetime bragging rights, and buy a new football and bicycle (reportedly his big plans for the reward money).

This is a quintessential demonstration of the power of an open-source knowledge economy. Maybe your organization does not have the resources to hire a full-time software genius, but you also cannot afford the potential catastrophe of having vulnerabilities in your code. In a traditional institution, you would be stuck. But in a collaborative framework, you can tap into the talent you need, get the one idea or technique that saves the day, and then never hear from that person again. That person can soak in his or her brilliance and claim a proper reward without being tethered to your company full time.

As Shirky points out, the fact that a single programmer, creative, or other genius can, without having to move into a professional relationship with an institution, improve a company once and never be seen from again is unprecedented and entirely unreachable in classic institutional frameworks. But that, friends, is the future of business.

Managing Freelance Talent

Anyone who has ever managed another person knows leadership is not easy. Every person is different and brings at least some of his or her personal life to work. Figuring out how to engage each unique person takes time and effort, both of which increase exponentially for every person you add to the team. Suddenly, team dynamics come into play, and everything gets more complicated.

Think of leadership like a maze. You begin at one end with an employee and together learn how to navigate to the other end by trying different strategies (with a lot of trial and error). Now, imagine doing it blindfolded. If you buy in to the widely held belief that more than 90 percent of communication is nonverbal, then you'll understand this analogy for managing freelancers.

You can't swing by a free agent's desk for a quick question. You can't rely on him or her being available during standard office hours. You have zero visibility into his or her overall workload with other clients and zero control over it. You can't engage him or her in the onsite activities of your office or hallway conversations. He or she has no desk. There is no hallway. And, chances are, that person is going to run to the grocery store or the gym when everyone else is at work.

So why bother? New types of work arrangements, like hiring free agents, will increasingly be the norm, as they should be, and demand we rewire our understanding of how to find, recruit, and manage the best people. The benefits of hiring and managing freelancers far outweigh the challenges. Not only is more top talent opting out of the corporate lifestyle, more companies are realizing how much an on-demand workforce saves them time, money, and headaches in the long run.

Case in Point: Creative Quarterback

At ExactTarget, one of Todd's best and brightest employees was a creative named Nicole Ross, who for 10 years rose swiftly through the ranks, donned dozens of corporate marketing hats, and produced some of our finest campaigns. After our acquisition by Salesforce.com, she elected to leave the company and venture out on her own. She launched a company built precisely for this new open-source knowledge economy. A virtual creative agency 100 percent powered by freelancers, Creative Quarterback has practically zero overhead, nimble turnaround, and impeccable talent, including designers, developers, writers, videographers, and other creatives. (Visit them at www.creativequarterback.com.)

Ross coordinates (or "quarterbacks") teams of freelance talent to remove the logistical burden from clients who want to embrace freelance talent but do not have the time or expertise to manage the creative process themselves. The majority of Ross's freelancers also had successful corporate careers but of their own accord opted out of that lifestyle for more flexibility.

Freelance talent is not a natural fit for every business, specifically those entrenched in traditional work patterns. Ross knows this firsthand because she manages up to 25 freelancers and an equal number of clients at any given time. Many organizations jump on the freelance bandwagon to save a quick buck, only to realize working with freelancers requires them to change the way they work too. Yes, you can save significant budget using freelance talent (often upwards of 50 percent). Yes, turnaround times are often faster than traditional agencies or overworked full-time employees. But Ross cautions against trying to manage freelancers like traditional employees. It isn't apples to apples. It's apples to penguins.

Embracing free agents may challenge you at first, as will any type of change. However, the challenges are few and the rewards are many. This is the future of work, so there's no better time to get on board.

Nicole Ross, founder of creative quarterback, shares these tips for managing freelance talent:

Intentionally Extend Your Culture

Culture matters just as much when you are trying to engage workers who are not full-time employees. Share your core values, onboard them, provide feedback, include them in team and project updates, recognize their contributions, and treat them like your own. You might be surprised how many short-term gigs can turn into long-term freelance relationships.

Change the Way You Communicate

Face-to-face meetings are few and far between, especially if your freelancer is located in another state or halfway around the world. You need to perfect the art of communicating virtually through email, text, Facetime, Skype, project management systems, and other nontraditional means. Expecting free agents to drive across town for meetings or hop on frequent calls is not realistic. Freelancers use technology so they are not tethered to someone else's schedule and can prioritize their lives. If you want to work with the best free agents, respect the choices they made and adjust how you communicate.

Set Clear Expectations Up Front

When your freelancer says you will have something by "end of day," he or she might mean midnight. Freelancers work nontraditional hours that change based on the demands of their personal lives; it's why many of them chose to freelance in the first place. Set clear expectations up front about when and how they will work for you, including time zones, communication preferences, and rate structures. And don't be surprised if they refuse to provide their cell phone numbers. Their lives, their terms. You have to respect that.

Chapter

Partnering with Purpose

(Or, Why Partners Must Mesh with Your Culture)

I n this new era of open-source talent and cooperative infrastructure, the lines we have traditionally drawn between personal and professional and between business and consumer are fading away. To the outside world, no one knows (or cares) who is your full-time employee versus who is your freelancer versus who is your partner. To everyone else, all your workers are created equal and represent your brand and culture to the world. Their actions speak to your brand, which is why it is so important to hire the right people—and partners.

What does this mean for the future of business?

Public Opinion about Your Brand Matters

Monitor your image and create brand ambassadors. Chief marketing officers (CMOs) monitor brand image and company reputation in public forums. Similarly, chief human resources officers (CHROs) must monitor public commentary and internal buzz about their organizations as employers. Negative public commentary about shabby work environments, lack of community involvement, and poor customer service repels talent, consumers, and partners.

Social media further raises the stakes of the game, for good or for ill. If you do something special for customers, and they tweet about it, their friends may come running. But if you mess up, the Internet can quickly spiral you into a viral fiasco. With increased opportunity comes increased responsibility. Your employees and consumers have a lot more credibility with the general public than do your executives. Leverage these people to become powerful brand ambassadors.

Kindness Is Remembered

We wish someone would have drilled this into our heads 20 years ago. People we competed against in high school athletics became friends in college, became colleagues in jobs outside of college, or became partners in current business ventures. Who you meet throughout your life and how you treat them will follow you into your future.

Keith Ferrazzi, author of *Never Eat Alone* and *Who's Got Your Back?*, writes on the importance of making other people successful (Ferrazzi, 2014). He gives the example of the familiar adage, "Build loyal relationships with your customers." He took this classic advice and said to 15 consultants, "Think of three of your customers who you authentically admire. Send them emails right now telling them that you authentically admire them and asking for a cup of coffee." That one new practice, embodying this age-old belief, created $258 million of revenue in less than two months, born of the simple, practical application of authentic kindness.

Culture Extends through All of Your Partners

Be painstakingly intentional in selecting who you work with—board members, independent contractors, real estate brokers, third-party vendors—anyone and everyone who could possibly be associated with your brand. We cannot tell you how many organizations we have seen go to scrupulous lengths to hire employees that fit their cultures, only to turn around and work with any old outside partner who comes knocking on their doors. Your customers, constituents, and the general public do not distinguish between the legal definitions of employee and nonemployee; they just see someone associated with your company who is presumably acting on your company's behalf.

Screening Outside Partners

Employees play an undeniable and crucial role in the cultural equation. However, it is high time we take a step back, expand our horizons, and shift our understanding of culture at its essence. Secret's out: It's about a lot more than us and our employees, or us and our freelancers.

Time and again, we see companies failing to consider the impact *outside partners* have when it comes to forming and nurturing workplace cultures. Companies spend countless hours recruiting and evaluating job candidates, straining to ensure each new recruit is a good "culture fit." Screening tools, interviews, personality assessments, and other methods are called in as reinforcements, all painstakingly applied to determine whether the candidate will fit in and contribute positively to the company and its culture. Some companies, such as Zappos and Pardot, have this process down to a science, and if even *one* interviewer vetoes a candidate in the culture category, it's over. No offer letter, period, the end.

Dramatic, but it makes sense. We certainly have all seen the impact of a positive or negative cultural fit on the broader work environment. Get it right, and you will reap higher employee engagement, job satisfaction, and bottom-line results. Hire a bad egg, and you are in for quite the rocky ride.

But now, consider how much time we spend screening our *outside partners* for culture fit. Most companies completely bypass any cultural assessment for outside influencers. Troublesome, to say the least. From third-party vendors to contractors, advisors to board members, these "outsiders" can still have a profound impact on workplace cultures. Some outside parties have some seriously significant exposure to your business, employees, and customers. Think roles like benefits and wellness partners, real estate brokers, and marketing agencies. In our experience, nearly every interaction between our outside partners and our employees has affected our culture in some way, for better or for worse.

Shifting Mindsets

We see the root issue paralleling the aforementioned shift toward a more borderless workforce. Many of us tend to not screen outside partners for culture fit because in the past we did not have to, and in many cases our mindsets are slow to catch up to our world. We try to operate from the industrial era perspective when we need to ground ourselves in the new realities.

We often refer to outside parties as "agents" of the company. But the reality is, to the outside world, agents *are* our company. Other employees, customers, and the general public simply do not differentiate between the legal designation of employee and nonemployee. They see someone associated with your company, and they therefore, logically and appropriately, assume that person acts on your company's behalf. Perception is reality.

Here are five tips to ensure outside parties are the right culture fits.

- Identify and understand the type and level of interactions your outside parties will have with employees, customers, and the general public. You will be surprised how much influence and access they have.

- Identify a key point of contact from each outside partner who will interact with your stakeholders and meet with that contact before you sign on the dotted line. You like their leadership team? Great, more power to you. That's not enough. Make sure the "feet on the street" align with your core values and culture, as well.

- Interview outside parties in the same manner that you would a potential job candidate. Have face-to-face meetings. Learn about how they would interact with your employees, customers, and prospects. Be thorough, and get multiple opinions from your team before making a decision.

- Check references. If potential partners cannot supply lists of references who vouch for their integrity, professionalism, and commitment, throw a red flag.

- Quickly eject any outside partners (existing or potential) who are cultural misfits. Like employees, one cultural bad apple can ruin the bunch. No person, regardless of résumé, is worth risking the culture you have built.

No doubt, outside partners can be a huge value-add and are often a business necessity. We love our outside partners, we interact with them nearly daily, and we could not do business without them. For those very reasons, we insist on applying the same rigor to our relationships with and expectations of our partners as we do to our relationships with and expectations of our employees. Enter those relationships with your eyes wide open. Your partners *will* influence your culture.

FirstPerson (www.FirstPersonAdvisors.com) partners with employers, augmenting efforts to drive employee engagement. CEO Bryan Brenner and his team have worked diligently to foster a distinct company culture that serves the people needs of companies that share their values.

From hiring practices, onboarding initiatives, and nurturing of community engagement, we have come to realize that we partner best with those who align with our particular business philosophy and style of delivering products that enhance working teams. Business partner relationships are just like any other relationship. Those partners that have similar belief systems, ethical views, and styles are the ones that create mutually beneficial, long-standing business relationships.

Just as you would check potential members of your own team for culture fits, you must do the same for outside partners. First, take time to identify your expected deliverables and your definition of a dream partner. Equip yourself to choose a partner that will fit your company style and approach. Ends do not justify the means. An outside partner that delivers the desired result but does not do so in a manner that fits your company culture is not a good partner.

Next, focus on the individuals within your company that will interface with the partner organization. Does the employee own the partner relationship to the same level that he or she would own an employee relationship? Does the employee take the time to invest in and develop the partner relationship? Does the employee communicate regularly to the partner, ensuring alignment on goals and strategies?

Partner engagement, similar to employee engagement, is something that needs to be unlocked and nurtured. When activated, partner engagement can yield tremendous results for an employer. Hone your skills in communicating your culture and what you value to your employees first. Then communicate the same to your partners. Amazing results will follow.

Chapter

Trending Telework
(Or, Why Coffee Shops Are the New Corner Offices)

We looked at the changing profiles of who is working. But the new era of work also brings with it a vastly different definition of *how* we are working—where work gets done, how we measure it, what we expect from it, and how technology has changed all of it. Many of our traditionally held beliefs about these concepts derive from the industrial era and will soon be obsolete.

In the industrial era, we had to be physically present in the workplace to do our jobs. We could easily clock our production, and we could mentally detach when we left the building. Your supervisor could take one look at you to know whether or not you were working, and it was impossible to work outside of work. This is the world our constructs fit, but it looks nothing like the knowledge economy in which we now live.

Where Work Gets Done

First on our list is our understanding of where work gets done. In a factory, you absolutely have to be physically present to do your job. When your work is on a Wi-Fi–enabled device, you are no longer confined to a physical space.

Even inside the physical office space, our traditional notions of where work gets done are falling by the wayside. Wi-Fi, laptops, and now mobile devices have completely untethered us from the confines of a physical workstation.

Take, for instance, the cubicle. In a tragically comic *New York Times* article, Nikil Saval, author of *Cubed: A Secret History of the Workplace*, opens with the words, "'I have known the inexorable sadness of pencils,'" quoting from Theodore Roethke's poem "Dolor," on the grayness of the American office. Saval traces the history of the fateful cubicle back to Frederick Winslow Taylor, who pioneered efficiency in office design (Saval, 2016).

We eventually, of course, came to the cubicle, brought to eager management and unwitting employees everywhere by Herman Miller in 1967. It debuted under the gloriously misleading name "Action Office II," proclaiming, "A workstation for the human performer [designed] to give knowledge workers a more flexible, fluid environment than the rat-maze boxes of offices" (Lohr, 1997). It was praised, validated, and copied. Its head designer, Robert Propst, sought to investigate how the world of work operated, and he concluded, "Today's office is a wasteland. It saps vitality, blocks talent, frustrates accomplishment. It is the daily scene of unfulfilled intentions and failed effort" (Action Office System, 2016). In his 1968 book, *The Office: A Facility Based on Change*, he also wrote, "we find ourselves now with office forms created for a way of life substantially dead and gone." Oh, the irony.

As Saval notes, the cubicle quickly decayed into a favorite tool of economical drudgery, fine-tuned at "squeezing more people into less space for as little money as possible" (Saval, 2016). Reflecting on his innovation years later in 1997, Propst lamented that "the cubicle-izing of people in modern corporations is monolithic insanity" (Lohr, 1997). Happily, though, their supreme reign has already begun its decline.

As an executive in past workplaces, Todd scored many a dream corner office with a view. He was admired, he was conspicuous, and he was lonely. Nothing says, "Enter at your own risk, you lowly underlings" like an intimidating, secluded office. That is the farthest possible cry from the message he strives to send as a leader.

Now, at Emplify, he does not even have an office. He works from communal couches, he works from coffee shops, and he works wherever his people are. Yes, sometimes people interrupt him, and sometimes he gets distracted. But as a leader, those people and their well-being rank as his highest priority. As a leader, he wants to be among and enmeshed in the company activities, to keep his finger on the pulse of the culture, and to be readily available for his topmost responsibility: the people he leads. He will never have an office again.

Even more notably, the devices we use have revolutionized our cognitive relationships with our work. We can no longer detach ourselves when we leave the office because we can now access our files, inboxes, and communications anywhere. The cognitive state of "work" that used to be barred to a singular place has encroached on even our least professional spaces, like vacation, bed-time stories, or family dinner. Who among us has not cast an email while lying in bed? Let's acknowledge the reality that a lot of knowledge work can be done anywhere, and this affects how we understand and design workspaces for performance.

Sam Julka, founder and president of DORIS Research, runs a design research organization that enables people to understand themselves and co-create solutions to workplace challenges using design thinking.

Researching physical workspace changes is a fantastic opportunity for employee engagement. Oftentimes, businesses are searching for meaningful ways to engage their employees in something beyond their day-to-day jobs. In an effort to build stronger teams, organizations do things like service projects or retreats. But instead of manufacturing projects with which teams engage, we think engaging employees on the front end of a physical workspace change project is one of the most meaningful things an organization can do.

A wonderful example reflecting the positive outcomes of a people-centered design research project happened at a small product distribution warehouse. This organization had a mix of front office and warehouse employees. Through research, we found their biggest problem was the division of the office and warehouse staff. Each group of stakeholders had knowledge to contribute and share with the other, yet the physical layout of the office prevented the groups from coming together. Based on the layout, over time negative cultural behaviors and beliefs developed. The warehouse employees, at times, felt like second-class citizens to their office-working colleagues. Meanwhile, the office employees had no idea they felt this way.

The groups needed some common ground to come together and break down the literal and figurative wall between them. When they ideated together on how this might be done, they came up with simple solutions that were tested and proved before implementation. One inexpensive solution was moving their mail bins to one centralized location. Moving their mail bins together created new serendipitous opportunities for both groups. Additionally, other supporting physical features surrounded their mail bins, like standing-height tables for the two groups to lean on and gather around to talk about their product knowledge. Lastly, another simple idea that came from within was to remove solid doors separating the warehouse from the office and replace them with transparent glass doors. Changing the doors changed the psychological connectivity between the groups.

If all organizations would take time to address their real challenges by engaging their own workforce, they would have the ability to make their physical office spaces tools for good.

Working Remotely

One of the first pioneers of the telework movement was a women-only U.K. tech company back in the 1960s. Stephanie "Steve" Shirley founded the software company Freelance Programmers in 1962 with an initial capital of £6. Of her first 300 employees, only three were men. Everyone worked from home, being mostly women with children. Despite society's best efforts to confine females to domesticity, they continued to have significant science, technology, engineering, and mathematics talents.

Stephanie adopted the name "Steve" so people would not automatically write her off from the beginning. She says, "When I started my company of women, the men sort of said, 'How interesting, but it only works because it's small.' And later, as it became sizable, they sort of accepted, 'Yes, it is sizable now, but of no strategic interest.' And later, when it was a company valued at over $3 billion and I'd made 70 of the staff into millionaires, they sort of said, 'Well done, Steve'" (Shirley, 2015).

Shirley embodies the perseverance and imagination of the best disruptors. At five years old, she fled Nazi Europe with her nine-year-old sister on the lifesaving kindertransport to England and says that her whole being stems from that event. She explains, "I decided to make mine a life that was worth saving, and then I just got on with it." And that she did. Shirley went on to become a celebrated businesswoman, information technologist, and philanthropist. She also raised a child with autism, and most of her philanthropic work centers around that. She's won numerous accolades for her magnanimous contributions, and her proper title is actually "Dame" (Shirley, 2015). Indeed, well done, Steve.

And alongside all of that, she demonstrated how mutually beneficial and profitable teleworking can be for employees, businesses, and stakeholders. From the beginning, teleworking has offered flexibility, incentives, efficiency, and creative solutions.

Even more so in today's technologically infused world, the case for teleworking is easy: It saves time, money, and resources, and it can be a huge benefit to employees who demonstrate that they are just as effective, if not more effective, working from home. All kinds of people want work flexibility—parents, millennials, military spouses, retirees, freelancers—and teleworking opens up a much larger recruitment pool. The fact is, between 20 and 30 million U.S. workers are already working from home at least once a week (Guthrie, 2013). Eighty to ninety percent of workers say they would like to telework at least part time, and just more than a third would choose it over a pay raise (Telecommuting Statistics, 2016).

In a research study from the *American Sociological Review* titled "Does a Flexibility/Support Organizational Initiative Improve High-Tech Employees' Well-Being?" sociologists Phyllis Moen, Erin Kelly, and colleagues investigated the perks and repercussions of telework policies at an anonymous corporation. They randomly assigned half of the employees to a control group, operating under business as usual, which at this company essentially entailed flexibility at the manager's discretion. They assigned the other half to the experimental group, permitted and encouraged to work whenever and wherever they wanted, results-based only (Moen et al., 2016).

Moen and Kelly assessed that the experimental group met their work goals just as reliably as did the control group but with the added benefit of a significant increase in happiness. Those employees experienced improved sleep, improved health, and reduced stress, and the benefits even cascaded down to the employees' children, who reported similar increases in happiness and rest. At intervals of both one and three years later, employees in the experimental group stated less interest in leaving the company.

Of course, teleworking is not sunshine and daisies for everyone. But significant increases in employee (and family) health, happiness, and retention should not be imprudently brushed aside. Teleworking proves a fantastic option if the following four specific factors are present, but trying to make it work well outside of these stipulations may likely leave you hanging in a less than ideal situation.

- *The job fits.* Some professions, like receptionists, childcare workers, portrait photographers, or dentists, inextricably require some solid face time to execute properly. The knowledge economy tides are shifting these physical presence jobs into rarer occurrences, and we happily anticipate that the workplace of the future will only continue to bend in that direction. For now, though, step one remains that the nature of the job must allow for or be conducive to teleworking.

- *The employee is a responsible and productive person.* We certainly hope you can place a confident "check" in this box as something you already factor in when hiring and developing your people (and if not, please do revisit and completely chuck those strategies).

But acknowledging the lamentable reality, we choose to reemphasize this point that the employee must be fully capable of effectively self-managing and producing steady, stunning results from outside the office, as well as from inside it.

- *The manager can handle it.* Undoubtedly, managing teleworkers adds a layer of complexity. And undoubtedly, some managers, especially those less experienced or less favored, may not be quite adept enough for the job. It is an unfortunate scenario, to be sure, and again one that you may already work adamantly to counteract, but for now the reality may have to stifle some would-be well-suited teleworker freedoms.

- *The organizational culture does not inadvertently impugn teleworkers.* The concept of teleworking has not yet quite gone mainstream, and until more people and businesses hop on the telework wagon, some cultures, managers, and coworkers may harbor certain biases, hidden or outright, against those who do it. If you are going to embrace telework policies, follow through. Flexible work environments should not hinder the professional success of employees who telework.

When all of these items are present, teleworking can be an effective and enticing option. Check out these appealing perks:

- *Productivity.* Today's office environments are rife with distractions: meetings, hallway noise, unannounced visits from coworkers. An informatics professor at the University of California, Irvine, found that some office workers are interrupted or switch tasks every three minutes, hardly enough time to accomplish anything of substance (Caldow, 2009, 5). Free from these distractions, the average teleworker produces 43 percent more business output than his or her in-office counterpart (Love, 2014). Teleworking minimizes wasted meeting time and allows virtual collaboration without logistical hassle. Organizations with telework options see a 63 percent reduction in unscheduled absences (Telecommuting Statistics, 2016).

- *Engagement.* In short, telework options are seen as big perks and elicit higher engagement levels. Of employees who telecommute, 82 percent note lower stress levels, 80 percent report higher morale, and 70 percent experience increased productivity (Love, 2014). The flipside confirms this: 46 percent of companies that allow teleworking say it has greatly reduced attrition (Telecommuting

Statistics, 2016). Additionally, telecommuting helps to equalize personalities (the loudest voice in the room is no longer the only one heard) and to reduce the potential for discrimination (many workers never meet face to face).

- *Savings.* With the growing weight of corporate social responsibility and increased pressure to mitigate costs, leading companies are looking to teleworking as a viable means of financial and environmental savings. The average real estate savings per full-time teleworker is $100,000 per year (Telecommuting Statistics, 2016). After transitioning 40 percent of their employees to full-time telework, IBM has saved $100 million annually in the United States and at least that much in Europe (Caldow, 2009, 9). Employees also can save $3,800 annually in gas and commuting time by teleworking two days per week (The Yin and Yang of Telecommuting, 2013, 5). Traffic jams rob the U.S. economy of $78 billion per year in lost productivity and idle away 3 billion gallons of gas annually (Telecommuting Statistics, 2016).

Despite these upsides, some companies have changed previous arrangements and called for workers to be physically present in the office. Marissa Mayer, CEO of Yahoo!, cut work-from-home policies because internal data indicated that fewer employees were actually logging in from home (Broder, 2013). Similarly, Hewlett-Packard asked teleworkers to start showing up at the office every day, saying they were in a critical turnaround period and needed to strengthen a culture of engagement and collaboration (Eha, 2013). Some companies cite more difficulty establishing connections with coworkers or finding a sense of purpose in work. Others report loss of strategic direction or continued innovation.

The pitfalls of teleworking fundamentally come down to an issue of culture, which is all important, unique to each company. A small company with limited resources may prefer teleworking to keep costs low and incentivize recruiting. A software startup might want all three engineers in the same garage to create synergy for ideas. A leading, innovative company might use carrots rather than sticks to entice people to come into the office. Who wouldn't show up for gourmet meals, yoga sessions, and free day care? Ensure that your policies make sense for the type of work your employees do and align with company goals and vision. Teleworking is maximized only when employees are fully equipped to perform their job duties outside the office. It seems obvious, but many companies initiating telecommuting programs do not get this right.

Ellen Humphrey, senior vice president of human resources at Appirio, talks about how she views and ensures telework success:

Connectedness is the key to operating an international, remote team successfully. In fact, most business professionals would agree that connectedness is vital regardless of whether a team is widely dispersed or centralized in one location. Strive toward connecting your team to one another, to the mission of your organization, and to the greater purpose of the work each of them performs.

As humans, we need to feel like we are a part of something bigger, and we need to know what we're working toward. For a remote team, it is vital to be purposeful in creating opportunities to share and discuss your vision and connect the work to it. Team meetings and one-on-one conversations are a must in a dispersed team. You cannot rely on a chance encounter in the hallway to spurn a creative thought or spontaneous brainstorming session. Tips to make virtual meetings more effective include the following:

- Allow space at the beginning of phone calls and meetings to socialize and engage in water cooler talk that might naturally occur in a physical office.

- Talk more frequently in team calls about team goals and corporate goals. Make it interactive, and give different people the opportunity to speak or present.

- Webcams are a must. Make them mandatory! Being able to see one another and read body language can make a huge difference in the effectiveness of the meeting.

Thanks to modern technology, we have many more tools today that we can leverage to create a sense of community among dispersed teams, among them social collaboration platforms, live chat/instant messaging that facilitates quick conversations, meeting forums, webcams, and document collaboration software. My team members use these tools every day with their colleagues across the globe.

Equally important in the connectedness equation is what I call a culturally courteous team. This means both understanding one another's cultural norms and regional practices and being mindful of those in every aspect of team interactions. Very simple examples of cultural courtesy include the following:

- Schedule meetings that accommodate time zones as best as possible. Try alternating which time zones have to join in the early morning or late evening. Acknowledge on calls those for whom it might be morning, afternoon, or evening.
- Take care not to schedule team meetings during holidays in other regions.
- Be aware of team members who might not be participating in their primary language.
- Realize that slow Internet connections may cause delays. A slight pause in conversation could have much more to do with this than with intellectual or linguistic ability.

Finally, even extremely effective remote teams can benefit from an opportunity to interact face to face. If at all possible, find a reason and a way to gather team members together in one location. Maybe it is an annual team meeting or a celebration of accomplishments. It could even be a vendor conference or learning opportunity. Leave plenty of time for socializing, dining, and having fun together. The deepened connections that result will more than pay for the cost of the event.

Tips for Teleworking

Whether your organization is dipping its toe in the waters of teleworking or diving in head first, it's important to set up teleworkers (and those working with them) for success. Here are seven tips to most effectively reap the benefits of teleworking by engaging your remote workers and maintaining company culture:

- *Effective remote management boils down to effective remote communication.* Telecommuting often erases the little moments—the jokes, the random thoughts turned into big ideas, the easy collaboration. Spend an extra few minutes on the phone to catch up. Put extra effort into personalizing your electronic communications. We don't mean multiple exclamation points, but we do mean a little humor or the occasional emoticon. (Think of it as affording you the luxury of nailing the joke you normally come up with 3 minutes too late in the office meeting. Finally, you have time to craft the ultimate pun!)

- *Get to know each other beyond work.* It's no secret that teams operate best when they know and like each other. Find ways to simulate this "water cooler talk" but without the distraction of having people gossiping 2 feet away from your workspace. Few things substitute for hanging out with your coworkers, and one quick fix is to simply make intentional time. You very well may be able to get more out of 1 hour of intentional time with your boss at a bar (or on the phone) than intermittently seeing her around the office all week.

- *Assume goodwill.* The loss of nonverbal communication is a huge downside. Considerably more than half of communication is done nonverbally (Pease & Pease, 2006). This rings especially true in business settings, where body language accounts for up to 80 percent of the impact made around a negotiating table (Pease & Pease, 2006). Despite our best efforts, sometimes people are rushed and send unintentionally snippy remarks. In your work, especially internally, always assume goodwill on your team's behalf. Give people the benefit of the doubt.

- *Establish clear, quantitative metrics for performance.* Without the psychological comfort of managers seeing subordinates and subordinates being seen in the office every day, performance can easily become dubious. In many ways, teleworking makes employees more focused, results oriented, and accountable. Harness that from the outset and determine how you will measure and communicate performance.

- *Create space for brainstorming.* There is something uniquely powerful about being able to lean over to the person next to you and bounce an idea off of him or her, and this loss of innovative potential is perhaps one of the most impactful downsides of teleworking. Be intentional about creating space using online forums, scheduled brainstorming sessions, or virtual "suggestion boxes" to replicate the infectious nature of synergy and idea flow.

- *Implement real-time employee engagement surveys.* When you go days or weeks without seeing your team in person, tuning into engagement levels becomes more crucial than ever. Teleworkers can quickly slide into feeling overlooked for future opportunities and underappreciated for their work. This will wreak havoc on your company. As fortune would have it, there's an app for that. (Disclaimer—This is the business we are in. Visit us at www.Emplify.com for details.)

- *Use technology to your advantage.* Work flexibility wouldn't be where it is today without the unprecedented advances in technology we have seen. Extend this further by automating HR and administrative functions to be fully accessible online, including health insurance, 401(k)s, supply orders, and development training. Take advantage of the incredible means available to maximize virtual teamwork. A few of the ones we favor are here:
  - For file sharing and storage: Google Drive, Dropbox, Evernote, Box.
  - For project organization and collaboration: Basecamp, Asana, Trello, Teamwork Projects.
  - For group communication: GoToMeeting, FreeConferenceCall .com, Google Hangouts, Uber Conference, Join.me.

And finally, effective telework programs necessitate a certain shift in company culture and language. The 2016 *New York Times* article "Rethinking the Work-Life Equation" reported that although up to 96 percent of employees agreed that they have some flexibility at work, only 56 percent actually believed their organization supported that option, and many employees believed those who requested more flexible schedules were less likely to get ahead (Dominus, 2016). Citing the previous research study, the author explains, "Workplace stress often is more accurately described as workplace guilt."

Moen and Kelly, the researchers of the earlier telework study, argue that when flexibility relies on manager discretion, it deters people from taking advantage of it, tied too closely with ever-impending workplace guilt. Alternatively, companies should strive to embed flexibility into the structure of the workplace and to make it a "default mode rather than a privilege." To be most effective, and most effectively used, ensure that telework policies are clearly understood, readily encouraged, and widely viewed as cost and sanity saving for the organization. Remove the guilt, and incorporate flexibility as a natural, necessary facet of our busy, blurry lives.

10
Chapter

Culture-Friendly Policies
(Or, Why Overlegislation Rarely Pays Off)

G iven the seismic shifts in how we work these days, you would expect workplace policies to be in line too. Sadly, we have found this is rarely the case. Adding to the list of industrial era leftovers, we now present our traditional and outdated notions of how we account for policy administration. A change in policies is overdue for two primary reasons:

- Policies manifest your culture.
- Policies should be relevant to the work they gauge and regulate.

Take a look at these companies that have stripped away traditional beliefs to create something more natural, more sensible, and more successful.

Case in Point: Patagonia, Inc

Blurring the lines between work and play works for them because their employees love the outdoors. Patagonia's reason for being is to build the best product, cause no unnecessary harm, and use business to inspire and implement solutions to the environmental crisis (Us).

They are famed for a rather unstereotypical culture you might expect of outdoor enthusiasts: minimalist style, bias toward simplicity and utility, and a love of wild places, exemplified in founder Yvon Chouinard's book, *Let My People Go Surfing* (Chouinard, 2005). Their sports entail risk, require soul, and invite reflection, and these qualities are demonstrated in their organization. Workers set their own hours, the headquarters is locked on weekends, and people surf during lunch.

They encourage time away with company-sponsored climbing trips, two-month paid parental leaves, and two-month paid sabbaticals to work on environmental projects (Schulte, 2014). They spend significant time outdoors because they believe that to think outside the box, sometimes you need to get outside the cubicle.

Chouinard has coined the term *MBA,* or "managing by absence," as his leadership philosophy (Hamm, 2006). When at the office, he's all in, but he does a lot of business traveling around doing outdoor things and talking to outdoor people. Last year, he and the CEO were together on a fishing trip when they noticed that their feet were cold and their Patagonia waders weren't quite up to the job, so they launched a series of product improvements to remedy them (Hamm, 2006).

They have little interest in mediocre products or fast profits, and they champion environmental preservation. Their unorthodox approach to growth is perhaps best exemplified by their famous 2011 Black Friday ad, "Don't buy this jacket," which took up a full page in *The New York Times* (Don't Buy This Jacket). The company is a talent magnet and receives an average of 900 résumés for every job opening (Hamm, 2006).

Case in Point: Netflix

The Netflix Culture Deck is famed for how effectively it strips and rewrites standard policies (Hastings, 2009). They believe in hiring stunning people and giving them freedom and responsibility as they tackle hard problems. Seems generic enough to be applicable to many companies, but their policies radically reflect those values.

They insist on high performance, not hard work: Sustained "B" level performance, despite an "A for effort," gets a generous severance package, with respect. Sustained "A" level performance, despite minimal effort, gets more responsibility and great pay.

Because they do not track hours per day or per week, they rewrote their vacation policy: "Netflix Vacation Policy and Tracking: There is no policy or tracking. There is also no clothing policy at Netflix, but no one comes to work naked. Lesson: You do not need policies for everything." Similarly, their policy for expensing and travel simply reads, "Act in Netflix's best interest." Rather than try to control, they create a context of freedom and responsibility in which high performers can do great work.

They do not do formalized development like career planning or rotations. They give people the opportunity to develop themselves by surrounding them with stunning colleagues and big challenges. They believe that with the right people, they can have a culture of creativity and self-discipline instead of a culture of process adherence, so they seek qualities like "self-motivating, self-improving, and picks up trash lying on the floor." In their creative-inventive market, the ideal growth model allows for failure and rapid recovery, and too many processes inhibit that. Minimum restrictions generate maximum growth.

Case in Point: Semco Partners

Even among like-minded companies, Semco is on a level all its own. Their deviation began 30 years ago, initiated in large part by owner Ricardo Semler, author of a slew of bestsellers, guest lecturer at Harvard and the Massachusetts Institute of Technology, and by all accounts a brilliant eccentric. He believes in responsibility but not hierarchy, and he thinks strategic planning and vision are barriers. He disputes the value of growth, control, and measuring success in numbers at all. He says they're looking for wisdom: "We've all learned how to work on Sunday night, but very few of us have learned how to go to the movies on Monday afternoon" (Semler, 2015).

Suffice it to say that with thousands of employees, they had only two people in HR, and thankfully one retired (Semler, 2015). There are no organizational charts, no five-year plans, and no values statements, much less a vacation policy. Workers set their own pay, subordinates hire and review their supervisors, and employees initiate moves into and out of businesses. No one knows how many people they employ, and they never bother to find out because they say employment contracts are too much trouble and it is useless information anyway (Semler, 2014).

In a corporate world of tireless pursuit of growth, they seem unconcerned with it at all. If you and Semco agree you will sell 57 widgets per week and you sell them all by Wednesday, Semler would like you to "Please go to the beach and start again on Monday. Don't create a problem for us and for manufacturing, so we have to buy new companies because you sold too many widgets" (Semler, 2015).

What's more, instead of waiting until retirement to do all the things you've been wanting to do, "Why don't you go and do them next week?" They'll sell you back your Wednesdays for 10 percent of your salary.

Semler says, "I own a $160 million company, and I have no idea what business it's in. I know what Semco does—we make things, we provide services—but I don't know what Semco is. Nor do I want to. Once you say what business you're in, you put employees into a mental straitjacket. It's a ready-made excuse for ignoring new opportunities: 'We're not in that business.'" (Semler, 2014)

Rather than dictate from on high, they let employees shape growth through their individual interests and initiatives. They create conditions for people to get involved and exhilarated, to get to do things their way and see if it works. They give freedom because they've found that with autonomy, people act in their best interests, and by extension their organization's best interests, and that forcing change is the surest way to frustrate change.

When it comes to aligning your rulebook to fit your company, be intentional and strategic, even if it goes against conventional corporate wisdom. If you trust your employees, if you want to give them autonomy and space for creativity, if you want to get the best out of the top talent you've worked hard to get, then structure a context that reinforces and supports the culture you strive to create.

Work Expectations

Changes in work constructs naturally bring corresponding changes in expectations. New values, new motivations. Cognitive work requires a different kind of motivation than manual labor, and many organizations have not kept pace with this. Although obviously not comprehensive, because we are individual people and rows of books already exist on these topics, allow us to present here some top examples.

Flexibility

See Chapter 9, regarding telework. Holistically, though, we are talking about an overall change in language around flexibility as we feebly attempt to squeeze everything into our lives. Let's face it, work-life balance is probably impossible and at the very least precarious and fleeting. We know firsthand about trying to run a company, be involved in community and church groups, spend time with family and friends, and maybe read a book once in a blue moon. We know life can be crazy, and we know how frustrating and unconstructive it is to dwell on this ever elusive muse of "balance."

Many organizations are shifting the terminology from "work-life balance" to "work-life fit," and we find this a much better and more heartening reflection of the needs of our modern business landscape and livelihoods. Our nonwork lives are not an inherent inconvenience, nor a distraction. They should serve as the basis of our existence, enjoyment, and purpose. Work should not deter from nonwork, it should intertwine with it, correlating positively, where well-being with life drives well-being at work, and vice versa.

Acknowledgment of Hard Work

Behavioral economist Dan Ariely conducted several studies on what makes us feel good about our work (Ariely, 2012). In one experiment, he gave subjects a piece of paper with a simple written task to complete. Ariely and the other experimenters reacted in one of three different fashions when the participants handed in the completed assignment. In some cases, they took the paper, looked it up and down, gave a satisfied "uh-huh," and put it on a stack of other papers. In other cases, they gave the paper a brief, noncommittal glance and put it on the pile. And in the third case, they did not even look at the paper. They put it directly through a shredder.

Participants were offered money to complete the tasks, and the amount steadily decreased with each repetition. This continued until participants declined to complete another task, ultimately determining how low they would go before deciding that the money was no longer worth the task.

The people whose work was acknowledged ("uh-huh") continued working until the payout dropped to 15 cents per page. Those whose work was ignored and placed on the pile continued until the payout dropped to 27 cents per page. Finally, participants whose work was immediately, unceremoniously shredded stopped at 30 cents per page.

There are two significant takeaways here: (1) Simple acknowledgment made substantial difference, and (2) ignoring people's performance was essentially the same as shredding their work right in front of their eyes. They conducted numerous similar experiments, and in each, the finding was the same: People clearly derive motivation from more than just money. Provide adequate compensation, certainly, and get the issue off the table, but know that a lot of employees do not go to work just for the paycheck.

Intrinsic Motivation

So we know money is not the only motivation driver or even the biggest driver for employees. Many people place higher value on motivators like meaning, progress, advancement, creativity, challenge, ownership, and pride—intrinsic motivations. If we only took action in return for payment, no one would climb mountains, start companies, or take risks. As humans, we are naturally drawn to challenging ourselves in the hopes of achieving a sense of progress, accomplishment, and self-worth.

We hope that many of you have watched, or at least familiarized yourself with, Daniel Pink's popularized push for autonomy, mastery, and purpose (Pink, 2009). Essentially, he argues that there is a "profound mismatch between what science knows and what business does" when it comes to motivating people at work. In several experiments, monetary incentives proved not only to be ineffective but actually to dull creativity and block thinking. Bonkers, right? So much for our performance bonuses.

Contingent, extrinsic motivators work really well for many industrial age tasks, but, alas, we find ourselves in the industrial era no more. Those contingent, extrinsic rewards narrow our focus and restrict our possibility thinking, which is the last thing we want for competitive innovation and problem solving.

Researchers have replicated these experiments the world over and have consistently found that when tasks call for "even rudimentary cognitive skill, a larger reward leads to poorer performance." Therefore, we need to not just create sweeter carrots and sharper sticks, we need to overhaul the whole approach.

Meaningful Work

Wharton management professor Adam Grant has done extensive research around the importance of mission and connecting work to something meaningful. In his research on "outsourcing inspiration," he found huge gains in productivity when workers were able to see how their work positively impacted other people (Grant, 2010). In some cases, enabling employees to meet one person who benefitted from their work led to a boost in productivity of 400 percent.

Grant proposes that instead of leaders striving simply to motivate employees with their own words, they should instead seek to serve as a "linking pin" to connect employees to the actual people who receive that impact, what he calls "giving the microphone to customers."

To understand these motivations in the workplace, let's flashback to Psychology 101 and Abraham Maslow's Hierarchy of Needs. First published in his 1943 paper "A Theory of Human Motivation" in the *Psychological Review,* Maslow's five-tier pyramid showed a series of needs that could be met only when the one below had been satisfied. Consider the bottom-most level: physiological needs like water, air, food, and shelter. Moving up, we can address safety needs like personal security, financial security, health, and well-being.

Love and belonging needs are interpersonal, like intimacy with friends and family. Esteem is the need to feel respected, accepted, and valued by others, including both self-esteem and self-respect, established through a sense of contribution and value. Self-actualization is the realization of your full potential, or the ability to "be all that you can be" (Maslow, 1943)

So, historically, businesses have met only the first two tiers of our human needs. This is good, but now we need more than that. In order to glean the best imaginable from our minds and compete in a knowledge economy, we need to hit and motivate those upper levels, as well, which is why we see rising trends toward things like community, respect, and mindfulness in the workplace.

One classic example of this: Google developed a leadership program called "Search Inside Yourself" that promotes self-actualization and transcendence at work (Search Inside Yourself Leadership Institute, 2016). They realize that self-actualized people tend to exude characteristics such as innovation, mindfulness, humor, compassion, and creativity, all of which are highly profitable for business. Google is proving that you do not have to choose between inspired employees and financial success. Inspired employees lead to financial success.

Integration and Engagement of the Whole Person

The lines have blurred between personal and professional, and anyway they were false constructs to begin with. We concede that those dichotomies were at least functional in an industrial age, but now they are outdated, counterproductive, and weird when you actually think about it.

According to Yext chief marketing officer Jeff Rohrs, it all comes back to leadership by example. "You should listen more than you talk. You should hold both scheduled and impromptu one-on-ones to gauge the unique needs of both individuals and teams. You should empower and inspire individuals to go beyond their job descriptions, which only happens when you know and show compassion for not only the professional but also the person" (Jeff Rohrs, 2016). Wil Boren, former vice president and general manager at Zimmer Biomet, reiterates the need to lead with love and a servant attitude. "It is easy to default to a leadership style of fear and intimidation, especially in difficult times," says Boren. "But the more your team knows that you will support them in every situation, the more deeply they will engage" (Boren, 2016).

Basically, people need to be seen as humans, not as cogs in a machine. At its extreme, this concept is perhaps best exemplified by women in war zones, as told by humanitarian and entrepreneur Zainab Salbi, founder of Women for Women International (Salbi, 2016). When she went into

Sarajevo, Bosnia, during its nearly four-year siege (the longest siege of a capital city in the history of modern warfare), Salbi asked the women what they wanted her to bring them upon her return. They said "lipstick."

She was baffled. Did they not want vitamins or food or some essential survival items? But they insisted on lipstick, explaining, "It is the smallest thing we put on every day, and we feel we are beautiful, and that is how we are resisting. They want us to feel that we are dead. They want us to feel that we are ugly." One woman said, "I put on lipstick every time I leave because I want that sniper, before he shoots me, to know he is killing a beautiful woman." For these women, resistance swells from staking their humanity. They choose joy, laughter, music, beauty, hope; they refuse to succumb to the midnight of their impossible circumstances. At its core, war dehumanizes us, so to resist is to be human (Salbi, 2016).

By no means are we trying to heedlessly draw comparisons between war and work. War is awful; we do not take it lightly. We merely mean to illustrate the unshakable nature of the human spirit, radiant even in the grimmest of circumstances. If humans in war refuse to be seen as cogs in a machine, then how on earth could we ever presume to impose such scenarios on people in the workplace? It is utterly nonsensical, and it will never work. We are simply too feisty a species. Businesses must engage the whole person because the whole person will shine through in the end.

Community and Corporate Social Responsibility (CSR)

Among these varied, alternative motivators, we want to specifically highlight contributions to the community. People are inspired when the work they do and the people they work with are inspiring. This rings particularly true among millennials, who do not yet face mortgages or childrearing, and who already care more about meaningful work than high pay. We see more and more employees minimizing the emphasis of financial remuneration in favor of an overall outstanding experience.

Here is why this works: Matthieu Ricard is by far the happiest man in the world ever measured by science (based on the relative activation of the left prefrontal cortex as noted in functional magnetic resonance imaging testing). His happiness measures are off the charts. After earning his PhD in molecular genetics, he became a Himalayan monk. And the thing is, this French scientist-turned-Buddhist-monk happiness guru is happiest of all when he is thinking about compassion.

This has tremendous implications. Compassion and happiness go hand in hand—good for our own well-being, good for society, and good for business. And it fundamentally works. Our brains actually change when we train in altruism (Ricard, 2015). Does it take 10,000 hours of meditation? Nope, not even close. Twenty minutes a day, for four weeks, of caring, mindfulness meditation already brings a structural change to our brains. (They even tested it with preschoolers and got them to all like each other—a feat, truly).

Grassroots efforts driven by compassion are popping up all the time. At many companies, the whole social responsibility team begins with two employees who simply want to do it, and the company says, "Okay." You don't need a big budget or hundreds of employees to make a difference.

Case in Point: Pass It Forward

At Creative Quarterback, community involvement takes the form of a grass-roots effort called Pass It Forward. Because the company has zero employees (everyone is freelance), and its small business budget would not allow the level of direct monetary giving that founder Nicole Ross aspired to, she did what she does best—she got creative.

She launched Pass it Forward, a win-win program that dramatically improves the marketing and online presence of animal welfare nonprofits through teamwork. (Learn more at www.creativequarterback.com/passit forward.) Through an innovative combination of freelancer discounted and donated services, plus a $15,000 fundraising campaign, the virtual agency took it upon itself to "build a marketing budget" for the only open-admission, truly no-kill animal shelter in Indiana.

Over the next six months, The Humane Society for Hamilton County received an agency-quality marketing facelift, including a new brand suite, marketing collateral, photography and videography, and a complete website overhaul that they would never have been able to afford otherwise. (See it at www.hamiltonhumane.com.) Creative Quarterback clients who sponsored the effort received discounted marketing services and publicity. Freelancers were paid for their services. Though Ross personally bypassed any financial incentive, she received the greatest gift of all—knowing her small business helped advance a cause about which she is passionate.

Compassion incites vibrant, energetic communities where people respect and admire each other. It promotes collaboration, initiative, and creativity. In other words, it promotes highly effective companies. What could be more of a win-win than that?

Chapter

Recruiting Revolution
(Or, Why Hiring for Intangibles Makes a Tangible Difference)

Innovative, community-minded workers abound in the workplace of now. Companies have realized that hiring top talent with these traits (and more) will affect not only their bottom line but their communities at large. Employers have started expecting and hiring for these new qualities. Although many traditionally held notions like strong work ethic, integrity, intelligence, and communication skills still carry significant weight, they're no longer enough. Today's workforce needs more.

As Brad Morehead, CEO of LiveWatch Security says, "In order to create a compelling culture, you must have a passion for something. Your true passion may not be home security, vinyl replacement windows, or finance contracts. So how do you find passion in more mundane industries? We try to find people with a passion for helping customers or beating the competition. They can become passionate about almost any product or service."

Here are several characteristics employees need in the workplace of now.

A Lifelong Desire to Learn

The world moves at rapid-fire pace, and the truth is, probably no knowledge worker today will use only the information gleaned from a degree for the rest of his or her career. That person would be shoved into irrelevancy within the decade, maybe sooner. Hire not just for knowledge, but for potential knowledge—for the proven ability to develop and self-teach, for the desire to learn and grow.

In the midst of new innovations sprouting like weeds, poise yourself and your organization to be in a constant state of learning. Compared with other animals, humans have bigger brains relative to our bodies (Gopnik, 2013). We are smarter, more flexible, more adept at learning, and far better at adapting to and surviving in varied environments.

For whatever reason, many people live under the notion that adults cannot learn as well as children, but recent research contradicts this belief. The prevailing thinking used to be that adult neuroplasticity was slow and ultimately insignificant, but bring out the books and bubbly, because it turns out adults are actually much better at learning than we often think we are (Okell, 2015). No more excuses to not be lifelong learners because even the oldest of dogs can still learn new tricks.

Insatiable Curiosity

"Passion" has been trending lately in cover letters and interviews, and we feel it is a little overrated. What really drives lifelong learning, innovation, and sustained motivation is not actually passion, but curiosity. Passion ebbs and flows. Passion intimidates. Passion is rare, and honestly a fairly unreasonable expectation for many fields. If you are a single-minded, wildly talented, successful jazz musician, then sure, passion likely played a big role in getting you to that point.

But for the rest of us, oftentimes passion can be hard to decipher, much less to follow. Can we really ask employees to be passionate about their work when their work is just not that invigorating? Would you be passionate about balance sheets, or data analytics, or phone calls with disgruntled customers?

Instead, focus on curiosity. Curiosity is accessible, and multidimensional, and sustainable for the long haul. Curiosity invites open-minded discussion, critical thought, and inclusive cooperation.

Adaptability

In the face of such a turbulent, wildly unpredictable business environment, being able to react quickly is highly valuable. Closely tied to curiosity and learning, adaptability entails the foresight to anticipate change, the confidence to believe you can change, and the independence to see it through swiftly and efficiently.

Let's take a peek at how adaptable we humans can be. Daniel Kish was born with an aggressive form of retinal cancer and had both of his eyes removed by the age of 13 months. Instead of resigning himself to "hapless exposure to the ravages of the dark unknown" that we as a society so often believe about blindness, he has adapted, and he has done so tremendously. In fact, Daniel Kish, navigates the world using echolocation, which he calls FlashSonar, by clicking his tongue and listening to how the sound echoes off the surfaces of his surroundings (TED). He is so acutely attuned to the specific acoustics of his environment that he can ride a bike along a busy street and recognize a building from up to 1,000 feet away (Finkel, 2012).

He says, "I have always regarded myself much like anyone else who navigates the dark unknowns of their own challenges. Is that so remarkable? I do not use my eyes. I use my brain. . . . We all face the dark unknown which is endemic to most challenges, which is what most of us fear. But we all have brains that activate to allow us to navigate the journey through these challenges" (Kish, 2015).

Kish does not have supersonic hearing, and he insists that anyone could learn FlashSonar. He founded a nonprofit, World Access for the Blind, that has disseminated his methods and courage to more than 10,000 students in 40 countries. Our brains are naturally inclined and designed to adapt; do not underestimate what they are capable of.

Learning Agility

How quickly can employees learn and master new tasks? Decades ago, we generally believed that our brains were largely static, unchanging masses. Intelligence, ability, discipline, creativity, compassion: We either lucked out and had them, or we didn't. But relatively recently, neuroscientists have started discovering just how much the brain is capable of changing.

In one case, a five-year-old boy had his left cerebral hemisphere removed, which houses the language centers of our brain and enables us to both understand and produce speech. In spite of this, his right hemisphere compensated by rewiring to form the necessary substrata, and the boy developed above normal adult language and intellectual capacities (Smith and Sugar).

The human brain can do that, and yet we sometimes find it difficult to break bad habits, or pick up new tricks. Happily, mental discipline is like a muscle, and exercising it actually makes it stronger. In our brains, we have neural networks made of neurons communicating with other neurons in circuits, and we can create and affect these circuits for ourselves. The more we employ certain thinking patterns, or neural circuits, the more impetus those circuits have to run again with less external stimulation (Taylor, 2010).

So what is first a conscious decision, when repeated, can become rewired as an unconscious circuit. When we learn new things and develop habits, our brain is essentially carving out new pathways. It takes a while to carve them deeply enough, but eventually we can work to reroute our circuitry by directing a willingness to change it. Our minds are highly sophisticated "seek and ye shall find" instruments. We are designed to focus in on whatever it is we are looking for.

Mental Discipline and Clarity

In a world made "always on" by our devices, mental clarity makes all the difference, for everything from critical thought to emotional intelligence, focus and productivity to proper disagreement, and a host of other useful and highly coveted abilities. What we are learning is that these abilities are extremely malleable through intention and discipline. Experts say that mindfulness—awareness and discipline of the mind—is "self-directed neuroplasticity."

One area in particular in which we find the positive effects of mental discipline pertinent and fascinating is creativity. Traditionally, many of us hold the view that creativity is some abstract, untamable thing bestowed on the lucky few, simultaneously exalting and dooming them to a life of tortured artistry. And maybe that bears some truth in part, that there is something ethereal about it.

But interestingly, a doctor, researcher, and musician by the name of Charles Limb has set out to study the creative brain like any other complex neurological process. While observing musicians' brains in action, he found something intriguing: One area of the brain was significantly suppressed in activity level, whereas activity in another area shot through the roof (Limb, 2011).

As he summarizes, the findings are fascinating because they show a simultaneous "turning off" of an area that is thought to be involved in conscious self-monitoring and a "turning on" of an area that is thought to be autobiographical or self-expressive. His research indicates that in order to be creative, we have to be uninhibited enough to make mistakes, for it is in that state of flow, free from repressive conscious self-monitoring, in which we can best generate novelty.

Why does this all matter? Because we can practice it. We can practice entering the flow state; we can practice suppressing our inhibitions in order to maximize creativity. At its core, we are inhibited by fear: fear of failing, of looking foolish, or of having nothing worthwhile to contribute. Creativity innately invokes uncertainty, and that can be scary stuff. So a huge part of creating is just getting out of our own way, and that is a discipline we can craft. And in a world run by innovation and human capital, it is a discipline we should expect from and seek out in others.

Imagination

Beyond people who excel at learning, organizations also need possibility thinkers—those who dare to dream bigger than everyone else. Like the other qualities we have outlined, imagination becomes more important as knowledge becomes more accessible. The information is out there, and now we compete on how to best channel it.

Scott Barry Kaufman, a psychologist at the University of Pennsylvania, characterizes the imagination quotient as the ability to envision new realities by forming mental representations of things not immediately palpable to our senses. It is something we use in processes like planning for the future, empathizing with strangers, reading an audience, outwitting an opponent, and creating something beautiful or useful. Growing evidence suggests that traditional intelligence testing does not quite capture this coveted skill, and that imagination actually springs from a different part of our brain entirely (Llewellyn, 2014).

Sir Ken Robinson, a prominent thinker and innovator on the realms of education and creativity, advocates for revamping our education systems to parallel the needs of our evolving, postindustrial society. He defines creativity as applied imagination, or the process of putting our imagination to work (Robinson, 2014). Imagination allows us to enter other people's worldviews, to empathize with circumstances and frameworks other than our own. And again, creativity invokes a certain suppression of our own self-monitoring and a preparation to be wrong.

Willingness to Be Wrong and the Humility to Learn

We have all seen it, in religion, in politics, and in boardrooms: the dangerous and polarizing nature of absolute, heartless conviction. Have an opinion and stand your ground, sure, but oftentimes we find that people who are so convinced of their absolute truth are disconcerting and, frankly, a little terrifying.

There is nothing wrong with not knowing, with asking questions, with voicing dissent. We are human, and therefore we are imperfect. Companies want to hire workers who have let go of this demand for certainty and embrace that sometimes we have to discover and learn together.

There are many hazardous side effects of cultures in which people are afraid to voice doubt or dissent. Management consultant Margaret Heffernan expands on one that she dubs willful blindness. In studies of corporations across the United States and Europe, she found that 85 percent of people said there were questions or issues at work they were afraid to raise—they recognize that there is a problem, but they neglect to say anything about it. She found that the numbers remain consistent across countries and demographics, and that under certain circumstances we are all guilty of and prone to being willfully blind (Heffernan, 2014).

In many organizations, change stems from people just deciding to do or say differently and discovering that they are actually far less alone than they feared. The real danger in organizations, she poses, is silence, with "all those brains whizzing around full of observations and insight and ideas that are not being articulated" (Heffernan, 2014).

12

Technology Revolution
(Or, Why Technology Turned the Tables on How We Work)

N ot surprisingly, qualities like imagination and exploration have been a driving force behind the technology boom of recent years. Technology is moving at a blazing pace, and if harnessed well, it can have huge impacts on your people management strategies by fostering collaboration. Financial outperformers are 57 percent more likely than underperformers to use collaborative and social networking tools to enable teams to work more effectively together (Working Beyond Borders, 2010).

Digital Transformation

Pierre Nanterme, CEO of Accenture, identifies three phases of digital transformation: digital customer, digital enterprise, and digital operation (Nanterme, 2015). We have already seen the rise of the digital customer, in how we learn about and engage consumers through technology. Now we are seeing this same hyperpersonalization emerge in the second phase, the digital enterprise. Within companies, we are going digital in how we run operations like HR and Finance. And we are already beginning the final phase, what Nanterme dubs "digital operation," and what most people know as the Internet of things, where physical objects will be able to collect and exchange information instantaneously through the cloud.

Similarly, Michael Porter delineates three waves of information technology (IT)–driven competition that have radically shaped the past 50 years. The first wave, in the 1960s and 1970s, "automated individual activities in the value chain." This included things like order processing and payroll. The second wave flowed from the rise of the Internet in the 1980s and 1990s, enabling coordination across geographic and time borders. And now, the third wave unleashes IT as an integral part of smart, connected products themselves, or the Internet of things (Porter, 2014).

Going digital is a hot topic right now, but, like engagement and culture, people often toss the idea around abstractly, without really knowing how to actually dive in and get started. It's not about adding a digital board member, or a chief technology officer, or a sleek new website, though of course those can all be good and worthy things. It's also not a magical solution to all your problems. It's about leveraging technology to run a leaner, smarter, more agile, more engaged, more *fill in your blank here* business. It's not necessarily changing your end goal, it's opening up new creative possibilities.

When "being digital" in and of itself is not the end goal, no industry is excluded. You may never offer a specifically digital product, but that holds no barrier to digitizing your HR systems. As Wharton Professor Eric Clemons states, "Digital transformation is probably about as big a deal as the invention of credit. It changes the way we do everything. That's not to say there have not been digital transformations before, but those are localized. What makes today's modern, digital transformation different is that it's practically all-pervasive. It's not transforming a part of the business. It's transforming the structure and the strategy of the entire business" (Clemons, 2015).

Technology Trends

As with most trends, we can look at the digital transformation positively or negatively. We can emphasize its volatility and complexity and defend ourselves against it. Or we can highlight its innovation and potential and focus on how to leverage its energy to create value for our constituents. As with most disruptive innovations, it can be a little shaky starting out. But soon enough it will be mainstream, and improved, and scalable. We choose and control our mindset, and in order to stay competitive, we have to choose to embrace these changes early and figure out how to make them work. Here are three key technological trends in the works.

- **Trend A: Systems of record → Systems of engagement**
  - Geoffrey Moore coined this term in a 2010 report called "Systems of Engagement and the Future of Enterprise IT: A Sea Change in Enterprise IT." He focused on how Internet access and expanding mobile use are driving what he calls the consumerization of IT (Aiim, 2016).
  - Now HR is undergoing the same radically disruptive shift, propelling us toward the consumerization of corporate systems.
  - It's a repurposing of HR software, a shift from back office data automation used by HR people to self-service platforms used by everyone.
  - Users do not want more features and functions; they want convenience, engagement, and ease of use.
- **Trend B: Separation → Integration**
  - As knowledge workers, we do not innately separate work and life in our minds.
  - Our old social constructs did that for us, because industrial life was pretty distinct from family life. But now we think about all of it all the time. I am one person, with one brain, and if I am stressed about work I will probably be stressed at dinner too.
  - Work and life are very much intermingled. It's not about keeping them separate, it's about keeping ourselves feeling like we are in control.
- **Trend C: Longer sessions → Shorter, more frequent intervals**
  - We first noticed it in our food.
    - In the late 1970s, only 10 percent of Americans snacked three or more times a day (Akst, 2014).
    - In 2014, 90 percent of consumers reported snacking multiple times throughout the day (Snacking Opportunities, 2015, 5).
  - Then we noticed it in our communication.
    - We used to call friends once in a while and talk for a good chunk of time.
    - These days, we talk with our friends in assorted little anecdotes via texts throughout the week.
    - Now we notice it everywhere—long-form journalism to blurb articles, quality clothing pieces to disposable fashion, albums to

songs, Facebook rants to Twitter quips. This, short-attention-span readers, is the snackification of life. And it is absolutely happening in our work as well. We seek real-time collaboration, immediate feedback, and quick turnarounds. We juggle multiple work items interspersed with a steady stream of checking our email. We work throughout the day at home, in the office, and everywhere in between.

Some of this snackification can be attributed to our devices. Interestingly, Phil Libin, CEO of Evernote, notes that screen size actually matters much less than session length. On a desktop computer or laptop, we may easily sit for a couple hours at a time. On a phone, we spend probably 5 minutes, but we do it 20 times a day instead of once. And on a watch, we may spend 5 seconds (Libin, 2015). Fundamentally, this comes down to an issue of design. How do we best make someone productive during 5-minute sessions 20 times a day?

Let's take corporate learning as an example. In their 2015 Global Human Capital Trends report, Deloitte reveals that 85 percent of companies said learning was "important" or "very important," up from just 21 percent in 2014. And alarmingly, the capability gap between importance and organizations' readiness to deal with it erupted by 211 percent from 2014 to 2015 (Global Human Capital Trends 2015, 25). Corporate America is still trying to catch up with the way people learn and consume information.

How do people want to learn? In personalized, bite-sized chunks, on demand. Sound familiar?

As we have touched on before, we can't just take previous classroom materials and awkwardly shove them into a mobile learning platform. We have to design for the mobile experience. Most people can more fully comprehend information in bite-sized pieces than in a one-sitting blitz, which makes mobile an ideal tool for corporate learning. This style reflects our natural orientation to mobile versus desktop. No one wants to stare at their phone for 3 straight hours the way we so aptly relish time with our desktop computers. We are naturally inclined toward shorter modules, maybe 5 to 20 minutes, and mobile devices lend themselves perfectly to those expectations.

Mobile learning also gives the opportunity to be extremely personalized. It is on-demand learning at its finest. We can choose where and when we learn, at what pace, by ourselves or with a group. We can cherry-pick topics that are especially pertinent. Individual learners suddenly get much more flexibility and autonomy to learn in the way that is best for them. It also grants us just-in-time learning, essential for success in our dynamic environment. We cannot afford to wait until next quarter when HR will give a group training session; we need the information now. Ultimately, e-learning gives employers and employees scalability and accessibility.

Technology Upended Work

Technology has turned work on its head. Technology entangles us in a hyper-connected workplace, it affords us improved means of collaboration, and it reshapes our whole relationship with and conception of work. Here are a few examples of this influence.

Office Space

The traditional office space is dying. Previously, we discussed how our devices have untethered us from the confines of a desk and revolutionized our cognitive relationships with work. Instead of just being physically present at work during designated hours, we are mentally present with work virtually non-stop. Technology tears down our disparate silos between people within the workplace and between our personal and professional lives. The nature of the technology we use shapes the way we work, for better or for worse. We see this in our modern day struggles to navigate work-life balance, and we also see it in the way teams are adapting and improving collaboration—how we communicate, brainstorm, make decisions, and produce.

Teams

Interestingly, the collective intelligence of a group exists separately from the sum of members' individual IQs. Putting all the smartest people together will not necessarily produce the smartest answers. Consequently, many firms now are transitioning to studying, analyzing, and improving not just individual performance, but teams'. With the collaborative, team-based nature of today's workplace, competitive companies optimize not just how people work, but how they work *together*.

A recent Harvard research study found that instead of simply being the sum of individual IQs, the main predictors of group collective intelligence are social sensitivity, the distribution of conversational turn taking, and higher proportions of female group members. Social sensitivity, defined as the ability to empathize with and appreciate someone else's point of view, proved the most powerful correlation, in *both* face-to-face and virtual settings, based on tone of voice, expressions, and other nonverbal cues (Evidence from a Collective Intelligence Factor, 2010). Even when we cannot actually see our fellow group members' faces, our ultimate collective success depends on our ability to perceive and keep track of what other people feel, infer, and believe (Woolley, Malone, & Chabris, 2015).

Similarly, a recent *New York Times* article traces the efforts of Google's Project Aristotle, which sought to uncover the building blocks of a perfect team. After studying and analyzing hundreds of Google's teams, they found that the "who" mattered much less than the "how," paralleling the study mentioned earlier. Project Aristotle researchers turned to group norms in how participants treated each other, and they settled on the concept of "psychological safety," which basically surmises the same social sensitivity and communication abilities unearthed in the other research findings. It boils down to interpersonal trust and respect, which, when we really think about it, is almost painfully obvious. Work occupies so much of our time, mental faculties, and well-being that we need to be able to feel some degree of psychological safety there (Duhigg, 2016).

Indeed, competitive innovation in today's world demands more than one-to-one collaboration. We are seeing a significant, more than welcome shift from channels designed for one to one (email communications) to channels designed for many to many, another example of how technology shapes the way we communicate, ideate, and produce.

Email

The end of internal email—can we get an amen? Internal communication is outdated and inefficient. Check out these nauseating figures on the leech we strangely hold so dear:

- In one day, more than 100 billion emails are exchanged, and only one in seven is critically important (Global Human Capital Trends 2015, 87).
- For the average interaction worker, 80 percent of email is just following up, copying, and forwarding (The Social Economy, 2012).
- McKinsey dissected the average work week and found that 28 percent is spent reading and answering email, 19 percent searching for information, and 14 percent collaborating internally, which leaves only the remaining 39 percent for actual, role-specific tasks (The Social Economy, 2012).

It is archaic. Email is the ultimate democracy, where a solicitation from a random outsider and a pending action item from the company senior vice president are awarded the same bit of space, in order of arrival. Maybe that worked in 1995 when email was novel and fun, but when managers get hundreds of emails a day, it's completely unsustainable. As company executives, we receive hundreds of emails each day, and, if we're honest, we read only a sliver. Something has to give.

We understand intuitively the power of social technologies to track consumer data, gather insights, and bolster customer support. Seventy-two percent of companies already use social technologies in some way, but we're still barely scratching the surface of their full potential (The Social Economy, 2012). Twice as much potential value lies in using social tools *internally* to enhance communication, knowledge sharing, and collaboration within and across the organization, proven to raise the productivity of knowledge workers by 20 to 25 percent. A central, searchable, internal record can reduce by 35 percent the 7+ weekly hours employees spend hunting for company information (The Social Economy, 2012).

Case in Point: Luis Suarez of IBM

Luis Suarez, a knowledge management consultant at IBM, epitomizes this perfectly, so much so that he earned the nickname "the amazing email-less man." In 2008, Suarez returned from an offsite event to the welcoming arms of several hundred unread emails, and he knew he had to figure out a better way.

As an in-house social software expert, he suspected he could skirt email almost entirely and hatched a self-experiment. From 2008 to 2012, he reduced his email inbox by a whopping 98 percent (The Social Economy, 2012). The secret to his success? He stopped responding to emails with emails, and he started transferring his would-be email replies to IBM's social sphere instead.

Suarez estimated that 80 percent of his, and the average interaction worker's, email volume was just from following up, copying, and forwarding (The Social Economy, 2012). He reasoned that if more of his communication was in the open, he would spend less time communicating. Brilliant. In addition to saving his own sanity, he credits the social platform replacements with increased knowledge sharing, improved discussions and interactions, and a consolidated, searchable base of information (McMillan, 2012).

Chapter 13

Mobile Revolution

(Or, Why It's Okay to Leave Early for Your Kid's Soccer Game)

Technology, as a whole, has clearly changed the nature of work in a massive and irreversible way. However, one particular subset of tech space has contributed far more than its fair share. Mobile technology has completely changed how we live, interact, and work.

Apple released the first iPhone in 2007 (Apple Reinvents the Phone with the iPhone, 2007), and eight years later 85 percent of young adults in the United States had a smartphone subscription (Smith, 2015). From 2012 to 2015, mobile marketing grew from a $139 billion business to a $400 billion industry (Bennett, 2014). People expect what they want when they want it, and it's transforming the fundamental underpinnings of how we do business. Smart companies are embracing these trends and seeing bottom line results as the market continues to explode.

Comparing original Internet growth to mobile growth is very telling of the impacts. In 1990 the Internet began amassing mainstream consumer appeal. By 1999 more than half a million websites had fundamentally changed consumer behavior (Total Number of Websites, 2016). Previously, when consumers were searching for information, they would search in print in publications like the Yellow Pages and find data in libraries. In just a decade, the Internet changed that instant impulse of where to look for information from print to online.

Then along came mobile. In 2011, a little more than two years after the birth of mobile apps in 2008, we already had about 500,000 apps. It took only two years to significantly change consumer behavior. What Internet did in nine years, mobile apps did in two. We now begin a majority of our searches through mobile apps (Apple, 2011). We input an address into a mapping app. We hail a cab through an app. We take photos with an app. We communicate with loved ones in other locales through an app. Essentially, we live out the majority of our digital lives through mobile apps.

Analysts call the world we live in today the post-PC world. In 2011, for the first time ever, smartphones outsold personal computers (Smart Phones Overtake Client PCs in 2011, 2012). Every year since then, smartphone sales have grown exponentially and are leaving PCs in the dust. Smartphones reached a billion people significantly faster than PCs did (Dover, 2012). And by 2020, 80 percent of adults on earth will have a smartphone (Benedict).

In fact, many countries and demographics are electing to skip the PC revolution altogether and simply go straight to smartphones. It makes sense. Smartphones are more affordable and more portable, use less energy, ship cheaper, and overall skirt many barriers to market entry faced by PCs. They are unquestionably becoming the standard means of communication and access.

In the United States, TV reigned supreme for more than 50 years as the dominant device on which Americans spent the most time per day. In 2012, mobile surpassed PCs in daily usage by the average American, but TV maintained its strong lead. But in 2014, mobile phones outstripped TV as the one device on which Americans spent the most time per day. Smartphones have officially knocked TVs off their 50-year pedestal and become the most used technology in our lives (Khalaf, 2014).

The average U.S. worker spends more time on a smartphone than on any other technology: 3 hours and 40 minutes per day, on a phone (Khalaf, 2015). Eighty-eight percent of consumer mobile Internet time is spent in apps, with only 12 percent browsing the mobile Web (Apps and Mobile Web, 2014, 3).

And it's not just the portability, it's the experience. We see change in two significant dimensions: (1) breadth, becoming ubiquitous across the world, and (2) depth, driving individual usage, engagement, and time.

Reaching Your Audience

Mobile communications through apps are the best way to meet audiences. Employees *are* consumers, and those consumers are on their smartphones, already communicating inside apps. Organizations who want to communicate with their consumers (i.e., their employees) need a relevant way to meet those consumers in their smartphones.

We already turn to mobile phones for "just-in-time" information, such as turn-by-turn directions when driving, breaking news and world events, and upcoming social activities. They're time critical, responsive, accessible, and interactive, and our brains cannot get enough. Mobile is barging into the work scene hard and hitting the ground running. By 2017, there will be an estimated 328 million workers worldwide using their own smartphones at work. Enterprise app activations are growing at an exponential rate even from quarter to quarter—for example, a 42 percent to 54 percent increase in one quarter in 2013 (Fried, 2014).

Eighty-seven percent of millennial smartphone users say their smartphones never leave their side, day or night. Forty-one percent of millennials say they are likely to download applications in the next year to use for work purposes and use their own money to pay for them. Forty-five percent of them already use smartphones for work purposes, compared with 18 percent of older generations. And nearly two-thirds agree that in the next five years, everything will be done on mobile (Meeker, 2016).

Which naturally raises the question, how do we prepare for this? Tempting though it is, we cannot just take everything from our desktop computers and transplant it into a mobile app. "Mobile friendly" does not equate to "mobile first." As users, we interact with mobile fundamentally differently than we interact with desktop Web. User interfaces and user experiences (UI/UX) for mobile entail some face-value enhancements, such as integration with phone functions (i.e., easily calling a number listed on a Web page), or the design elements of a vertical versus horizontal screen orientation. Some aspects seem insignificant but in actuality contain a vastly different experience and design. Some examples are listed next.

- *Content prioritization.* Spatially, we cannot present as much information on mobile, yet we still need to figure out how to present everything that is pertinent to the user.
- *Shorter session lengths.* On a desktop computer, we could sit and sift for 2 to 3 hours at a time. On a smartphone, that shrivels to around 5 to 10 minutes.
- *One thumb versus 10 fingers.* Given how transient most mobile-goers tend to be, we can assume users will be holding their phones in one hand, clicking and swiping with one thumb.
- *Gesture actions.* Beyond the classic touch and click, mobile users intuitively know to do things like swiping to go back, and these fine-tuned motor functions enhance UX.

- *Simplicity, functionality, and usability.* When time is scarce and space tight, the best mobile experiences eliminate all unnecessary elements that could potentially detract from the ultimate goals of simplicity and usability.

- *Minimalist color schemes.* Simpler designs with a splash of color or other enhanced features draw attention to the key content and ideal flow.

Cutting through the Clutter with Mobile Apps

Mobile apps are perfectly positioned to meet the ever-changing needs of the workplace, optimizing organizational effectiveness and providing the best means of communicating with employees. Why?

- *Mobile apps engage.* Meet employees where they are, which is largely on their devices. Mobile apps present a single, focused, purpose-built tool for internal communication teams.

- *Mobile apps integrate.* In a world plagued by infobesity and inundated inboxes, employees need a central hub where they can readily access information. Email is losing relevance and effectiveness.

- *Mobile apps snackify.* They provide a way to gather feedback, promote recognition, boost productivity, increase transparency and alignment, and centralize communication and resources—all in short, frequent, on-demand bursts.

Mobile apps take these marketing principles, take these overarching workplace shifts, and readily apply them to employee needs. They can be leveraged internally just as successfully as externally, and that truth should be unequivocally intuitive to us as businesspeople. Like for your customers, internal mobile apps provide a beautiful product that fits seamlessly with the reality of the lives of your users, who in this case happen to be your employees.

Employees Connect to HR via Mobile

Outdated HR system, meet smartphone. HR is going mobile, and it's working. Employees are two to five times more likely to access HR applications on their smartphones than on their PCs (Bersin, 2014), and they find them 60 percent more engaging (Mobile Apps Infographic, 2014). This is the consumerization of corporate systems, which essentially means treating employees like we treat customers (Global Human Capital Trends 2014, 100).

Mobile, with its one-click, one-swipe ease, will become HR's primary interface. People expect to get what they want, when they want it. Speed and ease are ever on the rise. So we're talking here about real engagement, material improvements intermingled in daily work, enabling them to do their jobs better. HR is seeing a major shift from static, one-way communications toward a real-time, mobile dialogue of engagement. With the rise of social media, consumers and employees expect two key things from brands: transparency and dialogue. People want a one-stop, easy source to check in, stay up to date, and connect (2014 Mobile Behavior Report, 9).

Mobile Impact on Performance Reviews

Take, for example, the standard annual performance review. First, it's expensive. Adobe found that their performance management process took 1.8 million person-hours per year to complete (Global Human Capital Trends 2015, 89). But mostly, it's archaic.

We live in a world where we can know in literal minutes how many people like our random musings or the wittiest 140 characters we can muster, yet we're expected to wait a year to know if our boss is approving of our work performance? Please take a moment to consider just how outrageous it is that I can get more immediate, measurable feedback on the aesthetics of my lunchtime sandwich than I can on my performance.

This obviously carries weight in the digital native world of millennials, but it rings true for people of all generations. We like to be able to understand how we are doing, what that means, and what to anticipate for the future.

So what if we take this antiquated process and translate it to shorter bursts of real-time feedback on a mobile device? What if we get feedback after each project or presentation, instead of feebly attempting to recall details from 11 months prior that everyone's forgotten and no one cares about anymore?

Nearly all companies want their employees to use their internal networks, and poor HR or IT is accorded the hopeless task of attempting to finagle people into using something no one actually wants to use. Turns out only 13 percent of employees participate in their company's social intranet daily, and 31 percent rarely or never do (How a Mobile First Strategy Can Increase Employment Engagement, 2014).

Some managers express concern with employees using phones at work or working from home. "But how can we know they're working?" they protest. To that we say two things: (1) The lines are already blurred. We cannot ask someone to check their work email on the weekend if we don't also let them call a doctor in the middle of the day. (2) Treat people as adults. If you don't trust your employees to act in your company's best interest, you shouldn't have hired them in the first place. Go rethink your hiring and engagement strategies first, because you have bigger fish to fry.

The reason those are the wrong questions is the distinction between voluntary and involuntary distractions. Tweets, walks, texting—those are voluntary distractions, which means they're not even really distractions, they're just little breaks. Involuntary distractions, on the other hand, often come in the form of ill-timed meetings or taps on the shoulder, actually interrupting you from the task at hand.

We love the way Jason Fried, cofounder of 37signals (We the Basecamp) and author of *Rework*, puts it: "Now, managers and bosses will often have you think that the real distractions at work are things like Facebook and Twitter and YouTube and other websites, and in fact, they'll go so far as to actually ban these sites at work. Some of you may work at places where you cannot get to certain sites. I mean, is this China? That's why people aren't getting work done, because they're on Facebook and Twitter? That's kind of ridiculous. It's a total decoy," (Fried, 2010). He likens today's social media to modern-day smoke breaks, and if no one used to care about letting people take a 15-minute smoke break, why does anyone care about a sporadic YouTube video? Of all the culprits preventing efficiency in today's workplace, Twitter should not be public enemy number one.

The Best of Mobile

Now that we've hopefully freed mobile usage from its rogue miscreant status, let's delve into why we love it and why it's uniquely positioned to meet the demands of our future workplace.

- **It reflects the current state of how people access the Internet and go about their lives.**
  - Ninety-two percent of full-time U.S. workers already use their smartphones for work purposes (BYOD Insights 2013, 4).
  - Of those who use their phones for work, 70 percent are expected to read work emails after hours.
- **Apps are easier to secure for storing and centralizing important information, rather than scattered elsewhere throughout a phone.**
- **Brands with the most seamless, easy-to-access content win.**
  - The top two reasons consumers download mobile apps are "convenient access to information" (65 percent) and "quick access to information" (51 percent).

- Eighty-three percent of consumers said that a seamless experience across all their devices is somewhat or very important (2014 Mobile Behavior Report, 17).

- People want the content they want where and when they want it. Fifty-four percent say mobile-optimized websites do not give enough information (2014 Mobile Behavior Report, 7).

- It's becoming the preferred method of accessing content, and many brands aren't addressing or catering to that.

- Ninety-one percent of consumers say that access to content however they want it is somewhat or very important (2014 Mobile Behavior Report, 17).

- **Apps are not just for games anymore.**
  - Forty-nine percent of consumers have downloaded a business-specific (not gaming or utility) app to their phones (2014 Mobile Behavior Report, 14).
  - Of those who use them, 92 percent say they're useful (2014 Mobile Behavior Report, 23).

- **Consumers follow companies who lead the way.**
  - Sixty-eight percent of consumers say it's important that the brands they interact with are seen as technology leaders (2014 Mobile Behavior Report, 18).
  - How much more potent is this for employees?

- **Social technology holds an almost primal appeal.**
  - We are hardwired to share stories with friends and family, form groups, define relationships, and embrace the stories of others.
  - More than any of our other devices, mobile carries particular emotional attachment. It represents our communities, our plans, our shared information, in a way encompassing all of our daily lives.
  - When asked how social and communication activities on smartphones made them feel, people most commonly reported, "Connected, excited, curious/interested, and productive" (2016 Internet Trends Report, 2016).
  - Already, 85 percent say mobile devices are a central part of everyday life (2014 Mobile Behavior Report, 33).
  - We're talking about major connectivity to our world: 89 percent say mobile helps to stay up to date with friends and family and ongoing activities (2014 Mobile Behavior Report, 6).

- **Mobile apps are the perfect tools to leverage our cloud-based, hyper accessible world.**
  - If Salesforce hasn't yet officially ushered in the "end of software," surely its demise is near at hand.
  - When was the last time you bought a CD of a program and installed it on your computer? Cloud technology has allowed for software, endless amounts of storage, games, and programs of all types to be housed and accessed from the cloud, transitioning our world to one of hyper accessibility.
  - Mobile apps are less costly and more user-friendly when compared with other modes of audience engagement.
- **Mobile is infinitely scalable.**
  - Ten employees, or 10,000 employees? Sure.

According to *The Wall Street Journal* (and every worker we have ever spoken with), "Fight it all you want, but employees *are* going to be bringing their own smartphones, tablets, and other technology to work with them. So it's time to stop resisting and start preparing" (*Should Employees Be Allowed to Use Their Devices for Work?* 2011).

Chapter

Resulting Challenges
(Or, Why Too Much of a Good Thing Is a Bad Thing)

In this information age, many workers are always on the clock (and their phones), doing mentally engaging work, with social media only a touch away. We see more sides of each other in today's workplaces than ever before. In such a collaborative marketplace, innovation is more than a single person's creative application of skills; it's the sum of an organization's capabilities, experiences, and knowledge. Innovation hinges on an organization's ability to streamline processes and technology to adapt to the needs of a quickly changing marketplace.

The real struggle comes not from figuring out how to turn on the technological fire hose but figuring out how to turn it back off when workers reach the tipping point of mental and physical well-being. The workplace is changing, and that's a good thing, but it's affecting us considerably, and we need to learn to properly address these seismic shifts before they swallow us whole.

Infobesity

First, let us discuss one of the most troubling issues technology-loving workers face. Infobesity is an epidemic, and it infects us all.

Blair West, director of corporate communications at Cummins, Inc., explains that in an effort to drive engagement, many organizations have a tendency to hit people over the head with a plethora of programs, offerings, logos, and slogans that only serve to overwhelm their workforce. They are not driving engagement, but adding frustration and unnecessary distraction. We need to help people decipher meaning out of the information overload. Set the tone with a simple, strategic vision that gives people a reason to care. From there, your content should be compelling, easy to navigate, and in bite-sized chunks that allow a person to consume as much as he or she needs. Empower your people with information that they can consume at will, and make it compelling to ensure they do.

IBM released these stupefying figures in 2013: 90 percent of all the world's data had been produced in the past two years (Bringing Big Data to the Enterprise). Computer Sciences Corporation (CSC) examined these numbers and said that in 2015, 90 percent of all the world's data will be equal to approximately 7.9 zettabytes (Computer Sciences Corporation, 2015). That's right, zettabytes. One zettabyte is one trillion gigabytes.

As a leader, your role is to sift through the barrage of information thrown not just at you but also at your employees, customers, and prospects. It's your responsibility to distill the necessary from the noise.

Here are four ways you can help your team avoid infobesity.

- *Not everyone needs to know everything about everyone.* Cross-functional teams are only helpful until they become counterproductive. At some point relaying all information becomes excessive and actually clouds important messages. Wharton professors Massey and Grant dub this phenomenon "collaboration creep," when too many meetings and emails balloon interdependence and end up overwhelming everyone (Grant & Massey, 2015).

- *Personal time does not equal work time.* Just because you *can* check work email first thing when you awake and right before you fall asleep does not mean you have to, or should. Give yourself and your employees some free, restful mental space to recover. Set clear expectations about when employees should be accessing data and when they can be disengaged. Allow employees the opportunity to be freed from the electronic ties that bind them.

- *Lists, lists, lists.* Whatever's distracting you, write it down somewhere so you don't have to remember to remember it. Staying organized frees your brain to focus on those things that are important right now. Don't hesitate to create lists for your employees either. By doing so, you and your employees can better discard the excessive noise and focus on your goals.

- *Too many choices make it too hard to choose.* People who are overwhelmed by choices often choose nothing at all (i.e., analysis paralysis). Consider cutting the bottom 10 percent of your products—they're probably just distracting people from your best goods. Studies show that people are much more likely to buy things when their options are more clear cut. If you need help determining which options are important, ask your employees. If they cannot articulate the value, neither can your consumers.

By implementing some or all of these best practices, you can stave off infobesity in your workforce and customer base and enhance overall engagement.

JP Rangaswami, a self-described "accidental technologist" who now works as chief data officer at Deutsche Bank, theorizes and blogs on information. He presents the idea of information as food, where the fundamental issue is not production but consumption (Rangaswami, 2012). Energy and information are our two forms of input, one fueling our body and the other our mind. So, just as we regulate our diet and exercise (some better than others), we ought to balance our information intake and protect our mental faculties. Like food, information can have toxins, sell-by dates, and mashups. We have found it to be a helpful, familiar framework as we wrap our heads around the relatively new, rather indigestible concept of infobesity.

Overworked Employees

Coupled with the rise of infobesity, organizations around the world identify "the overworked employee" as an urgent workplace challenge, and nearly half of executives aren't prepared to deal with it (Deloitte, 2014). Employees face an onslaught of organizational complexity, increasing demands, emails, and information, so much so that 40 percent of workers believe it is not possible to simultaneously succeed at work, make a good living, and have enough time to contribute to family and community, which is honestly one of the more troubling workplace statistics we have seen (Deloitte, 2015).

Extraneous Complexity

Peter Drucker wrote that "much of what we call management consists of making it difficult for people to work." And indeed, 74 percent of HR leaders say their workplaces are "complex" or "highly complex" (Global Human Capital Trends 2015, 10). Boston Consulting Group (BCG) has found that complexity among Fortune 500 companies has increased sixfold since 1955 (*Businesses Must Fight the Relentless Battle against Bureaucracy*, 2014).

Bad Meetings

Where do we go when we really need to get work done? We go to the library, to a coffee shop, we come in 2 hours before everyone else. What we certainly do not do is slot our peak productivity for the middle of the day in the middle of the office. But productivity is exactly what the office is for, right? For many of us, our workdays in the office have deteriorated into more of an extended series of work moments. We do a lot of tasks, but we do not actually do any meaningful work, because we can never quite snag a long enough stretch of uninterrupted time.

Prominent venture capitalist Paul Graham originally coined the distinction between makers' schedules and managers' schedules (Graham, 2009). Managers dissect their days into 1-hour intervals where by default they shift gears every hour. In contrast, makers—people like programmers, writers, designers, or developers—prefer and require much larger blocks of time. They tend to think in half days at least because 1 measly hour is barely enough time to cognitively get settled, focused, and rolling. Consequently, for makers, a single 1-hour meeting can be a noisy distraction; it could disrupt and despoil a whole half day of productivity and creativity. Maker spirits positively soar at the prospect of an entire day to do work, unblemished by meetings or interruptions.

In a comically poignant *New York Times* article titled "Meet Is Murder," Virginia Heffernan swoons with us over maker hours that "blend childhood summer-day vagueness with a thick coat of artistic entitlement." She laments with us that most of us worker bees are "managers or managers' minions, ineligible for stretches of solitude, destined for lives of video conferences and call-in codes. We were to return to days chopped, like hot dogs for toddlers, into meetings" (Heffernan, 2016).

Even as managers, we crave those unspoiled, resplendent maker hours. Ever since his days at ExactTarget, Todd has developed the habit of getting up early each day just to get his "work" done before everyone else crowds the calendar. In fact, the only time he really gets anything done in the day is from 6:00 to 9:00 AM. The rest of the day will undoubtedly succumb to the needs and whims of other people and steady workplace demands.

The average white collar U.S. employee spends 15 percent of his or her time in meetings, many of which have no clear purpose. Senior executives spend two full days a week in meetings (*Businesses Must Fight the Relentless Battle*, 2014).

Arthur Angotti, president of Artistic Media Partners, agrees that short meetings are critical: "If you can't make a decision in twenty minutes and delegate execution to the right people in that time, either you have a bad idea or the wrong people" (Angotti, 2016).

We are not saying meetings are inherently vile. We love a well-run, positive meeting with actionable results. We couldn't have written this book without meetings. We are saying that time is the most precious resource we have, that bad meetings are rampant and miserable, and that better meetings are possible, so choose them wisely.

- Try cancelling whatever meeting you have coming up. Not rescheduling, just cancelling. Honestly, most meetings are extraneous, and you'll probably be fine.
- Limit meetings in expectations, participants, and time. A handful of people is ideal, probably no more than seven. Ban fancy PowerPoints internally. Do not try to impress each other, just address what you need to do, respect each other, and get back to work.
- Insist on some blocked off hours. For you, or for your company as a whole. Maybe set aside an afternoon where no one can meet, or email, or talk.

We all know how crazy work can get. Between an inundated inbox, meetings all day, and a carking swamp of routine tasks, before you know it it's time to go home, or it's Friday, or it's next year. Be intentional about leaving some room for the unimagined. Set aside half a day each week to work on big picture projects, to strategize for the future, to envision how you will tangibly get where you are trying to go. This clutter-free, big picture mental space is where our best ideas originate. More important, give your team vision (not just a list of tasks) and empower them to take ownership of getting there.

Emails

We get it, the irony is thick. Todd spent eight years helping send billions of emails as an executive at ExactTarget, the world leader in targeted email communications, and now he works toward helping businesses cut through that email clutter.

But the total number of external communications that managers receive has increased from 1,000 per year in 1970 to 30,000 per year in 2014 (*Businesses Must Fight*, 2014). Divided by 261 working days per year, that's 115 emails per day. Do you have time for that? Neither do we. In one day more than 100 billion emails are exchanged, but only one in seven is critically important. The average employee now spends more than 25 percent of the workday reading and answering emails (Global Human Capital Trends 2015, 87). Something has to give.

Overall Complexity

Despite the barrage, 72 percent of employees say they still cannot find the information they need within their company's systems (Deloitte, 2014). Simplification is dire and overdue, and HR can take the initiative to streamline processes for maximum efficiency, productivity, creativity, and collaboration. The phase of investing in technology because it was trendy is over. Employees today have not one iota of care for any technology that does not materially make their lives better. Whole industries have been rocked by innovations that simplify the way we live, and the workplace is next in line.

HR has a regrettable reputation for being more of a hindrance than a help. Instead, HR should aim to be a catalyst to make people more productive and engaged, to rethink our underlying models of how work gets done, and to enable people by optimizing systems for how they want to work. It's high time for entire organizations to declutter and simplify communications, disentangle processes, and consolidate information.

Treat "time capital" with the same gravity you allot financial capital, and start by simplifying complexity through integrated technology. Time is the most valuable resource we have. No one can buy more, we can only more effectively maximize it. Declutter needs to be a top priority. Knowledge workers spend a great deal of their time, 41 percent average, on discretionary activities that offer little personal value and could be handled competently by others (Birkinshaw & Cohen, 2013). We instinctively cling to tasks that make us feel busy and important. Think consciously about how you spend your time and what adds value to your organization, and drop or creatively outsource the rest.

In today's global, volatile, uncertain world, the best business leaders stand out as catalysts. They set the vision, they create a high level of engagement to motivate people, and they make change possible to execute.

The director of BCG's Institute for Organization, Yves Morieux, proposes several rules for dealing with complexity:

- *Understand what others do.* Beyond their stated job description, what is their real, everyday work?
- *Remove layers.* When there are too many layers, people are too far from the action and need to supplement with key performance indicators and metrics, poor proxies for reality.

- *Empower people.* Give people enough authority that they can use their own judgment, intelligence, and skills.

The real battle, he poses, is not against competitors. "This is rubbish, very abstract. When do we meet competitors to fight them? The real battle is against ourselves, against our bureaucracy, our complicatedness. Only you can fight, can do it" (Morieux, 2014).

Potential Solutions

What are companies doing to fight this issue? Some ban emails on Fridays, others forbid internal PowerPoints. Coca-Cola shut down their voicemail to "simplify the way we work and increase productivity" (Global Human Capital Trends 2015, 90). Another company saved the equivalent of 200 jobs by halving the default length of meetings to 30 minutes and limiting number of attendees to a maximum of seven people (*Businesses Must Fight*, 2014).

The methods look different for different organizations, but the motivation of simplifying work and the outcome of more focused, less stressed employees are the same.

People realize more than ever that what they do outside of work profoundly affects their work itself. Our physical health lends nicely to this point. But especially in recent years, concern for mental health has taken off full speed ahead. Mindfulness, meditation, sabbaticals, and yoga have become commonplace at many organizations.

We seem to have reached our brink of information and work overload, and now we are entering an era of "doing less better" rather than "doing more with less." Instead of continuing to work more, we are learning to improve the work process itself.

Smartphones will be, and are already, one of the most important tools invented for increasing the productivity of knowledge workers. They are time critical, responsive, and accessible anywhere. We can leave the office without the fear of missing an important memo.

The biggest downside? They're taking over our mental rest space. We unlock and look at our phones 150 times a day (Global Human Capital Trends 2015, 87). When we work past 9 PM, into the evening, we deplete our productivity for the following day (Barnes, Lanaj, & Johnson, 2014). They compromise our sleep and squander our downtime, even more so than television, laptop computers, and tablets. Smartphones are uniquely unyielding when it comes to our attempts to psychologically detach.

Leslie Perlow, a Harvard Business School Professor of Leadership and author of *Sleeping with Your Smartphone*, has taken a special interest in the detrimental effects of smartphones and how we can best circumvent those. "Let's face it," she writes, "when that phone buzzes, few of us have the mental fortitude to ignore it." She suggests that most of our frenzy around smartphones stems from what she dubs the "cycle of responsiveness." Our jobs are legitimately more unpredictable than they used to be, stretching across time zones and physical workspaces, and so we adapt our devices and our habits to meet these demands (Perlow, 2012).

Once others see that we are responsive, they expand expectations accordingly. Under the mounting pressure to be always on, our conscientiousness perpetuates the cycle, and soon we're trapped. "When we are trapped," she says, "we don't think about better, faster, more effective ways of working. Rather, we just keep working more and more, perpetuating and amplifying the bad intensity in our work, which includes those unnecessary iterations, the lack of communication and alignment, the last-minute, late-night changes, and those weekend 'emergencies' that get in the way of doing our best at work and having time for life outside of work" (Perlow, 2012).

In her book, she conducts an experiment with some of the most high-strung workers imaginable: the weary dynamos of BCG. By bringing teams together to cover for each other, she gave each person a predictable, agreed-on chunk of time off. In the experiment, 54 percent of participants with paid time off (PTO) reported satisfaction with work-life balance, versus 38 percent of participants without it. Similarly, 72 percent of those with PTO reported satisfaction with the job itself, versus 49 percent of those in the control group (Perlow, 2012). Incremental, self-instigated changes achieved surprising improvements on a stubbornly embedded system.

The good news here is that smartphones in and of themselves are not our enemies. Rather, it's about reconfiguring our relationships with them, taking back some semblance of control. It's about turning off more, while improving the work process itself. Technology, for all its benefits, can amplify the pressures of our jobs, making them feel more overwhelming, more demanding, and less fulfilling than they need to be, not to mention less effective and less efficient than they *could* be. Break the cycle, mitigate the pressure, and free employees to spend time in a way that is more desirable to them both personally and professionally.

Cyborg anthropologist Amber Case examines the way humans and technology interact and evolve together. With the rise of social networks and limitless information, we are developing a sort of entire mental exoskeleton. Our devices demand full attention, to the extent that they interrupt primary, human tasks, like driving, walking, and talking to someone face to face ("Screen Time Part I," 2015).

As strange as it is to think about, we basically have whole second selves online, and people interact with those second selves even when we are not there. Case calls it "ambient intimacy," where though we are not always connected to everyone, we could, at any time, connect to anyone. Psychologically, this is a huge adaptation from how humans have always lived. And consequently, we have to learn to maintain those virtual selves, present them well and congruously with our analog selves. And we need to be intentional about taking time for mental reflection, for slowing down, for disconnecting from all that ambient intimacy in the same way we disconnect from present intimacy.

Chapter

HR of the Past
(Or, Why Manufacturing and Unions Forged HR)

By now, you are probably asking yourself, "How does HR fit into this whole work revolution?" As we have mentioned, HR is not solely responsible for your culture. However, HR plays a massive role (or should) in the future of culture and engagement. Before we examine the future of HR, and how you should evaluate your own, it's important to understand the function's history and evolution. We will briefly highlight the key events to give us the perspective we need to see how we arrived at where we are now.

The Rise of HR

HR as we know it emerged from the Industrial Revolution, first in eighteenth century Europe and then in the United States, from a simple, ceaseless desire to discover better ways to create business value through strategic management. During the Industrial Revolution, labor was one of the many factors of production. In fact, people were interchangeable, even expendable, to some extent, and much more so than expensive machines.

The Bureau of Labor and Unions

Unions arose in resistance to this notion, people naturally demanding to be seen as more than cogs in a machine. Although workers had randomly, briefly unionized throughout the late 1700s and early 1800s in order to accomplish specific goals, unions really began to surge with the founding of the National Labor Union in 1866 and the Knights of Labor in 1869 (National Labor Union, 2016).

In response to calls from the strengthening unions for a national labor agency, the federal government created the Bureau of Labor Statistics in 1884, purposed with collecting, analyzing, and disseminating essential information on labor market activity, working conditions, and price changes in the economy. The Bureau's first commissioner, Carroll Wright, spoke of "the amelioration of unfavorable industrial and social relations wherever found as the surest road to comparatively permanent material prosperity." He viewed the period's perpetual unrest in labor-management relations as a basic essential to improving the human condition, and believed it was the government's duty to provide information to educate those in the midst of it (Goldberg & Moye, 1985, 8).

Interestingly, he was also adamant that facts, not theories, be the cornerstones of constructive action, and that those facts be obtained by "only the most faithful application of the statistical method." Apparently we still have much to learn from this HR pioneer. The Bureau managed to achieve cooperation both from businesses, who provided a significant portion of the data to be distributed, and from unions, who sought investigation and exposure of industry conditions.

In 1911, Frederick Winslow Taylor, perhaps the first notable management consultant, recognized labor as a key factor in the success of the manufacturing process, and saw that improved employee well-being led to improved work. In 1913, largely fueled by the growing power of the unions, the U.S. government created the Department of Labor (DOL), which encompassed the Bureau of Labor Statistics and in a sense promoted it to cabinet-level status. The DOL was tasked with promoting the welfare of workers, improving working conditions, advancing employment opportunities, and ensuring work-related rights. HR began to morph into a means of advocating for and protecting employees (Taylor, 1910).

Unions continued to gain traction through the early 1900s. They briefly veered toward irrelevance in the blinding economic success of the roaring '20s, only to resurge quickly in the Great Depression. Particularly with FDR's New Deal policies in the late 1930s and passage of the National Labor Relations Act of 1935, unions gained clout, membership, and legal rights, and many of the workplace laws and regulations that were won by unions still apply to this day. Employer-sponsored health coverage began during World War II (WWII) as a recruitment and retention tool, a workaround when employers were restricted by federal wage and price controls. In the early 1950s, unions reached their peak prowess, with membership encompassing 35 percent of the total workforce (Rubis et al., 2005).

The Growth of HR after WWII

Naturally, HR grew alongside the unions as companies sought to navigate the requirements of collective bargaining and maintain production amid strikes. Additionally, the U.S. economy as a whole faced the post-WWII era of recovery and isolationism, striving for efficiency improvements, competitive production, and organized personnel administration. We also expanded our understanding of how work best gets done. Abraham Maslow published his hierarchy of needs in 1943, and society began to see labor as not just a factor of production, but as something that could be psychologically improved and harnessed.

Couple this with the fact that many workers (think the traditionalist generation here) went to work for one company for life, so their careers were largely determined internally by HR (sans analytics, mind you) and perhaps based more or less on personal relationships. In the 1950s a poll of executives actually voted HR as the most glamorous business function (Cappelli, 2015). Needless to say, the glory days did not last for long.

The Civil Rights Era and Transition into the 1980s

During the civil rights era of the 1960s and 1970s, companies faced a barrage of new and precarious employment laws, from equal pay to age discrimination to affirmative action, that brought a host of litigation and compliance issues. HR evolved as a means to prevent lawsuits and in a way became much more essential to business functioning, but also more begrudged by the rank and file.

The 1970s also brought a decline in unions, hitting an unceremoniously definitive pitch in 1981. After months of negotiation with the federal government, 13,000 air traffic controllers went on strike (Society for Human Resource Management, 2015). President Ronald Reagan ordered them to return to work, and, after 48 hours of the strike, he fired those who refused: 11,350 workers (Schalch, 2006). The era of labor union strength was officially ended. Membership fell to 17.4 percent by 1985 (Mayer, 2004), and as of 2016 sits at 11.1 percent (Union Members Summary, 2016).

The current notion of "HR management" really started to take shape in the 1980s with the development of new theories on change, motivation, and team building (Duggan). The decade was fraught with massive corporate lay-offs, and HR efforts turned to areas like mergers and acquisitions and employee training. Employee loyalty plummeted, company policies and processes spiked.

Age of Technology

The 1990s and early 2000s welcomed a new age of technology, with computer usage transforming the workplace (Hunt, 2011). Newly automated systems and outsourced administrative functions freed up more room for HR strategy, and leaders began focusing on a more talent management role. This included things like goal setting, competency training, and structured interviews, enabled by the integration of technology.

However, this era also marked a shift toward a perception of HR as more promanagement (Is Your HR Department Friend or Foe?, 2005). Many of those most basic, mundane administrative functions, such as help with medical insurance and family leave, were appreciated by employees and bolstered the image of HR as an advocate and protector of the people. The automated dearth of those day-to-day support roles contributed to the perception of HR as a necessary evil, instead of an ally.

Decline of HR's Popularity

The post-2008 economic recession brought a new wave of bemoaning HR, as employers faced tough decisions around compensation, a huge talent surplus, and the difficulty of investing in people when all other areas of business were trying to cut costs (Human Resources Management in Recession, 3). A tight labor market meant increased workloads and trying to do more with less. In many cases, HR was made to play the role of antagonist, or at least bearer of bad news, continuing to burden employees already reluctant to complain and unable to quit.

When there are labor problems, business leaders call HR for help. At the height of union membership, HR was deemed glamorous. But when the economy suffers and unemployment rates rise, HR seems irrelevant, even nagging, because most people are in no position to quit their jobs. Peter Cappelli, director of Wharton's Center for Human Resources, notes, "Basically, in every generation or so there is a new popular article complaining about HR, and the complaints are all from people who are in other parts of the business and HR is making them do things they do not want to do" (Cappelli, 2015).

Even in 1998, business leaders debated the question of whether or not to do away with HR altogether, voicing serious doubts about its contributions. Renowned HR guru Dave Ulrich himself wrote, "It is often ineffective, incompetent, and costly; in a phrase, it is value sapping. Indeed, if HR were to remain configured as it is today in many companies, I would have to answer the question above with a resounding 'Yes, abolish the thing!' . . . But the question is not 'Should we do away with it?' but 'What should we do with it?' HR should be defined not by what it does but by what it delivers, meaning results that enrich the organization's value to customers, investors, and employees" (Ulrich, 1998).

Current Role of HR

Now, nearly two decades later, Ulrich's words ring even more true. What should we do with HR, in our ever-turbulent business landscape? Among the slew of changes HR faces, past and present, these stand out:

- *Diversifying demographics.* Humans have changed dramatically in the past 60 years. In 1955, minorities made up only 13 percent of the workforce (Society for Human Resource Management, 2005), and women only 27 percent. In 2005, 33 percent were minorities and 59 percent were women. And that is just the beginning. We are now seeing a more multigenerational and globalized workplace than ever before, with four (soon to be five) generations working together and an exponential spike in freelance and borderless work (Society for Human Resource Management, 2005).

- *Technological changes.* In 1913, the agricultural sector comprised almost one-third of the workforce and white collar workers only 20 percent. In the 1950s, nearly half of the workforce was in manufacturing, construction, and mining, whereas the services-providing sector was just 30 percent (Society for Human Resource Management, 2005). In 2014, less than 2 percent of the workforce was in agriculture; just more than 10 percent in manufacturing, construction, and mining; and a whopping 80 percent in the services-providing sector. Technology did not just automate processes, it completely changed the game (Employment by Major Industry Sector, 2015).

- *Rise of knowledge workers*. Last century, workers were literally a cog in the wheel, a small part of the larger manufacturing process. Now, employees often *are* the process, forging with their own minds the wheels that drive business. This means less money invested in equipment, but it also means that investing in people is now everything, and HR needs to rise to the occasion as a strategic partner to the business. Experts call it the decade of human capital, where value accrues to those who creatively innovate and where talent reigns supreme.

As Reed Hastings, CEO of Netflix, points out, "As a society, we've had hundreds of years to work on managing industrial firms, so a lot of accepted HR practices are centered in that experience. We're just beginning to learn how to run creative firms, which is quite different. Industrial firms thrive on reducing variation (manufacturing errors); creative firms thrive on increasing variation (innovation)" (McCord, 2014).

Strategic Shifts in HR

Leadership is becoming more strategic across the board, and HR is following suit. Chief financial officers moved from generic to strategic. Chief human resources officers are doing the same thing, because although largely administrative, no talent means no growth.

The business world needs a human capital maestro, someone able to harmonize all of the evolving workplace dynamics, disparate business needs, and valuable talent resources entwined in our systems and structures today. This people maestro role could be called chief human resources officer, chief talent officer, chief people officer, vice president of human resources, or even your hoi polloi aficionado. Organizations need a strategic partner seated squarely at the proverbial "executive table" to lead the honorable functions of people selection, motivation, and management.

That presence has been historically lacking for many decades, but fortunately, we in HR are not left to forge completely anew this path toward relevance and executive standing. Thankfully, our brethren in the historically neglected, recently resuscitated areas of finance and marketing have already tackled the trailblazing challenge of carving out and sustaining a seat at the executive table. And like any quality brethren, they have bequeathed us a roadmap of how to trace that transition from what was long considered a purely administrative, generic function into a strategic, differentiating role, essential to future business success.

For the human capital maestro, we propose that this shift will entail three key factors:

- *Diversifying demographics.* HR of the future adeptly navigates the diverse and disparate global workforce of an open talent economy, in which people move freely from job to job, across geographical and organizational borders.

- *Technological changes.* HR of the future seamlessly incorporates analytics, data-backed research, and scientific rigor into people decisions.

- *Rise of knowledge workers.* HR of the future cultivates qualities like creativity, innovation, and collaboration, rising to compete on intangible assets such as talent instead of on tangible assets like machinery and capital.

HR may not be widely viewed as the most forward thinking of functions. Yet history shows a persistent value-add to business, openness to change, and expansion in duties. The field of HR is reinventing itself again, alongside the workplace of now. And there's never been a more exciting time to be involved.

Chapter

HR of the Future
(Or, Why HR Is More Than Forms, Filing, and Firing)

Now that we have explored the history of the HR field, we can more clearly look toward the future. A lot has been learned through our past experiences, and HR professionals are now in a unique position to lead in the workplace of now. It's HR's time to shine.

The War for Talent

The World Economic Forum states that talent, not financial capital, is the "key to innovation, competitiveness, and growth in the 21st century" (Jackson, 2015). The Economist Intelligence Unit found that more than anything else right now, organizations need people management strategies (Plugging Skills Gap Shortages Among Plenty, 2012). CEOs around the globe named human capital as their most critical challenge (The 2015 Conference Board CEO Challenge, 2015). "These days, the scarcity impeding firms' growth is not of capital; it's of talent" (Benko & Volini, 2014). According to a 2013 survey by Deloitte, nearly 40 percent of executives said they are either "barely able" or "unable" to meet demands for the talent required to effectively run their organizations (The 2013 Deloitte Global Finance Talent Survey Report, 6).

The need is paramount, no question. But when we couple that with the sheer lack of readiness, we start to get antsy. These are the kind of thoughts that keep people like us up at night.

According to a 2014 survey of CEOs, HR is overwhelmingly viewed as the least agile function (Global Human Capital Trends 2014). Nearly half of business leaders agree that HR is not ready to lead (Benko & Volini, 2014). And most telling, HR executives graded *themselves* a C-minus for overall performance (Global Human Capital Trends 2014, 16). So, at least we are all on the same page. HR has literally been in a static state for decades, and we are on the cusp of a major transformation.

Talent underscores success, and ample supply is no longer a given. In fact, 75 percent of executives say the most important challenge for today's chief human resources officer is attracting, retaining, and developing talent (The Changing Role of the CHRO, 2015). Trying to scope out just how extraordinary top talent can be? Google's people analytics team calculated that their exceptional employees can perform as much as 300 times higher than their average employees (Sullivan, 2013). Keep in mind, of course, that on average each employee at Google produces $1 million in revenue (or $200,000 profit) each year. Sounds like a pretty compelling business case to us.

Now more than ever, people determine business success. And when a talented, productive, and engaged workforce is the competitive advantage, HR must take the lead. The "soft stuff" like culture, emotional intelligence, and intellectual capital matters. We shouldn't even call it soft stuff anymore. Traditional forms of competitiveness, including cost, distribution, and product features, are assumed and can be copied. But it's the organizational capabilities, such as agility, human capital, and culture, that distinguish the goods from the greats. In the past, value derived from material and financial assets. But now, 85 percent of corporate value creation stems from brand, intellectual property, and people (Benko, 2013).

HR Leaders

Can we all take a moment to agree that the name "human resources" is terrible? Todd dubbed himself chief people officer. Let's define it as a talent function, because real business value lies in talent and people management. HR is charged with some of the most indispensable, profit-building roles in an organization: How to get talented people, how to keep them, and how to motivate them to do their best work, not to mention being responsible for a huge portion of workplace costs (70 percent of an average company's expenses) (The Changing Role of the CHRO).

HR is not a place for average graduates who want to do rank-and-file work. In today's open source, transient, hypercompetitive knowledge economy, we need to recruit the best and brightest to HR in order to get great results. Naturally all eyes are on HR, and expectations are mounting as we look to HR leadership to play a much more critical role in driving business outcomes.

It's not enough to have top talent, you also have to engage them to drive top performance.

HR is the caretaker of the largest investment of the company and tasked with nurturing that investment and making it grow. The collective intelligence of your people (intellectual property, brand, talent) accounts for the largest share of market valuation for publicly traded companies (The Decade of HR, 2014, 2). How you engage your collective talent matters and can have a huge impact for your bottom line. Companies with high employee engagement have 3.9 times the earnings per share of their competitors (Walter, 2013).

Alarmingly few organizations are prepared for this future of human capital. HR leaders themselves cite a huge capability shortfall, with 77 percent of respondents ranking the need to reskill the HR function among the top quartile of their priorities (Global Human Capital Trends 2014, 15). Yet despite both awareness and prioritization, most organizations have taken no steps to help HR get better at contributing analytical, data-driven, strategic value.

Quite a lot has changed in HR over the last several years. The economy rallied, the workforce expanded, and companies began losing top talent. We are realizing the need to dethrone some old ways of doing things. Ten years ago marketing was where HR is now, using intuition rather than data to drive big decisions and strategies. They changed, and HR must too.

Move from simplistically saying "our people are our greatest asset" to being able to tangibly describe the value that asset brings in a way that helps investment decisions. Find new ways to connect people to each other and to information, both internally and externally, through your organizational culture. And ultimately, remember that when we talk about talent management, it's your employees' talent, not yours, and they are loaning it to your company.

Marketing, operations, and financials are table stakes for today's CEO. More than ever, CEOs are being evaluated on their ability to manage organizational challenges like talent, agility, and culture. HR leadership should be experts on those and can provide deep insights while owning the business plan to fuel growth and development.

What does the future demand for HR leaders? The new stars of HR will be strategic, data-driven, innovative, and proactive and will play a more significant role as advisor and driver of business results. HR leaders have strikingly similar profiles to CEOs and chief operating officers in three vital categories: leadership style, thinking style, and emotional competencies (statistically closer than the profiles of chief marketing officers, chief information officers, or chief financial officers) and are uniquely positioned to serve as chief advisor and confidant to the CEO from the perspective of human capital (CEOs and CHROs, 2014). No matter what business you're in, you're always in the people business, and in the age of human capital, you cannot afford to get that wrong.

Experts have been talking about culture, talent, and engagement for a couple years here. People want these changes, they want better workers and better work. What's missing, and what we hope to offer, is the practical, actionable application. The Engagement Canvas, detailed in Part 3, addresses this need.

Wave of the Future

In the words of John F. Kennedy, "Change is the law of life. And those who look only to the past or present are certain to miss the future" (National Center for Biotechnology Information) As we have seen, the workplace of now is a far cry from the workplace of yesteryear. How employees are working is evolving at a pace unrivaled in human history. Employees of all ages (not just millennials) expect employers to understand their ever-changing needs and preferences and to act accordingly. Employers are expected to proactively implement teleworking plans, leverage alternative work schedules, embrace multinational workforces (actual employees or otherwise), and communicate using tools that are native to employees.

The way we work, the places we work, and the *why* behind our work are shifting in major ways. We must shift with them. We must embrace change for what it truly is, a catalyst for greatness and possibility. We must develop new ways of thinking about work and new strategies for engaging today's enlightened workers. The next part provides you with a powerful framework to do just that, and it's called the Engagement Canvas.

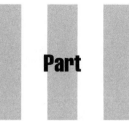

Part

III

The Engagement Canvas

Chapter

Engagement Canvas and Emplify Score Overview

The workplace of now is changing. It's not enough to nod along and twiddle your thumbs. It's not enough to point to your HR leaders and wish them luck. If you work with people, culture and engagement are your responsibility. Organizations who fail to respond to the tectonic shifts in the work world will fall behind others and lose the war for talent. The good news is that culture and engagement are finally seeing their day in the sun and earning a seat at the big kid's table. According to Deloitte's 2015 report (Global Human Capital Trends 2015, 35):

- A significant 87 percent of organizations worldwide cite culture and engagement as a top business challenge.
- Only 7 percent rate themselves as "excellent" at measuring, improving, and driving engagement.
- Only 12 percent rate themselves as "excellent" at effectively driving the desired culture.
- Only 22 percent of organizations report that they have either a poor program for measuring and improving engagement, or no program at all.

We clearly have work to do, and it should not come as a surprise. You cannot open a business magazine, pass by a bookstore, or browse the Internet without unearthing a new discussion or theory on workplace cultures and the importance of employee engagement. Lots of talk, but far less action.

Unfortunately, most organizations that tout culture and engagement as top priority challenges have no tangible strategy to improve them. And we are all well aware of what happens when we have an admirable goal but no roadmap: absolutely nothing.

In this section, we introduce a new concept called the Engagement Canvas and a corresponding measurement tool called the Emplify Score. These tools are intended to help organizations of all sizes, industries, and sophistications surface fundamental pieces of their workplace landscape and create specific strategies to cultivate a culture that fuels employee engagement.

The Rise of People Analytics

Like all professions, HR has a running list of things filed away under "needs improvement." Near the top of the list (if not at the top) is learning to use and demonstrate the return on investment of HR actions, decisions, and procedures. Finance started the trend, exploring rationale behind investments, risk, and revenue. Marketing picked it up next, studying and adapting to consumers, trends, and campaigns. Instead of taking tradition at face value, people started questioning, "Why do we do it that way?" and stopped accepting, "Because that's how we've always done it" as a reasonable answer. Best practices are no longer accepted at face value; they must be proven and measurable. People across industries and across departments have gotten in the habit of measuring and analyzing every move they make and using those learnings to plan their next moves.

HR, though, has lagged behind when it comes to embracing measurement and analysis. This is ironic because HR typically controls the principal cost of most organizations. No wonder other areas of the business are chomping at the bit to see some numbers that explain why we hire, fire, promote, and reward the way we do. Often, HR is unprepared to give those answers. Ten years ago, marketing was where HR is now, using intuition rather than data-based foresight to guide big decisions. They revolutionized their profession by leveraging data, and HR must do the same.

Increasingly, companies contract out routine HR administrative tasks (compensation, benefits, retirement) to third parties so internal HR staff can focus on strategic talent acquisition and development. The problem is that many HR departments that were good at and accustomed to the routine tasks of the past are now ill equipped to take on strategic talent acquisition and development tasks.

An executive poll by Harvard Business Review found that the biggest obstacle facing HR today is a lack of analytical skills and the ability to use data to drive strategy (Harvard Business Review, 2015, 1). Seventy-five percent of companies believe that using analytics in HR is "important," but one-third of respondents (Harvard Business Review) indicated they are doing nothing to address HR analytics gaps, and only 8 percent believe they are strong in this area (Demand for HR Analytics Roles Strong, but Slowing, 2015).

The policies created surrounding our people—hiring, engaging, incentivizing—are some of the most essential policies a company can create. People analytics seeks to bring some more critical thought, data-based insight, and deeper understanding to these crucial areas. The things is, we make bad decisions without even realizing it. As much as we love to tout our own sound judgment, our intuition is often misguided, and we should probably trust it less than we do. In any given moment, we have somewhere around 11 million bits of information coming at us, of which we are aware of and processing only about 60 (Martin, 2009). Our brains do this out of kindness, so we don't have to think about things like how our socks feel on the tops of our feet or what the roofs of our mouths taste like. Pretty handy most of the time, and we certainly would be overwhelmed otherwise. Unfortunately, this can also lead us to make ill-informed decisions without realizing it, otherwise known as unconscious bias. People analytics is our attempt to bring some more facts to these traditionally intuitive processes.

Another gap in the people analytics space is measurement. Mostly we measure things that run parallel to people issues, without really capturing the heart of organizational culture. We look at salary, turnover, and tenure. Although those are certainly important, they are not comprehensive.

Enter the Engagement Canvas and Emplify Score

We created the Engagement Canvas and Emplify Score to provide a robust strategy construct and measurement tool that enhanced objectivity in employee engagement, minimized the shortcomings of our own gut feelings, and offered a more complete tool for such an elusive concept. By effectively quantifying and analyzing employee engagement, we become better able to improve it.

Bear in mind, however, that although data support research sensationally, they don't have to dictate the conversation entirely.

- *Complement humans, but don't replace them.* Our model, however robust, is still influenced by our inherent human biases.

- *We are constantly improving.* These processes and measurements are a significant step up from our intuition, but they are still imperfect solutions. That is why we are constantly improving them.

- *Humans are hard to measure.* We produce a final number with the Emplify Score, but we must still expect some imprecision because of our highly variable humanness, where not everything is perfectly quantifiable.

Engagement Canvas Inspiration

As most of you have probably guessed, we modeled the Engagement Canvas after the popular Business Model Canvas proposed by Alex Osterwalder in 2008, which pioneered the way for organized, straightforward, comprehensive mapping of businesses.

We also credit Eric Ries and his acclaimed Lean Startup methodology for building and launching new products. He introduced a way to shorten product development cycles through iterative releases, focusing on streamlined production philosophies and overall reduction of waste, and influenced the way many of us think about culture.

Steve Blank, creator of the Customer Development methodology and investor, advisor, and previous professor to a young Eric Ries, describes the difference well in his 2013 *Harvard Business Review* article, "Why the Lean Startup Changes Everything" (Blank, 2013). By favoring "experimentation over elaborate planning, customer feedback over intuition, and iterative design over traditional 'big design up-front' development," the Lean Startup methodology transforms conventional wisdom. It helps us intuit fresh perspectives and approaches, even formerly evaded tactics like failing fast and learning or improving ceaselessly. It works because it reframes our challenges and centers us on a path forward. In his article, Blank outlines the fallacy of the traditionally held "perfect business plan," a static, tedious, hyperdescriptive document that presumes to predict in detail wild unknowns like success five years in the future. He argues that business plans rarely survive first contact with customers anyway and that trying to predict too far in the future, particularly in such a fiercely turbulent business landscape, is largely pointless.

In a similar vein runs the Lean Canvas, invented by Ash Maurya, which we have used and benefited from on numerous occasions with multiple companies, including at Emplify (Maurya). The Lean Canvas focuses on stating hypotheses, revisiting and testing assumptions, and finding viable and proven processes. It encourages logical, focused thought and simplifies otherwise complex planning tasks. Asking the right questions in a specified order allows intentional consideration of each component of an otherwise hazy concept. The canvas layout channels this process spectacularly, while simultaneously keeping it simple and able to be completed in a single sitting.

Likewise, in order to sustain employee engagement, culture must be repeatedly revisited, adapted, and improved on to meet changing needs and opportunities. We intentionally styled the Engagement Canvas to be a living document. Cultures are amorphous because without continuous tending to, they naturally degrade. Thus, they require flexible execution and continuous improvement.

Naturally, as we searched for the best way to enable our customers to digest the challenges they faced formulating an employee engagement strategy, we found that the concept of a single-page canvas presented the most logical, viable approach. Most business people are already acquainted with the way our canvas forefathers approached challenges and objectives. So, rather than create something entirely new, it made more sense to adapt the canvas approach to the world of employee engagement.

Navigating the Engagement Canvas

We designed the Engagement Canvas as a one-page worksheet to help you develop a more engaged workforce. It has 10 sections that are straightforward to complete and easily understood, articulated, and improved. At the highest level, the Engagement Canvas is divided between two halves: (1) elements driven by the company, and (2) elements relative to or descriptive of the employees (Figure 17.1).

Working through the Engagement Canvas provides insights into what organizations can control and adapt and what kinds of employees do well in a particular culture. Both parties, the organization and the individuals, contribute both good and bad elements toward engagement, and these vary from organization to organization. The Engagement Canvas therefore seeks to parse those two drivers, clarify engagement, and help organizations articulate their culture to employees who will embrace it.

The bottom three boxes give insight into the current reality of employee engagement within your company (Figure 17.2). On the bottom left we have tangible actions taken by the organization to improve engagement. If culture is recognized as a strategic advantage, we should expect to see meaningful investment made here, beyond mere lip service. In the middle, you'll put your Emplify Score (more on that later). And on the bottom right you'll record key employee needs. These can be initially populated by anecdote, gut

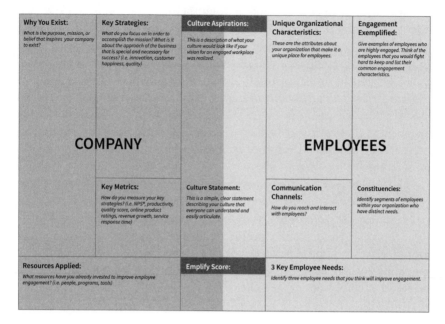

FIGURE 17.1 Engagement Canvas Halves

ENGAGEMENT CANVAS

Company				Employee(s)
Why You Exist:	Key Strategies:	Culture Aspirations:	Unique Organizational Characteristics:	Engagement Exemplified:
	Key Metrics:	Culture Statement:	Communication Channels:	Constituencies:
Resources Applied:		Emplify Score:	3 Key Employee Needs:	

CURRENT REALITY

FIGURE 17.2 Current Engagement Reality

feeling, and any recent surveys. Then after running the formal Emplify Score Survey, you can further tease out what engagement conditions are not being met and why.

Unlike many of the more antiquated predecessors, the Engagement Canvas process does not necessitate a slew of lengthy meetings only to leave you dejected and void of business value. Rather, the Engagement Canvas offers a holistic and simple way to evaluate your culture's current state, describe your desired future state, and chart the path to achieving increased employee engagement for your unique organization.

Completing the Canvas

Although there is no absolute order in which you must complete the Engagement Canvas sections, we've arranged them in a natural flow that tends to yield the most effective outcomes (Figure 17.3). The earlier boxes help you lay a foundation and formulate ideas for the later ones.

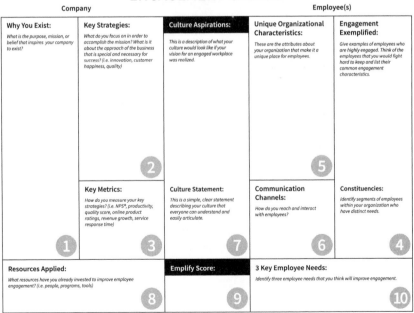

FIGURE 17.3 Engagement Canvas

In the following chapters, we detail each section of the Engagement Canvas, complete with underlying rationale and general guidelines. Please follow along and begin inputting your immediate thoughts using the online, printable Engagement Canvas at www.AgileEngagmentBook.com. You will also find additional resources and tools on the site.

Remember to respect the process and complete the Engagement Canvas in its entirety. When you do, you will gain both deeper clarity about the identity of your organization and strategic, actionable steps you can take moving forward.

Why You Exist
Engagement Canvas Box 1

At the core of most ultrasuccessful businesses is a clear understanding and expression of why the business exists. As Simon Sinek, author of *Start with Why*, explains, "People don't buy what you do, they buy why you do it. . . . The goal is not to do business with people who need what you have, but with people who believe what you believe." Sinek notes how most organizations start with what they do, then how they do it, and end with why—if they get there at all (Sinek, 2009).

The most influential organizations, on the other hand, reverse that thought process. Sinek uses Apple as an example: "Everything we do, we believe in challenging the status quo, in thinking differently. The way we challenge the status quo is by making our products beautifully designed and simple to use. We just happen to make great computers. Want to buy one?" What you do serves as the proof of what you believe. And what you believe, *why* you do what you do, is what provides focus, engages employees, draws loyal customers, earns the faith of investors, and inspires true transformation.

Scott Kraege, CEO of Mobi, understands the importance of outlining your why:

> At all levels and size of an organization, a clear vision is the first step in building momentum around a team. We must know why

we do what we do before we can effectively do what is necessary to accomplish our goals. The vision and purpose an organization has is what jumpstarts the energy of its people, a company, or team. Without a vision, we won't start our journey and we'll never reach our destination. If we're surrounded by people who share the same vision and have the same passion, we will move faster toward our goals. If we are surrounded with those who do not share our vision, at best we will be distracted and threatened, at worst we will come to a grinding halt. (Kraege, 2016)

Sadly, few companies expend the energy to drive the "why" behind the business. We see this phenomenon exemplified in the classic case of a hospital that fails to regularly draw the nexus between every single job in the hospital and the provision of necessary, life-altering, medical care to members of the community. Caring for the sick—you can't get a much more noble endeavor than that, one that employees can easily, authentically get behind. It's one thing to dwell on why it's important for housekeeping to maintain clean patient rooms. It's another thing to go the extra mile and explain that clean patient rooms result in a significant decrease in the transmission of multidrug-resistant infections. Housekeeping should be lauded for performing at a high level, resulting in shorter patient stays, higher customer service, and more expeditious patient treatment.

Often companies do not take the time to surface the compelling aspects of their work, the makeup of their workforce, or the nature of their industry. Consequently, they mistakenly take these unique characteristics for granted and fail to leverage them when developing employee engagement. Employees yearn to be drawn into the "why" around what they do. Like all of us, they want to feel that they have a purpose and are contributing meaningfully to achieving a shared vision or goal.

And so in the Engagement Canvas, we choose to start with *why*. It is our foundational business wellspring from which everything else flows. If you find yourselves struggling with other sections of the Engagement Canvas, we would point you back to reexamine this core tenet, to ensure that it is clear and believed and sincerely undertaken.

Many organizations already have clear, concise statements describing why they exist in mission statements and company values statements. If they ring true, then by all means, pull from them. This section may be easy. If, however, you aren't as confident in your "why," take some time and mental energy to reflect, discuss, and really make sure you nail this section. It may be difficult to proceed with the Engagement Canvas, or effectively engage employees for that matter, if you don't know why you're doing it.

Tips for Crafting and Communicating Your Why

Communication and Consistency Matter More Than Content

In their classic *Built to Last*, Jim Collins and Jerry Porras describe a collection of 18 companies that consistently ranked at the top of their respective markets for more than 50 years. True to our point, these companies shared no common, distinctive cultural attributes. What they did share, however, was a tremendous ability to hire, develop, and retain employees along their unique, clearly stated mission, vision, and values. Prospective employees who know what they're getting themselves go into new jobs with eyes wide open. Employees who align well with the organizational culture will be more inclined to stay, engage, and promote a positive environment. There are enough organizations and enough people in the world that you can be incredibly specific and still find good fits—best fits, even.

Whatever you're going to be, communicate and embody it adamantly. A survey of senior executives at 20 of the top 25 ranked best places to work found that the most effective and valued benefits programs consist not of traditional perks like health insurance and family leave (only 15 percent), nor onsite perks like cafeterias, childcare, and volunteer opportunities (a mere 5 percent). Indeed, the programs that best retain employees during economic uncertainty are the ones that clearly communicate brand mission and provide career development opportunities, as reported by 75 percent of respondents (Campbell, 2011).

Discover What's Already There

We can all set aspirations and affect change, and we are here trying to help you do precisely that. But it must be done systematically and reasonably. You cannot sit down to write your core values and make up a list that sounds admirable and trendy. For good or ill, every organization already has existing values and a purpose. Figure out what your organization already embodies, and go from there. Out of the overflow of these core tenets comes everything else. Define your terms well, and keep doing so, because they serve as guiding principles for nearly everything you do.

Continually Practice Core Principles

Unless they underscore and augment everything else you do, they can quickly fade into the forlorn background. Many organizations begin with the best of intentions and perfectly wordsmithed statements, but unless they are continually, thoroughly practiced and manifested, they can quickly become meaningless.

Spread the Word

In order to ensure continuous and thorough application, everyone in your organization should understand and be able to articulate these fundamentals. It should be at the heart of every conversation, decision, and motivation.

Alignment

Which brings us to our next point: alignment. As Jim Collins highlights, too many executives spend too much time drafting, wordsmithing, and redrafting their mission, vision, and values statements, and they spend nowhere near enough time *aligning* their organizations with those statements. We implore you to make this Engagement Canvas useful and actionable for your organization, and we have designed it with precisely that intention in mind (Collins, 2000).

Whatever you do, do not spend days holed up in a room crafting the perfect culture statement just to post it on your website or wall or useless plaque and not think about it again until next year. Please, anything but that. Far too many executives dedicate a negligible amount of time and energy toward understanding the current situation and working to create alignment, and exorbitant time and energy toward perfecting the mission/vision/values/culture statements. Reverse those efforts, and you'll be well on your way. The perfect words can wait.

Now, the catch: Mission, vision, and values are not a substitute for a culture statement (see Engagement Canvas box 7). Although mission, values, and (to an extent) vision are timeless, culture is dynamic. Culture reflects operating principles and behavioral norms of the organization, and it represents the aggregate of your people. If you hire a ton of new employees, your mission, vision, and values will remain steadfast, but your culture may shift to match the changing constituencies. Don't be afraid to recognize, steer, and drive necessary cultural change in your organization.

Unlike values, culture is inherently unique. As we mentioned earlier, your values may resemble those of other organizations, and that's fine. As humans in functioning societies, we naturally espouse similar morals and qualities, and we would probably struggle to maintain order and cooperation without them. When it comes to culture, however, we can afford to be unique. In fact, therein lies our advantage.

Key Strategies
Engagement Canvas Box 2

ichael Porter, the man who quite literally wrote the books on business strategy, stressed that organizations need to develop a clear strategy around their unique place in the market (Porter, 2006). He posed that managers too often run into trouble when they attempt to compete head-on with other companies. In that kind of zero-sum game, no one comes out on top. Many companies set out to be the best in their industry, but in reality there *is* no best company in any industry. "What is the best car?" Porter asks. "It depends on who is using it. It depends on what it's being used for. It depends on the budget."

Of its many benefits, increased employee engagement spurs improved productivity, but if not effectively applied, that newfound productivity may go to waste. Develop these Key Strategies to define and clarify precisely where and how to direct the force of employee engagement. In this section try to articulate a few of the key strategies you pursue that help you reach your business goals. At any given time, you want employees who are ready to be engaged to know *how* to apply that passion and energy. What makes your overall business different than your competitors that can help your employees have clear, high-level direction about how to engage?

Clarity like this can be difficult, but again, the essence of strategy is choosing what *not* to do. Understandably, we want to be the best in everything. We want the best product, service, price, sales, you name it. Unfortunately, we must disillusion ourselves from "having it all" and instead hone in on one or two things we can do that manifest our mission—the "how" to our "why."

When Sam Walton founded Walmart, he chose to focus on low prices and widespread access. He built in rural towns. He lowered costs ruthlessly. In so doing, he also chose to *not* focus on quality or customer service. His clear mission was clearly executed in his strategy.

Now take Jimmy John's, for example: "Subs so fast you'll freak." They plaster their motto in advertisements and back it up in each experience. A bold and catchy statement, to be sure, and indeed one fateful substarved day, we went to a local Jimmy John's and, while gearing up for our freak out, engaged some employees in conversation. What made them so amicable, accurate, and productive? They shared with us that the company commits to firing and promoting quickly, based on performance. Speed seemed to be a pervasive business strategy—fast orders, fast preparation, fast delivery, and fast promotions. In that kind of environment, when engaged employees know exactly what is valued, they are empowered to direct that energy toward simultaneously benefiting the business, the customer, and themselves.

In that same spirit, consider for yourself: What are the *one* or *two* things that you do differently that demonstrate how you accomplish your mission?

Key Metrics
Engagement Canvas Box 3

Flowing directly from key strategies, we move to metrics. We set the strategy, and now we measure our progress. We measure to know if our strategies work, if our improvements materialize, if we've moved the needle at all—high hopes for resounding affirmatives. But practically speaking, we often see lack of tangible improvement stem from two primary reasons:

- An external factor causing the business to suffer
- Engagement not being directed in the right place

So in this box, list your key performance indicators, your executive scorecard metrics, or whatever else you use to gauge business success. Think about how you will integrate an engagement score into your larger business intelligence practice so that you can effectively monitor connections between increased employee engagement and improved business results.

The goal of this section is to drive clarity on what key metrics lie at the heart of overall business success. You can then effectively evaluate the impact your future engagement efforts have on the business. A return-on-investment discussion becomes infinitely easier and more impactful when you can correlate increases in engagement with business improvements.

Engagement Exemplified

Engagement Canvas Box 4

Thus far, we've focused on the organization side of the Engagement Canvas. This is what meaning drives our work, what strategies guide our direction, and how we gauge success. Now we turn to the employee side, because in order to improve engagement, you must also understand what it looks like for an employee to engage in your organization.

This matters because part of engagement is inherent in the individual and how inclined he or she happens to be toward engaging. Although much of engagement is certainly driven objectively by the organization, it also has to do largely with the fit between organizational culture and each individual. By recognizing, therefore, what drives an organization, how an organization executes strategies, and what kind of individuals thrive in that environment, we can gain clarity around what that ideal fit looks like. From that base, we continue to improve and construct culture. Building, shaping, and steering culture of course takes time. Repeated doses of altering leadership behavior, finding well-fitting candidates, and discerning what positives you can already draw on in the organization are important. Recognizing who the engaged candidates are and what makes them that way *now* can illuminate the path forward.

Think here first about those certain people who seem to epitomize the best things about your organization. They are the ones you would fight to keep if they considered leaving, the ones esteemed by peers and leaders, and the ones you want on your team. From that coveted bunch, think then about the employees who are passionate about their work and genuinely want to help the organization. In that overlap lives engagement exemplified.

These shining cultural stars may be founders, executives, long-tenured employees—really just about anyone. They tend to garner remarks like, "She bleeds <insert company name>" or "If we had a hundred of her, we would have the best culture in the world." What these casual comments really mean, and what you should infer as leaders, is that these people are your rare and admirable cultural cornerstones, and you want to study and repeat how they exemplify engagement. Regardless of official title or role, these people undoubtedly carry significant sway in your organization, influencing and setting examples for other employees. Don't be shy to single them out and specifically involve them in your engagement strategies. By all means, invite them to help complete the Engagement Canvas. They may shine light on perspectives and methods you wouldn't have otherwise considered.

Constituencies

Now that we have identified the primary engagement examples, let's take a few steps back and think more broadly about all of the distinct groups that need to be reached and engaged in your organization. As any good marketer will tell you, you need to understand your audience, or in the case of cultures, *audiences,* plural. Cultures comprise a multitude of employee types and classifications, including but not limited to exempt/nonexempt, headquarters based/remote, administrative/professional, go-to-market/nonsales, and manager/individual contributor, not to mention the host of nonemployee constituents like directors, advisors, external partners, and freelancers. Attempting to identify every last constituency is unnecessary. You should, however, dedicate some time to determining the main constituent groups so you can tailor your strategies and associated communications accordingly.

In so doing, bear these tips in mind:

- Different constituencies represent different sets of interests. It's great that you distinguish between groups, but don't forget to follow through in appealing to those groups differently.

- In some cases (such as interest groups), constituencies are defined by the constituents themselves, not the categories into which top management has segmented them for optimal convenience or business purposes.
- Each individual can belong to several different constituencies.

One quick, common example: We often see a constituency flag arise in the distinction between remote employees and headquarters-based employees. Although both groups technically fall under the umbrella of full-time employees, they remain distinct. One group maintains daily ties to the heartbeat of the organization and interacts face to face with team members on a regular basis. Conversely, remote employees fly somewhat solo from the mothership, oftentimes get overlooked in regular communications, and rarely have deep operational ties to the company. However, as we see the rise of teleworking, globally dispersed teams, alongside flexibility policies with work-life fit, remote employees definitely warrant consideration and revamped policies.

As you begin to differentiate, consider groups such as the following:

- New versus established
- Part time versus full time
- Millennials versus boomers
- Managers versus individual contributors
- Blue collar versus white collar
- Employees who travel frequently versus those stationed at headquarters

Hone in on groupings that necessitate the most significant customization in how you communicate and relate to them, based on their preferences and the nature of their work. We suggest listing at least three constituencies, depending on the size of your organization.

Unique Organizational Characteristics

Engagement Canvas Box 5

In today's knowledge economy, the battle for the best talent is fierce. In this section of the Engagement Canvas, capture one or two things you do to attract, retain, and engage employees, distinct from your competitors. Naturally, we place it here on the employee side because these unique characteristics are principally employee oriented and intended to entice them away from alternatives and toward your organization.

First thing's first: Don't try to take on the world; just take on your competitors. If you operate a progressive tech company filled with knowledge workers, you compete against those with similar employee compositions. If you own factories with physical laborers, you compete in an entirely different environment. If you manage several significantly different constituencies within your organization, you compete on multiple levels. Luckily for you, you filled out the constituency box already. Find at least one unique characteristic that will appeal to each group.

Now to the fun part: What makes a good unique characteristic? Here are some of our favorites:

- *Remote culture:* Work from anywhere you want. Some of our partners have built their entire organization around this core freedom. It's entwined in the way they work, the way they meet, and who they recruit. Even with all else held equal, they mushroom their potential talent base by a conservative 50x. Anyone in the world can work for them, and we do not know many other "perks" that reap such sweeping change. By no means is remote culture for everyone, especially if you already have a firmly built nonremote infrastructure that values things like desks and in-person meetings. Budgets look different and communication is more asynchronous, but it certainly classifies as a unique characteristic.

- *Required breaks:* Chevron believes that rest and focus are critical for safety, and they mean it. Every 45 minutes, they lock employees' computers to make everyone take a quick break. Extreme, perhaps, but certainly extremely unique. Forced breaks stimulate intense focus in the in between, leading to significant productivity gains. In completing the Engagement Canvas, Chevron might put: "We value focused attention and productivity, and we believe that to sustain these, humans need brief breaks. So every hour, we require every employee to take a five-minute break." This practice is not the only option, but it is their option. It aligns with their values and makes them stand out.

- *Big Dreams:* When your mission is to colonize Mars with 1 million people, we'd say you already have a pretty solidly unique organizational characteristic. Obviously not all companies can point to something so extreme or compelling as space colonization, curing a disease, or engineering solutions to climate change, but for some it is more than distinctive.

The risk when looking to highly lauded companies like Google or SpaceX for unique examples is that they themselves are unique. They may have funding, followers, and research the rest of us can only dream of, but that's kind of the point. Don't try to be Google. Deal with the reality of your current size, industry, and constituencies. Figure out how you can win employees from your closest competitors, and capitalize on those unique organizational characteristics.

We have been in this business for a while, and we have yet to find, research, or work with a single company that does not have at least something unique about its business, workforce, geography, or such. Whatever it is, identify those unique characteristics and accentuate them.

Some companies provide a world-changing service, such as Ecofiltro, an enterprise committed to providing clean water to rural Guatemalans (and expanding to other countries from there) using ecologically, socially, *and* financially sustainable models (Ecofiltro, 2016). Others involve cutting-edge technology, like machine-learning startup PatternEx, who partnered with the Massachusetts Institute of Technology's Computer Science and Artificial Intelligence Laboratory to develop a platform that has proven able to detect cyberattacks 85 percent of the time and to reduce false positives by a factor of five (PatternEx, 2016). Still other companies endure as a steadfast pillar institution of the community, such as Indiana University Health, a top nationally ranked hospital system that provides innovative, quality care to more than 1.3 million Hoosiers and invests upwards of $140 million annually in charity care (Indiana University Health, 2016). Work to uncover the particular characteristics that differentiate your organization and leverage those traits to your advantage.

Chapter

Communication Channels
Engagement Canvas Box 6

T he biggest issue we consistently see with engagement strategies is this: failure to communicate. For whatever reason, leadership teams often discount how they internally communicate and engage with employees. We continually see handbooks presented in hard copy format, requests for information to be sent via fax machine (do your millennials even know how to use those fossils?), information conveyed via corporate intranets, and hard copy memos placed in physical office mailboxes.

The world has undergone major shifts over the last two decades and as a human species we have evolved to meet and embrace our new habitat. We interact with friends, family, professional contacts, brands, merchants, academics, and everyone else in more streamlined, hyperefficient, aesthetic, finessed ways. Meanwhile, employee-related communications stalled out somewhere in the 1980s, and we are sick and tired of it.

Hear this loud and clear: One of the most important ways to improve engagement is by communicating well. If you fail to communicate, you fail to engage. Communication is the nexus that takes everything we worked on and externalizes it to employees, to prospects, to partners, and to yourself, in order to ensure culture is shared and understood. Talk to your employees consistently about why the company exists, why the work they do matters, and where you are heading.

And in particular, talk to them via channels they are already tuned in to. Allow us to let you in on some secrets when considering communication channels.

First, define effectiveness by consumption, not by reach. Exhibit A: email. Email typically serves as the easy default communication channel because every single employee has access to it. The problem is knowing who is actually reading it. Say you send a meaningful email about company direction to 100 percent of your population but only 20 percent open it. Is that really better than an alternative channel that only reaches 95 percent of your people, but where 75 percent read the entire message? According to our calculations, we think not. Seek communication channels in which you are actually *heard*.

Let's step outside the box for a minute and think through your opportunities for communication. We'll get you started with a few ideas. Although the defaults may be emails, phone calls, mail, or in-person meetings, we suggest alternatives like text messages, smartphone apps, internal communication platforms (enterprise social networks), VoiceThread, video messages, or even Snapchat.

Second, branch out. As in all of life, we form habits in our communication. Simply introducing a new channel, perhaps one used solely for employer-employee communication, can help establish a new cultural tone and bolster long-term success. Email is on the decline in the realms of internal effectiveness, growing cluttered and task oriented. Find a channel that works for your organization.

The truth is, every company we work with is focusing on providing a mobile solution for communications, given the reality that people spend a whopping (and ever-increasing) amount of time on their smartphones, they are the most personal devices we have, and we already bring them to work. So whatever channels you end up with, do make sure they work well on mobile. Smartphones are built and epitomized for communication, and there is no sense in not being where your people already are.

Chapter 24

Culture Statements
Engagement Canvas Box 7

ruth: All companies have a culture. It may be magnificent and drive engagement and draw the awe-inspired masses, or it may be lackluster. It may serve as a differentiator for recruiting and employee retention, or it may send prospects and employees running headlong in the other direction. Whether positive or negative, cultures emanate a palpable message tacitly felt by every person that comes in contact with your organization. Being able to accurately *articulate* that culture, however, is a whole different matter.

In the Lean Canvas, there is a box called Unique Value Proposition, defined by Steve Blank as "A single, clear compelling message that states why you are different and worth buying" (Blank, 2013). In the Engagement Canvas, we wanted to capture this same essence with the Culture Statement section. This section calls for you to reach consensus on how to describe your culture. You bear the responsibility of being able to effectively articulate specifics about your organization's culture. For this reason, we recommend you establish a generally held, intentional description of your culture (based on your unique characteristics and culture aspirations) in a Culture Statement.

In our experience, oftentimes recruiters seem to do the best job of describing and articulating organizational cultures. After all, they sell your culture to prospective candidates every day. They know how to phrase the ins and outs of your business, talk about your physical workspace, specify what it takes to be successful as an employee, and detail how work gets done. Ask your recruiters how they describe your company culture. You may be surprised, pleased, or even disappointed, but we are confident that you will be enlightened.

Given the importance of consistent communication and alignment when it comes to culture, Culture Statements are still surprisingly rare. The flipside, however, is that there is plenty of room for improvement. We put together the following tips to keep in mind when crafting your culture statements.

Make It Authentic

Don't make your Culture Statement an obtuse string of feel-good, warm and fuzzy words. What actually guides your day-to-day behaviors, actions, and decisions? A rambling list of generic virtues like "integrity" and "teamwork" does not count. Instead, be real about your cultural reality and reflect it accordingly. As Hank Orme, former president of Lincoln Industries, says, "What you say, what you do, and what you say you do, all need to be consistent" (Orme, discussion with Todd Richardson).

Whatever you do, do not simply mimic other organizations' Culture Statements. Culture statements must be specific to your unique organization. In the widespread exaltation of trendy tech companies, and the resulting mad dash to spice up company cultures that paled in comparison, we have created ourselves in each other's image. When we all compete on the exact same level and say the exact same thing, we create a zero-sum game in which we are indistinguishable to employees. Both the individual and the organization thrive and self-reinforce when culture aligns. Differentiate yourself, study the market, and identify those standout qualities to help the right people find you.

Make It Specific

Strive to outline supporting elements of specifically *how* the culture is manifested and evaluated in your company's context. The famed Netflix Culture Deck demonstrates this well (Hastings, 2009). Like many companies, they list a number of stated cultural values. Unlike many companies, they accompany each item with four descriptors of what that actually looks like.

For example, instead of merely proclaiming "communication," as many companies do, they materialize it by also stating: (1) You listen well, instead of reacting fast, so you can better understand; (2) You are concise and artic-ulate in speech and writing; (3) You treat people with respect independent of their status or disagreement with you; and (4) You maintain calm poise in stressful situations.

Beautiful. As a Netflix employee, you would know exactly what that otherwise hazy value of "communication" actually means for your day-to-day work. You would also know how you will be evaluated, and what you can expect from your coworkers.

In practice, remember that your Culture Statement isn't constrained by the arbitrary size of a box on the Engagement Canvas. Your words should carry weight, and if you create a Culture Statement that you love and that aligns with the unique qualities and goals of your organization, do not be afraid to write in the margins with wild abandon!

25

Culture Aspirations
Engagement Canvas Box 7

I f the key to the Engagement Canvas lies in being able to continuously measure and improve engagement (which it does), then one underlying assumption is that whatever your current cultural state, there is always room for improvement.

Take some time to review your unique characteristics, mission, and those who are most engaged within your organization. Seek first to truly understand your current state and then to visualize your desired culture. We all have "culture crushes" that make us swoon, cultures we want to emulate. What about those cultures sticks out to you? Ask yourself, How do you want to be able to describe and demonstrate your culture five or ten years from now?

This section calls for you to take a step back and think about the culture you want to achieve. What is the culture you want to be known for? How do you want employees to describe your work environment? Put into words what you aspire to culturally form. We are not saying that you have to have perfect clarity on your desired culture or fully understand how you are going to achieve that culture. What we are saying is that you have to have a general idea on the direction you wish to steer efforts and be willing to be both responsive and adaptive in pursuing that aspirational culture.

Create a Culture BHAG (Big, Hairy, Audacious Goal)

In their book *Built to Last,* Jim Collins and Jerry Porras popularized the concept of the big, hairy, audacious goal (BHAG, pronounced bee-hag). The power of a good BHAG lies in its ability to free us from thinking and acting on too small a scale. It propels us into our imagined futures. Collins and Porras characterize BHAGs as goals that push us, that we can throw ourselves into. They operate on time frames not of a quarter or a year, but rather a decade, maybe even three decades. They should be clear, compelling, and easily expressed in plain English. They provide an organizing and orienting construct for our lives. They are the kind of bold, lofty goals that challenge, inspire, and better us. (Collins and Porras, 2002)

Try applying BHAG principles when determining your own culture aspirations (think of it like a big, hairy, audacious culture goal). Be prepared to stretch to reach your aspirations. BHAGs are not supposed to be low-hanging fruit. This is not the time to cower and pad your future ego with easily achieved objectives. Bill Gates (and probably others throughout history as well) famously stated that as humans, we generally overestimate what we can do in a year and underestimate what we can do in a lifetime. In other words, don't be bridled by reasonableness. Dream big in creating your cultural BHAG.

Alan Eustace, former senior vice president of knowledge at Google, dared to dream so big that he became the only person to jump from the stratosphere (and live to tell the tale, we might add). The stratosphere lies above the troposphere, which is the layer in which we earthlings reside, along with Mt. Everest, our clouds, and our commercial jets. The stratosphere houses the ozone layer, which he actually surpassed. Eustace ascended to 135,890 feet over the course of a "meditative and breathtaking" 2 hours and 7 minutes, in nothing but a special suit attached to a helium balloon (sans capsule). From that staggering height of 25.7 miles above New Mexico, he could physically see the curvature of the earth (Eustace, 2015).

He then released (basically skydiving) into a 4 minute and 27 second freefall, hitting the smashing speed of 822 miles per hour. He broke the sound barrier. And at 10,000 feet, he parachuted the rest of the way down. The process took years of meticulous planning, a stunning team, and relentless commitment to safety. The lesson? A good BHAG will propel you into the future, challenging and inspiring you to be better and do more than you ever thought possible (Okell, 2015).

Now that we're all sufficiently awed, let's talk some key strategies for creating your cultural BHAG.

Make Progress Every Day

Set far-off goals, yes, but also act with urgency today. In the future you will scale some distant mountain, but this afternoon you will do 100 pushups. The bilateral nature of the BHAG motivates quite well. Precisely because it's so big and so audacious and so hairy, it increases our sense of urgency and mobilizes us to get rolling now.

As Jim Collins puts it, when we look at a BHAG, we can't help but say, "Oh my goodness, if we're going to bring the world into the jet age or transform education or put a computer on every desk, then we have to get to work today with a level of intensity that is unrelenting." BHAGs almost impend us with the need to start today and continue unwaveringly tomorrow and every day after that, for 365 days or for 3,650 days or however many it takes (Buchanan).

But for now, we start today. You know how to eat an elephant, right? One bite at a time. In a very real sense, our life is made up of all the things we do next. Sometimes all those things culminate in something interesting, or laudable, or, if we're lucky, maybe even important. But for now, all we can really control and celebrate are the small, daily victories of stubbornly showing up and making progress, however incremental it may be.

Believe in the Worthiness of Your Aspiration(s)

The best culture aspirations truly engage and excite people, stimulating creativity and persistence, and concurrently tend to be a little risky. I cannot devote myself to the noble, auspicious pursuit of revenue the same way that I can to exploration, innovation, or social change. Pick something you and others can honestly set your minds to, and work to shape reality around. Think back to some of the most awe-inspiring achievements like landing on the moon, summiting Everest, and taking flight.

Humans are such a remarkably resilient, resourceful, and adaptable species, overbrimming with potential. We owe so much of our modern comforts and knowledge to all those who went before us and pushed boundaries, challenged status quos, explored, and risked everything to bring us to this point. Find strength in your innate potential as a human being, and stretch yourself to think of an aspirational culture that will fundamentally change the lives of your employees. Put yourself out there, and embrace the battle scars that will likely ensue along the journey.

Culture Aspirations in Action

What type of culture do you strive to create? Here is what some of our favorite business leaders had to say.

- "A culture of growth, accountability, creativity, and winning together. Winning together means something different to me than to most people. Too often people strive for teamwork. You can create a culture of teamwork that keeps people working as a team . . . toward losing. Our goal is to win, and we want to win together."—Brad Morehead, Chief Executive Officer (CEO), LiveWatch Security

- "Honest, open, big goals, team-oriented, challenging, fun, hilarious, creative, results-oriented."—Nicole Bickett, Chief Administrative Officer, Mainstreet

- "The culture most suitable for success in our industry is a learning culture."—Rob Edwards, Director of Engineering & Race Operations, Andretti Motorsports

- "Proactive, critical, innovative thinkers, sweat the details, think process."—Tom Eggleston, CEO, RENU Management

- "I always try to develop a culture where each team member feels he or she was as important as the CEO and knows I will support him or her in good times and bad."—Wil Boren, Former Vice President and General Manager, Zimmer Biomet

- "I strive to create a culture where employees have meaningful work and the necessary support system to be successful. Because work comprises such a substantial amount of our time, it's important that the environment is conducive to laughter and enjoyment, as well."—Blair West, Director of Corporate Communications, Cummins, Inc.

- "I try very hard to lead in a way that encourages collaboration. The more team members understand why we are doing what we are doing, and feel comfortable challenging it and presenting their own views, the more they can understand their part of the whole. We value learning from failing and also try to find ways to help people sharpen the skills that make them the most happy."—Sam Julka, President, DORIS Research

- "We encourage an environment of fanatical collaboration, where people and departments work together to achieve our common goals. We encourage hard work, passion, and pride in workmanship."—Clay Robinson, Co-Founder and Owner, Sun King Brewing

- "We encourage creativity, but demand results. There are no stupid ideas, but we are always looking for ideas that ultimately contribute to our desired results."—Arthur Angotti, President, Artistic Media Partners

- "Culture is not created or driven from the top down. It should be defined, owned, maintained, and lived into by the collective team. I strive to have a culture where the team feels mutually responsible for living our core values and empowered to hold each other accountable. I strive to lead a team who cares about each other as people first, has each other's backs, and consistently operates with the best interest of kids, families and communities at heart."—Rebecca Thompson Boyle, Former Executive Director, Teach for America

- "A culture where in the midst of chaos or distractions our customers see us perform at our best."—Gary Reynolds, Owner and President, Reynolds Farm Equipment

- "Entrepreneurship is encouraged through the power of small teams while still leveraging the strength and scale of the enterprise."—Terri Kelly, President and CEO, W. L. Gore & Associates

26

Resources Applied
Engagement Canvas Box 8

Moving right along, turn your attention to the bottom portion of the Engagement Canvas. These three boxes help assess your current situation and establish clear next steps. Oftentimes we find that organizations initially feel pretty pleased with their efforts toward engagement, then realize there may be a decent breach between that effort and the reality among employees.

In this section, list what you currently do, in terms of time, energy, and money, to intentionally bolster engagement. Be as honest as possible with yourself even if you do not like the answer. Think about what you've specifically done as a leader to help employees engage with their work and the business, not just other actions that happened to bolster engagement as a fringe benefit.

Grand efforts require widespread support, and this section will show you whether your organization is truly committed to culture or simply says it is. Support can materialize in the form of financial resources, staffing, external resources, creative assistance, technical help, or a host of alternative viable options. If 87 percent of organizations worldwide cite culture and engagement as a top business challenge, then by all means, invest meaningfully in forming and launching your engagement efforts (Global Human Capital Trends 2015, 35). Much in the same way that we seek clarity in how we measure engagement and establish our plan to improve those measures, we should also ask ourselves what resources we're currently dedicating to achieve such improvements.

Chapter

27

Emplify Score
Engagement Canvas Box 9

W e have spent years bemoaning the widespread inability to objectively measure employee engagement. Sure, it's good for your ego to prove when you have built a culture of significance. But the true value of measurement comes in the ability to set a benchmark on which you can improve.

We have passed many wistful, arresting hours contemplating how the rest of modern business society has managed to successfully adopt a measure/improve/measure/improve cadence. Meanwhile, HR has sufficed to meagerly gather the leftover, second-rate tools that fail to yield effective measures—thanks for the crumbs, HR forebears. Alas, why has HR straggled decades behind other business functions when it comes to vital measures and improvements? Inspired by such a divinely gaping need, we anointed ourselves to set out once and for all to solve this quagmire.

With no reliable, robust measurement tool within HR's grasp, we took it upon ourselves to create one. We enlisted the help of Brian Deyo, a gifted product manager, marketer, and lifelong learner to lead our efforts. We then recruited the considerable academic forces at the Butler University Business Consulting Group and endeavored to provide a formula that all employers, regardless of size, geography, industry, or composition, could use to measure employee engagement and garner specifics of what and how to improve. Statisticians, mathematicians, and business theorists from Butler eagerly accepted our mission to develop a model that captures the heart of evaluating employee engagement. The result? A proprietary way to measure engagement (inspired and informed by HR gurus) that leverages employee sentiment, employer inputs, and machine learning to produce a scalable and flexible model of employee engagement. To learn more about how to deploy the Emplify Score Survey at your organization, visit www.AgileEngagementBook.com.

By unearthing your company's unique Emplify Score, you will discover a baseline metric that can henceforth be used as your company's true north. Not only can you use the Emplify Score outputs to help craft your Engagement Canvas strategic objectives, but you can more easily determine whether your strategic objectives have resulted in meaningful improvement. It is impossible to know for certain if you have improved something unless you have the ability to measure it, and the Emplify Score allows for precisely that.

The Emplify Score distinctly differs from the typical, traditional method of measuring employee engagement: the fateful, annual employee survey. Let us be rid of it once and for all, shall we? At Emplify, we have set our sights on no less than a fundamental upheaval of the way employers and employees engage one another at work. The ability to explicitly, accurately measure employee engagement is integral to this goal.

As Hank Orme, former president of Lincoln Industries, says, "In most organizations there is not equal status given to cultural metrics and financial or operational metrics because they are not viewed as important. But, the truth is cultural metrics are more important."

In this next section, we delve into some delightfully nerdy details about the science behind the Emplify Score. Be warned that this discussion is more esoteric than the rest of this book but yields a rich discussion around the meaning and measurement of engagement.

Though we do encourage you to wade into these deeper waters with us in order to understand the theory, measures, and deeper insights and challenges behind the Emplify Score, we also happily accept that it is not for everyone. Rest easy knowing that we recruited some brilliant left brains to thoroughly and accurately create this measurement tool. For our faithful data analysts, economists, statisticians, and otherwise mathematically inclined or curious readers, read on.

Summary of Engagement Construct

Employee engagement is tricky because we humans tend to be nuanced, varied, and often weird. Unlike measures of profit and turnover for which we can rely on hard numbers, employee engagement invokes the more challenging realms of human psychology, or how we think and feel. In psychology, such attempts to assess human emotion and thought are deemed "constructs."

This construct of employee engagement has thus far been studied primarily by industrial and organizational psychologists. Their conclusions have been varied, but foundational, and so before detailing our own theory, we will summarize some of the relevant thinking to date. We have incorporated several of these concepts into our theory as well, without relying too heavily on any particular one. So without further delay, we present our summary version of the differing views of engagement, what it is, and what it is not.

Four Views of Engagement

Engagement as Satisfaction

Probably the most popular and perhaps the most dangerous current concept of engagement equates it to satisfaction. Although satisfaction contributes to engagement, engagement envelopes additional components of passion, commitment, time, effort, and care. *Satisfaction* implies a sort of contentment, or a treading of the work waters, if you will. But competition today demands rejection of the status quo. Engagement supersedes satisfaction. It inspires, it challenges, and it drives results.

Flow

One of the closest concepts to engagement is that of "flow" (Csikszentmihalyi, 1990), defined as the "holistic sensation that people feel when they act with total involvement" (p. 36). When a person is in a flow state, the distinction between her and her environment goes away almost entirely. Engagement can feel very much like this, and we think people who are able to get into a flow state regularly are likely very engaged. However, flow is a sort of peak cognitive state, and we believe that engagement is variable and ranges greatly. If you think of flow as the ultimate work mind state, engagement is much more variable and involves all of mind, body, and emotions.

Engagement as a Trait

Some hold the view that engagement is a personality trait largely uninfluenced by external inputs. From this stance, measuring an individuals' emotions or behaviors is not actually measuring their engagement because their engagement remains consistent according to personality or disposition. Although we do acknowledge that some people are more prone to engagement than others, we disagree that it is so unmalleable. In our model, we incorporate the component of "engageability" to comprise this aspect of personality.

Engagement as Behavior Only

Management consulting firms have long operationalized engagement, and many have developed compelling theories and proven models that have offered much to this space. However, many of them assess *only* behavior, neglecting to capture anything related to individual feelings and affect, and we posit that this misses something fundamental about the engagement construct.

Okay, you ask—feelings? If we can assess desired behaviors, then who cares about feelings, right? Wrong. At the core of engagement resides a foundation of just and fair treatment. Engagement is an inherently balanced concept—an individual's investment of himself or herself in a role and meaningful value in return. Engagement extracted from the employee purely for the benefit of the organization is not sustainable. It is one-sided, and it is shallow. And if we are getting technical, it's not even really engagement; it's just short-term behaviors masquerading as such. True engagement serves *both* the organization's and employee's interests for the long haul.

Employee Engagement Model

Our model for employee engagement consists of four key elements:

- Organization, individual, and fit drivers
- Psychological engagement conditions
- Engagement feelings
- Engagement behaviors

Conceptual Model

Note here the flow of engagement through an organization, sprouting from individual employee, the organization, and fit between the two. Out of that environment, psychological conditions are created in employees that enable them to engage and act in ways that reveal that engagement. See Figure 27.1.

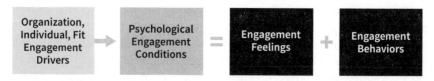

FIGURE 27.1 Conceptual Employee Engagement

Drivers of Engagement (Organization, Individual, Fit)

This is the most central and tangible section of the Emplify Score and the company's main stage for action. Essentially, it is this: You should create an environment where engagement can happen. If you follow half of what we have suggested elsewhere in this book, you will be better off than most.

We break down drivers into three key components: the organization, the individual, and the fit between them. Together, they lead to engagement. (Figure 27.2).

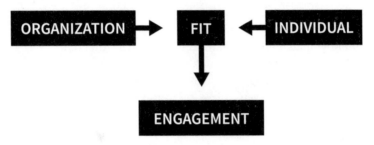

FIGURE 27.2 State of Engagement

First up, we have the organization component. Organizations carry inherently positive and negative traits that assuredly affect engagement. *Safety* is a big one here. If employees don't feel safe to engage without risking emotional distress or inappropriate relationships, you will obviously not see desired results. Also within the organization, we account for *meaning*. Do your employees believe their work and mission are important and worthwhile? Although nuanced to individuals, meaning largely arises from the organization.

On the other side of the model, we have individual employees. Although not everything, personality certainly plays a significant role in how engaged an employee can be, and the Emplify Score takes into account certain *traits* known to correlate with engagement. Doing so helps control for trait during organizational changes in employee composition and in engagement strategies, lending insight into whether your strategic actions actually moved the needle or if you are simply hiring people who are more "engageable." Neither is necessarily bad, but we want to distill what is working.

Also within the individual component, we examine their *capacity* to engage, influenced by everything from personal financial stability to quality of sleep. Some individuals may want to engage and may be perfectly positioned to do so but face restrictions in their personal life, such as health complications or marital problems, that constrict engagement. Understandably, gathering this sort of information can be problematic in terms of maintaining trust and privacy. This is why we think it is critical to involve a third party to more easily bear the challenge of protecting information and sustaining trust. We dream of a world where employees can be honest about their capacity to perform on any given day and where organizations can in turn help them recharge and produce the best work possible. Until then, you should use a third party to help create trust. Such trust can be difficult to earn but has vast potential to simultaneously spike well-being and productivity.

For individuals to engage in an organization, three psychological conditions must be present: capacity, safety, and meaning. In our concept of "fit," we aim to capture the complex intersection of these qualities between the individual and the organization.

All individuals and organizations have elements that objectively are neither good nor bad, just unique. Think anything from role differences to dress codes, perks, mission, leader styles, work space environments, and everything in between. When those stars align, we call it a good cultural fit. Although capturing all of these elements would be nearly impossible, we ask specifically targeted questions that solicit these elements from both the individual and the organization to isolate fit.

Fit is one of the most important elements to engagement. It already happens. Employees already self-select into companies based on surface-level understandings of culture, but we can and should make them better. Because clearly the better the fit, the deeper the engagement.

Psychological Conditions

In order to engage, we must first satisfy certain basic psychological needs. Picture employee engagement as a foot race. Before we can sprint, we first need the following:

- *Meaning.* How fast and how far are we motivated to run?
- *Safety.* How safe and sound is the path? Riddled with mud and tree roots, or clear and well-marked?
- *Capacity.* How strong and capable are we to swiftly go the distance? Have we trained? Are we in over our heads?

Likewise, for your employees to effectively engage, focus your efforts on the conditions surfaced by the Emplify Score and analysis and try to create a meaningful, safe environment full of employees with the capacity to engage.

Chapter

Three Key Employee Needs
Engagement Canvas Box 10

othing betrays a disengaged workforce quite so tellingly as an executive team that boasts a culture of positively flowering utopia, only to have employees grumble the ghastly realities of that "same" culture. Obviously we exaggerate to make a point, but in all seriousness, that juxtaposition flatters no one. This disconnect speaks to and should alarm you on many fronts, but, as always, acknowledgment is the first step to healing. Surface these incongruities as quickly as possible, for only when you come to grips with such an issue can you work to remedy it.

In this last section of the Engagement Canvas, we form the basis for personalized, actionable steps forward. If all this engagement fervor is new for your organization, expect a fairly drastic gap between what you put here versus the previous investments you listed in the Resources Applied section. The Emplify Score reveals which particular engagement drivers are lacking on your team, and you would do well to start with those. List the bottom three and have at it. If you don't have the Emplify Score, go with your gut for now, though be wary that although we tend to think we have a pulse on our organizations, we misdiagnose them shockingly often.

Good things come in threes: musketeers, stooges, little pigs, strategic priorities, you get the picture. For whatever reason, our human minds are naturally inclined to enjoy, comprehend, and act on a well-rounded three items. Similarly, when working to improve pressing matters like engagement, we've found that prioritizing three items reaps the best outcomes.

Complete this box with three employee needs that you specifically intend to address. If you don't have three, start with one or two, but make them targeted and actionable. Self-scrutinizing though it is, focus less on reinforcing what you're already doing really well, and more on removing barriers to engagement. For the simplest way to do this, force rank the questions from the Emplify Score or the driver categories. The questions will be specific and reveal categories of problems, while the drivers may unearth groupings of problems consistently mediocre across the organization.

Wondering what to do with different departments and teams? We like to start at the federal (company-wide) level as opposed to the state (team) level, because leadership often cascades through the organization, and because similar issues often emerge across teams. Jumping straight to the team level can also be fine, it just requires more work, more decisions around focus, and more disjointed campaigns, so we encourage such team level targets only for those organizations already doing fairly well with their Emplify Scores.

Chapter 29

Engagement Canvas FAQs

Who Should Participate?

We get this question a lot. And the predictably unsatisfying answer is: It depends. It depends on the unique makeup of your organization and the depth to which various players are involved. Probably, though, key players will involve some combination of the board (or select board members), executives, business leaders, HR representatives, and key team members who embody your ideal culture. Be choosy and strategic with whose inputs, opinions, and directions you take into account.

In decades past, as we have noted, HR was "keeper of the culture." A tool like the Engagement Canvas likely would have landed squarely, and solely, under their jurisdiction, far from the watchful or even remotely interested eyes of anyone else in the business. Thankfully, though, times have changed. Although HR should and will continue to play an important role in the Engagement Canvas process, other key leaders should also take vested interest in and ownership of the outcome.

Organizations are inherently political. To be able to accomplish wide-reaching objectives, you must be able to navigate the steadfast variety of occupational roadblocks and less-than-savory workplace personalities. Overcoming these obstacles requires an acute awareness of what it takes to be successful in your organization. Ask yourself, Who do we need to be part of the solution, not part of the problem? Who are employees that others listen to and respect on crucial issues? Which employees elegantly and effectively implement change? The names that arise from these questions are likely the same ones that should be involved in some capacity with crafting your Engagement Canvas.

Jim Collins offers a method for surfacing an organization's key players, which he dubs the Mars Group (Collins, 2000). If you had to re-create the very best attributes of your organization on Mars, and the rocket ship had seats for only a handful of people, who would you send? You would scout people with a gut-level understanding of the essence of your organization, who have earned impeccable credibility with their peers and demonstrate unmatched competence. Ask the larger group to nominate this select handful of exemplary people, and empower them to articulate the underlying pillars of your organizational culture and partake in this Engagement Canvas process.

Why Can't I Simply Complete the Engagement Canvas Myself?

As tempting as it may be for a CEO or chief human resources officer to lock the door and hash this all out solo, resist the urge. As a leader, you cannot take matters of culture and engagement into your own unaccompanied hands and attempt to impart an authentic or reasonable Engagement Canvas. Think for a second about the words *engagement* and *culture*. Pretty much nothing about those words happens individually. Solicit thoughts, points of view, input, and direction from multiple leaders, because a single person's perception simply will not yield the richness generated by multiple business people providing meaningful insights. Furthermore, strategic outcomes will be more readily adopted if a cross-functional group collaborates to drive the work. So basically, do not attempt to fly solo here because (1) it will not be an accurate representation, and (2) it will not be adopted, which means it would be a colossal waste of time.

We have had multiple leadership teams approach us concerning how to best address cultural challenges emanating from the CEO or other executives that cause troubles for the organization. So, chief X officer, you cannot do it alone because you might be a significant root cause of the problem. We suggest using this Engagement Canvas approach as a nonthreatening way to bring up, discuss, and work through concerns. Self-aware executives that participate oftentimes discover the need for changes in their own behavior in order to create positive impact on the business culture as a whole.

Rob Edwards of Andretti Autosports says it "should be more like a set of sailing instructions than a road map. The crew should be involved, and the process should be iterative and flexible" (Edwards, 2016).

What Does the Process Look Like, and How Long Does It Take?

We are all busy people with plenty of demands on our time and attention. Maybe you are luckier or more well organized than the two of us, but we certainly do not have the hours or the mental stamina, nor the faintest desire to sift through hordes of information to compile a 40-page culture plan. And in any case, we are fresh out of neglected, cobwebby drawer space in which to haphazardly stash and soon forget about it. We designed the Engagement Canvas intentionally as an insightful and intuitive exercise that yields meaningful results, not an onerous and ultimately pointless task.

Although circumstance specific, depending on the people involved and the depth of rigorous dialogue they undertake in the process, we expect actionable outputs in the matter of a few weeks.

The suggested process is as follows:

1. Determine the select team of leaders and employees to partake in the process.

2. Socialize the Engagement Canvas process with the selected team. Pro tip: You can access a brief introduction to the Engagement Canvas process online at www.AgileEngagementBook.com. Although we would obviously recommend that participants read the book to gain full context, the online introduction could also serve as an adequate primer.

3. Facilitate a discussion around the current culture state, mission/vision/values, unique characteristics, and employee constituencies.

4. Execute the Emplify Score process, or another true engagement measurement tool, to identify opportunities for engagement improvement. Find details about the Emplify Score at www.AgileEngagementBook.com.

5. Facilitate a second discussion to review outputs from the first meeting and discuss strategic objectives moving forward, including the communication channels and resources needed to execute those objectives.

Ultimately, the time it takes for those involved to diverge and converge will drive how quickly your strategic objectives manifest.

What Is the Expected Outcome of the Engagement Canvas?

The process of navigating the Engagement Canvas provides almost immediate benefits for your organization. The Engagement Canvas takes processes and key factors that organizations should be addressing anyway and streamlines them into a simple, concise, actionable, one-page game plan. For instance, leadership teams should regularly go through the exercise of identifying the current state of the organization and strategizing to improve their organizational alignment to those pillars.

More times than not, businesses continue operating from the same statements they originally created at the outset of the company. We have found, however, that as time passes, leaders and employees alike forget the core tenets on which the business was formed and continues to stand. Proactively reviewing and reminding teams of these fundamentals often yields productive discussions, enhanced alignment, and recasting of vision statements in particular.

Apart from simply prompting group interactions around the business foundations, the Engagement Canvas helps to clarify areas of employee engagement focus. Numerous and complicated objectives rarely get accomplished. The Engagement Canvas therefore drives clarity around those few key objectives aimed specifically at enhancing cultures and increasing employee engagement. The Engagement Canvas yields succinct and precise objectives that can be subsequently adopted across the organization.

Is the Engagement Canvas a One-Time Activity?

The Engagement Canvas is best used on an ongoing basis, following the classic cadence of continuous measure and improve. Given that cultures themselves are not static, sensibly they require regular visitation and attention. Overall, though, the process should become crisper and less time consuming with each subsequent occasion. A number of the sections allow for reuse of materials. For example, we would anticipate your Why You Exist section to remain fairly consistent, along with your Unique Organizational Characteristics, which typically linger around for reuse. Other sections, such as the Emplify Score and Culture Aspirations, are more prone to shift from year to year.

The framework we suggest is one that stresses a consistent and frequent cadence of measurement and improvement. Adopting the below engagement process ensures these key tenets are met.

In our use of the Engagement Canvas, both at Emplify and with our varied customers and partners, we have seen the most benefits when we conduct the exercise on a continual basis. Similar to other processes that maintain ongoing cadences of measurement and improvement accountability, having a real-time pulse is invaluable in charting our engagement strategy. With that

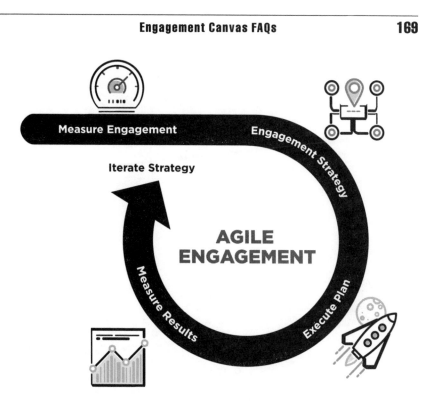

Agile Engagement Framework

said, most companies still conduct annual budget, goal-setting, and operational reviews, and tucking the Engagement Canvas in with these worthwhile activities would also be a satisfactory approach.

Part

The Practice of Engagement

Chapter

Speak with One Voice
(Or, Why Conformity Is Good Sometimes)

L et's pause. If you have been following along, you now have your very own Engagement Canvas, tailored to fit your organization. Congratulations!

We want to take a moment to invite you to peruse and join our online community at www.AgileEngagementBook.com. Because culture is a process, we want to be able to continue the conversation, share more stories and examples, and help you through the journey.

Now comes the fun part: execution. In your snazzy new Engagement Canvas, you unearthed several key strategic priorities. For the next six months, pick a few of them and focus your efforts there. The essence of strategy is already choosing what not to do, and even among what we do choose, we can't do it all. So start small. This will be an ongoing process. In six months, reassess, realign, and reboot. When it comes to culture, sometimes incremental, sincere progress is best. Take it in small strategic objective chunks, and you will make meaningful progress toward forming, enhancing, and cultivating your culture.

As you are carrying out these strategic objectives, roadblocks will surface. We have compiled a list of pointers, situations that may present themselves, and practical tips to help you to overcome them. The process manifests differently for everyone. Some of these may be irrelevant or already assumed in

173

your organization, and others may be your lifeline. But they are all things that we, or people we have worked with, have faced in the process of forging and tending to our cultures, and we choose to share them candidly because we believe they offer insight and guidance.

During the time we were writing this book, Todd asked a CEO how he would describe his company's culture. He replied, "You know, that's a good question, I have never been asked that before." To that we say:

- Even if you have not previously considered your culture, or been asked about it by pesky culture enthusiasts such as ourselves, the fact is, culture is becoming a recognized pillar of the workplace. Gallup released their study on the state of the global workplace in 2013, and many people hurriedly jumped on board the culture/engagement movement (Crabtree, 2013). In 2014, *culture* was Merriam-Webster's word of the year (2014 Word of the Year, 2014). It is becoming normalized, and more people than ever will be asking about it. If you are not already making this a priority, you should be.

- Furthermore, even if no one is asking you about it, that is no reason you should not be taking the initiative yourself to describe, cultivate, and promote your culture. At ExactTarget, we championed our culture like it was our job (. . . it was) and there were always a few naysayers who thought we were outlandish or did not realize the significance of culture. But we did. And when we went public, we included "culture" as a distinct differentiator in our initial public offering filing, which was the first time such a thing had been done. No, of course culture was not the sole reason for our success, but it was the foundation on which everything else was built.

We encourage you to talk about culture with investors. Take it into account when you interview employees and partners. We have already established it is important, so it is time we treat it that way. When describing your culture, you should do the following:

- *Be explicit.* Define your culture in specific terms. Don't say it is "good" or "strong," say what makes it that way. Show, don't tell.
- *Be consistent.* Is the elevator pitch that the CEO gives about the culture the same spiel that HR distills throughout the company

and that rank-and-file employees say to their friends and family? If executives tout your shining accolades while low-level employees bewail the inner horrors, who do you think people will believe?

- *Be empowering.* Beyond ensuring that everyone is on the same page of what your culture is, make sure each person understands his or her ability and responsibility to create and sustain it. Culture starts with each of us.

31

Brand What's Important
(Or, Why Marketing Should Live in HR)

By now, I'm sure we have you hoodwinked, thinking this was a book about HR, not marketing. But, these two departments go hand in hand (or at least they should) in order to truly engage employees and create a culture worth bragging about. Bye-bye jagged, hand-cut construction paper desk drops about open enrollment. Sayonara cheap starchy t-shirts for volunteer day. Adios 16-paragraph Outlook emails about tax documents (rife with typos).

Employees are like curious, spongy toddlers in the sense that they watch everything we do and listen to everything we say. They notice when we say something is important, but then turn around and refuse to approve any time or resources for the project. They notice when we only care about culture events that are sexy enough for a company press release. They notice when we boast a set of core values but act in exactly the opposite fashion when the going gets tough. They notice everything.

This brings us to the topic of branding. As organizations, we brand what is important to us, or in more general terms, we expend resources on what we value. Plain and simple, if you want to see what we value as people, don't listen to what we say, look at how we spend our time and our money. Same goes for organizations. Let's do a quick assessment. Look at your internal culture and communications budget. Is it miniscule? Do you even have one? Can you spot it tucked away somewhere on the balance sheet?

Recognize first how telling the numbers are as opposed to the lip service, and candidly acknowledge how much value you're actually giving your culture. That is not to say that all culture initiatives hit your pocketbook. Many do not. But executives who boast about their cultures all the live long day, while refusing to spend a dime to advance them, won't last. Culture requires deliberately investing in your people. It means taking resources like money, time, and sometimes even headcount to brand what you claim matters most to you.

Case in Point: ExactTarget

One of Todd's favorite examples of internal branding came from his time at ExactTarget. As the company continued to hire rapidly, the size and frequency of the onboarding program exploded. With so many new employees going through this process, and gleaning their first impressions of the company, Todd's team took a good hard look at the program's branding. Mismatched documents, confusing processes, outdated designs, and lengthy text emails did not represent the company's young, fun-loving, vibrant Orange culture.

Hence, Todd commissioned a full rebrand of the program using a mix of HR and marketing resources. The result was Officially Orange, a cohesive and beautiful program with its own professional logo, marketing materials, swag, branded emails, and professional head shots; a stunning participant workbook complete with crossword puzzles; an ExactTarget glossary; ads for HR programs and events; and more.

Not only did the program's facelift get the attention of new employees, who felt welcomed, invigorated, and Orange to the core, Officially Orange captured the hearts of the leadership team and helped change their view of HR as a department. As they continued to dedicate resources to branding high-visibility programs like the ExactTarget Cuties New Parent Program and the ExactWIN women's group, the leadership team and employees at large began to realize that HR was far more than forms, filing, and firing; they were culture beacons and brand-savvy communicators.

Chapter 32

Treat Employees Like Customers

(Or, Why We're All Created Equal)

onsider the Golden Rule: Treat others as you wish to be treated. In business, this has historically translated to treating our customers like our most valuable assets. Companies commonly invest upwards of 25 percent of their budget on customer service and customer communications yet dedicate less than 1 percent of their budgets to employee marketing.

To be clear, we agree that customer service and marketing are paramount to business success. If we do not execute well in these areas, no one will care how superior, polished, and well-positioned our products and services are. If customers do not feel valued, understand what makes our company unique, and fully commit to our product over competitors, our business will eventually flatline.

Amen to all of that. But it is not nearly enough. We advocate for extending this beyond *customer* service. As business leaders (and especially HR leaders), we need to approach *employee* marketing, measurement, and investment with the same tenacity as they approach their customer equivalents. In short, treat employees as well as you treat customers.

Howard Schultz, CEO of Starbucks, says it best: "You can't expect your employees to exceed the expectations of your customers if you don't exceed the employees' expectations of management" (Smith, 1998).

Brad Morehead, CEO of LiveWatch Security agrees:

> We found our culture and engagement were highly correlated with our customer satisfaction and retention. We measured customer satisfaction using Net Promoter Score and retention by looking at churn on a daily basis. In general, if we saw any issues in customer satisfaction or churn (and it wasn't related to an obvious product or service outage), then it was typically related to company culture, morale, management or training. Money is necessary, but not sufficient for motivating teams. While people do tend to do what you pay them to do, they are capable of so much more. Culture is an amplifier for productivity. When culture is positive, productivity is amplified. (Morehead, 2016)

As employees ourselves, we inherently want this to be true, we want to be treated with the same care and commitment as customers. Yet, head to your local bookstore's business section, and you will find dozens of titles about how to build, grow, and evolve your approach to customer service. Everyone understands that customer success begets business success, and we see this clearly demonstrated in how much time and money organizations spend on customer marketing, communications, and service.

Next, browse for books about corporate culture. You will find dozens of additional titles that promise to help you build, grow, and evolve powerful cultures like those of Zappos and Patagonia. We obviously applaud that also. Now, peruse the section related to corporate marketing. You will come face to spine with a plethora of books addressing every facet of marketing—how to target campaigns, how to study your audiences, how often to send messages, and everything in between. Awesome.

Finally, search high and low for books about how to implement world-class *employee* marketing and communications. We guarantee you will not find many, if any, titles on the topic. As business leaders and HR enthusiasts, we are beyond baffled by this gap. We all seem to accept the reality of *employees* serving *customers*. We spend countless hours reading, meeting, and speaking about how to deliver world-class customer service, as we should.

But what about the importance of *leaders* serving *employees*? How much time do we spend perfecting the noble craft of employee marketing? Sure, affordable, comprehensive benefits are a good start. Meaningful volunteer opportunities and gracious paid time off help too. But that's only the beginning. We are calling for a radical rethinking of every single employee touch point.

Consider your current customer communications (likely owned by the marketing team): scrutinized at length, designed with care, professionally printed or delivered through user-friendly channels. Beautiful. Now contrast that with your current employee communications, likely consisting of plain text emails, newsletters tossed together in Microsoft Publisher and printed ever so slightly off-center on the office copier, company meeting PowerPoints bursting at the seams with cluttered bullet points and cheesy animated gifs. Please, for the sake of all that's good and green in the world, get your head out of the 1990s and disavow tacky clip art forever.

We firmly believe that if you take care of your employees first, they will then take better care of your customers. Unfortunately, this belief is not widely shared in the business world, with actions not following the lip service it often receives.

So if employee and customer communications hold equal value to their constituencies, why, then, do we so often grant such superior design, messaging, and delivery to our customer audiences? The age of such foul inequality is over. The good news? Your organization already has a playbook for how to treat employees. It's the same way you treat your customers.

Here's how you can start.

Realize Looks Matter

Nonmarketers often believe it's the message, not the method, that matters most. In reality, it's both. Every email, every digital slide on an office TV, every sign, every desk drop, every mobile app notification, and every event needs to be executed at a high level of professionalism that *reinforces* the message. Employees respond to solid creative communications as much (if not more) than customers do. It lets them know they are important to the organization. It makes them feel part of something bigger.

Use a tone, style, and quality that you would award to customers. At ExactTarget, we took weary HR efforts and turned them into masterpieces. One year, instead of sending out a routine Outlook email begging for employees to sign up for a new benefits plan, we created video spoofs about open enrollment, including cinematic inspirations like *The Hangover* and *The Fast and The Furious*. We even spoofed *Office Space,* complete with clobbering an old copy machine, with baseball bats, on film. Did this effort take money? Yes. But it achieved the desired result and then some. We had 99 percent of employees enrolled within 48 hours of the deadline.

Secure Marketing Resources

We set the bar high for customer communications because the marketers executing those communications are uniquely qualified to develop compelling communications across design, messaging, and delivery. Employee communications, on the other hand, are typically planned, created, and delivered by HR team members who, though qualified in many areas, usually lack specific training in communications and marketing.

Fear not. You have options. Try giving your employee communications and marketing campaigns professional polish by (a) requesting design and creative assistance from the marketing department, (b) allocating HR budget to hire external marketing agencies or freelance creatives, or (c) cross-train your team members on design basics and tools via online and offline courses.

While at ExactTarget, Todd was so passionate about marketing well to employees that he recruited one of the marketing team's veterans to join HR full time. It was an unorthodox move, but it paid off. For the cost of a single headcount, every campaign, program, and communication HR executed looked like it came from the marketing team. Employees sat up and took notice. Leadership sat up and took notice. Best of all, other members of the HR team saw their hard work presented in professional ways that improved the way the rest of the company viewed their roles and contributions.

Create an Employee Advisory Board

Companies use customer advisory boards to understand needs and gather feedback about products and services. These groups provide customers with a unique sense of value, influence, and camaraderie. Unlike customers, employees rarely have a robust and regular forum to share suggestions, feedback, and ideas. Why should companies give customers more control over products, services, and overall direction of the company than their own employees?

Form an employee advisory board comprised of key influencers and your most engaged employees across the organization. Give the group direct access to company leadership and solicit their opinions on business and employee matters. Not only will this help increase employee engagement, it will also give you invaluable insights into the hearts and minds of your employees and prove that employee feedback is a critical part of the company's direction and evolution.

Regularly Solicit and Act on Employee Feedback

Most companies monitor and measure customer feedback on a constant basis. From postpurchase surveys to product reviews and focus groups, companies treat customer feedback data like gold. Employee surveys, on the other hand, are typically conducted annually, if that. When results are gathered, the feedback is rarely acted on. Or, worse, surveyors spend six months conducting, six months digesting results, and another six months communicating those results back. So 18 months later, the organization can start to address the issues at hand and make substantive change. But of course by then the issues at hand have resolved themselves or long since been swept into some forlorn corner, and all that effort was for naught.

Instead, let's try something that is actually useful. At Emplify, we conduct smaller, frequent, randomized surveys via mobile app tools to garner continuous feedback and improvement. Consider partnering with a third-party employee survey group or creating an internal employee survey cadence. Then share high-level results back with employees, tell them what actions you're going to take based on their feedback, and hold yourself accountable for following through on those promises. Make sure leadership communicates what will be done, and do not solicit more feedback until you respond to the first round.

Ask Employees to Drive Meaningful Change

The weight of the employee engagement world does not rest solely on your shoulders. Invite employees to help brainstorm opportunities and solutions, and then listen to what they say. Empower employees to affect changes themselves, and provide them the avenue and funding to make it happen.

Marc Benioff, CEO of Salesforce.com, gives a fantastic example of precisely this in his book *Behind the Cloud*: In the early days, Sue, a support analyst, asked what the company was doing about the environment. Marc said, "I'm not sure. You have six paid days to figure it out, I'll support you." She did and eventually went on to become the company's first sustainability manager (Benioff & Adler, 2009, 162).

Implement Employee-Related Change Management Strategies

Companies agonize over how to communicate important (and sometimes minute) business changes to their customers. Leaders take painstaking care to ensure they communicate key information clearly, concisely, and consistently. It's not uncommon for companies to deliver the message across multiple channels and measure engagement and reception.

Employee-related changes should be planned, drafted, and delivered with the same (if not more) intentionality as customer communications. Last-minute, half-baked, one-time, email-only employee communications don't cut it anymore. From leadership changes to process changes, use a thoughtful, cross-channel, measurable communication plan that gives employees the information they need in a format they can digest. Consider videos, live meetings, desk drops, text message or mobile app alerts, and FAQs. Make sure *every* communication includes a clear path for employees to ask questions or voice concerns.

Educate and Enlighten HR Staff

Whether you partner with your corporate marketing team, use external firms, or have the benefit of hiring dedicated communications staff within HR, make education a priority. Every member of your HR organization needs to understand the value of professional, polished employee communications and internal marketing. Spend time educating them about how and when to engage with marketing/creative team members. Explain how HR benefits from putting more time and resources into internal communications. Celebrate successes as a team to build momentum around effective campaigns. Only once every member of your HR team understands the value of marketing and communications will your team truly begin firing on all cylinders.

In the end, we push for this so resolutely because how you treat people affects what they believe about themselves and, in turn, how they treat others.

Case in Point: Manchester Bidwell

Bill Strickland epitomizes this concept in a profound way. He has figured out how to engage his constituents, transform their mindsets, and completely revolutionize their performance. He does not run a tech startup or a Fortune 100 company, yet we find his example even more telling. He takes high school dropouts from the Pittsburgh ghetto, rallies them with beauty, dignity, and hope, and sees more than 80 percent of them go to college. He runs an organization called Manchester Bidwell, which offers high school arts performances and various other programs to serve the community (OurHistory, 2016). These include high school arts education, adult career training, and jazz performances. They all operate on the fundamental principle that you have to change the way people see themselves before you can change their behaviors.

If you walk into their arts museum, one of the first things to catch your eye will be a lovely fountain in the courtyard. Strickland also serves on the board of the Carnegie Museum and noticed that they had a fountain because they think that the people who go to the museum deserve one. "Well," he says, "I think that welfare mothers and at-risk kids and ex-steel workers deserve a fountain in their lives." So he put one there, to set top-notch attitudes and expectations right from the start (Strickland, 2008).

They also keep real flowers in the hallways, and Strickland describes how so often visitors say to him, "Mr. Strickland, what an extraordinary story and what a great school. And we were particularly touched by the flowers and we were curious as to how the flowers got there." "Well," he responds, "I got in my car and I went out to the greenhouse and I bought them and I brought them back and I put them there. You don't need a task force or a study group to buy flowers for your kids. What you need to know is that the children and the adults deserve flowers in their life. The cost is incidental but the gesture is huge. And so in my building, which is full of sunlight and full of flowers, we believe in hope and human possibilities" (Strickland, 2008).

Every day, they have 400 high school students who were flunking out of the public school system show up for arts education. And for the last 15 years, they've put an average of more than 80 percent of those students in college. "We've made a fascinating discovery," he says. "There's nothing wrong with the kids that affection and sunshine and food and enthusiasm and music can't cure. For that I won a big old plaque for Man of the Year in Education. I beat out all the Ph.D.'s because I figured that if you treat children like human beings, it increases the likelihood they're going to behave that way. And why we can't institute that policy in every school and in every city and every town remains a mystery to me" (Strickland, 2008).

First and foremost, we applaud Strickland's transformative efforts and the tremendous work he and his organization continue to do. We assert his belief that people will show you world class behavior if you treat them that way. And we echo his question: Why can't we institute policies like that in every school, every city, every organization?

Trickle-Down Effect

If you need a purely business reason to follow this advice (and you shouldn't), remember that your employees' engagement will directly affect your customers' experience with your company. That, in turn, affects your bottom line and public image.

"All employees are ambassadors for your company," says Gary Reynolds of Reynolds Farm Equipment. "Most of your customers' interactions are with employees, not leadership" (Reynolds, 2016).

If you want a deeper reason to follow our advice (and we hope you do), consider this: Whether you deal with high school kids or stock brokers, welfare mothers or software developers, call center representatives, C-suite executives, customers, investors, or employees, treat them like you want to be treated, treat them like you treat customers, and treat them like world-class human beings.

Austrian neurologist and Holocaust survivor Viktor Frankl relays a similar concept in his book *Man's Search for Meaning* (Frankl, 1972). If we take people as they really are, he posits, we make them worse. But if we overestimate them, we promote them to what they really can be. Presuppose the spark in people, and you will elicit that spark from them. You will help them become what they are in principle already capable of becoming.

Chapter 33

Leverage Data

(Or, Why There's No Shame in Nerdiness)

The last thing you want to do is pour a lot of time and money into marketing to employees and have no way to prove whether or not it worked. Return on investment is measurable, even in people analytics. Back in the 1800s, physicist William Thomson (also known as Lord Kelvin, of the Kelvin scale of temperature) presented the view that "if you can't measure it, you can't improve it," (Lord Kelvin). Peter Drucker later commandeered those words to our familiar "If you can't measure it, you can't manage it." And we have continued to adopt that sentiment, incorporate it into various tools like Define, Measure, Analyze, Improve, Control (DMAIC) and Six Sigma, and apply it to fields from marketing to clinical health care trials to code quality to body composition.

We painstakingly measure so much in our businesses, including sales performance, search engine optimization, margins, and expenses. After all, you are what you measure. If a firm measures A and B, but not X and Y, people will naturally focus on A and B. Employees are smart; they know how to pay attention to what their leaders value. If I see my manager measuring and judging how much I can cut costs but not how satisfied consumers are, I will naturally prioritize expenses to the detriment of customer happiness.

Despite this, alarmingly few organizations apply the same measurement rigor to their cultures. We know it's important. We know it enhances employee engagement. The question is, how the heck are we supposed to gauge it? How can we measure the positive and negative aspects of our cultures and improve our shortcomings?

For perspective, check out these disconcerting employee engagement statistics from 2014 (The 2014 Employee Engagement Organizational Culture Report, 2014):

- 64 percent do not feel they have a strong workplace culture.
- 49 percent are not satisfied with their direct supervisors.
- 66 percent see no opportunities for professional growth.
- 25 percent feel they do not have the tools to be successful in their jobs.
- 21 percent feel strongly valued at work, generally because of lack of appreciation and recognition.
- 42 percent know their organization's vision, mission, and values.

Read those numbers again. Sobering, right? We're talking about a serious workplace gap here.

Of the minority of companies that do measure culture and engagement, most do so via annual surveys. An annual survey? Really? That's the best we've got, to check in on our greatest asset? By the time responses are collected, reviewed, and analyzed, there's usually been a change in leadership, an updated product, or a shift in technology or market opportunity, rendering the data outdated and ultimately unhelpful.

To stay on top of our game, we must reinvent employee engagement for the digital age. We must better gather, evaluate, and analyze our data, and this must be done through something more than an annual employee survey.

Happily, though, the answers are already here. We just have to learn how to properly leverage them. Twenty years ago, Tim Berners-Lee (inventor of the World Wide Web) asked people to put their documents online, and it completely revolutionized how we interact with the world around us. Where would we be without websites? Poring over encyclopedias and feebly attempting to navigate a card catalogue? No thank you. We certainly have him to thank for making this book possible, not to mention our companies and livelihoods. Berners-Lee reflected on that transformation: "I said, 'Could you put your documents on this Web thing?' And you did. Thanks. It's been a blast, hasn't it?" (Berners-Lee, 2009). Yes, indeed, it has.

Now Berners-Lee is calling people to put their data on the Internet. He had an audience chant, "Raw data now!" after lecturing on how he believes that the more pieces of data we connect, the more powerful they become (Berners-Lee, 2009). Considering his history of incredible foresight, we daresay he's onto something. Society is finally learning to take informational data and place it within holistic data schemes. On a global scale, people are using data to address mass challenges like feeding people, supplying medical care, providing energy, and averting climate change. If data can do all that, they can certainly help us keep top talent engaged in our organizations.

Relative to other disciplines, however, HR has been notoriously lagging in the general push to leverage data and analytics. Although just about every other area of business has been able to gather and evaluate data as a way to diagnose problems, chart out strategies, and otherwise set an actionable cadence, the areas of people and culture have proven mulishly impermeable to robust data and analytics. Though our need was dire with much at stake, given the hefty consequences of flying blind, we have lagged behind in the realms of people and engagement.

To meet this need, and to do our best to resist and reverse the bum leg reputation with which we HR descendants have been saddled, we created the Emplify Score. We sought to develop a statistically sound tool that would enable us and any organization to objectively judge employee engagement. The resulting Emplify Score measure provides the necessary analytics to inform business leaders how they can affect their workplace culture and resulting employee engagement.

Adding this analytics dimension to your HR team is necessary and attainable, but we certainly don't mean to say it is easy. Unfortunately, most HR employees have not had extensive, or often any, training in statistics, data science, or high-level math. Work to address that gap, by all means, but also do not hesitate to call in reinforcements. Properly leveraging data and analytics in HR could literally be made into a whole other book, and we do not presume to offer an adequate, comprehensive coverage of the topic in this chapter. That said, we will present a few tips and practices to garner an idea of what it entails and to demonstrate why it warrants additional consideration.

When you frame issues:

- *Ask the right questions.* Generally, we run into problems not with embracing the concept of analytics but with knowing how to focus it. Asking "How are we celebrating birthdays?" or "How many people signed up for our volunteer day?" will not create lasting impact. Instead, ask "How is top talent being engaged?" and "What if everyone were able to reach his or her full potential?" Measuring too many things (or too many of the wrong things) leads to watered down results. According to a 2015 survey, one of the least-measured HR metrics is "quality of hire," which is only being measured by 28.5 percent of organizations (Bruce, 2015). Of those, more than half ask only one question: how satisfied the hiring manager is with the new recruit. Actionable? Not so much. Data are only as good as the questions you ask.

- *Ask questions in the right way.* Seek continuous feedback and measurement. With all the tools currently available, there is no reason you shouldn't be continuously gathering data. If you wait until the end of a year to survey employees, you will probably get feedback on the previous month. Gauge in real-time, not in annual retrospect. Along with this, cater to the ADD generation. If you ask more than five questions, people start to lose interest or stop responding authentically.

- *Address the big picture.* Instead of asking each department to provide three measurements to add to the scorecard, focus on the whole—the why, the root cause—and let those strategies cascade through everything else. Imagine a hierarchy: strategic impact on top, effective processes in the middle, and transactional efficiencies on the bottom. Draw an organizational map to see how the concepts and outcomes relate. Those ground-level tactics may be similar across different businesses, but the top level is unique to your organization.

- *Think forward.* The beauty of analytics is that it helps us chart our future course, not just record the past. One of the most popular HR metrics is voluntary and involuntary turnover, measured by 78 percent of organizations (Bruce, 2015). But if you're not recognizing valuable talent until it's walking out the door, you're missing the power of data. McKinsey tells of an organization that used predictive behavioral analytics to learn that most employees were leaving because of inadequate recognition and limited training (Fecheyr-Lippins, et al., 2015). Unknowingly, management had been giving expensive retention bonuses that were "an ineffective and costly Band-Aid." The company redesigned training and recognition and consequently reduced its retention bonuses by $20 million and employee attrition by half. Be predictive, not reactive.

- *Make it personal.* There is no one-size-fits-all formula for data management. Walmart, Goldman Sachs, and Zappos might all measure turnover, but they're using results to address different questions. One reason Google's intensive people operations team has been immensely successful is because their strategy and tactics are so specific to Googlers (Bryant, 2011). They've learned that time off and exposure to senior leaders are more motivating rewards than cash or prizes. A study revealed that their people value even-keeled managers who make time for one-on-one check-ins and help their people solve problems. Using that information, they helped 75 percent of their least effective managers improve. Rather than try to replicate another company or adopt best practices, measure and understand what works for your organization.

When you whip out your calculators:

- *Bring in the right minds.* You need business people who address the right problems, statisticians who ensure there's rigor in the methods, and technologists who make solutions scalable and transparent. Some data collections and analyzations are huge undertakings: Statisticians often gather thousands of observations across hundreds of variables. They may need to code nonnumerical information (feedback, interview notes) in order to synthesize results and look for patterns. There may be random correlations that look significant but are actually just noise. There may be correlations that shouldn't be confused with causations. Make sure you have the right people on your team.

- *Complement humans, but don't replace them.* In the euphoria of new analytics tools, it's easy to think a few simple clicks will transform your business. But assumptions can be built into the metrics that are biased and discriminatory, or they could be measuring irrelevant or excessive information. We're still at the outset of the big data revolution and are learning how to handle it best. These processes require strategy, critical thought, and creativity.

When you get the results:

- *Make them visual.* As data visionary Hans Rosling says, "Let the dataset change your mindset." One of the best ways to do so is by visualizing the information. Design it so it makes more sense, tells a story, and lets patterns and connections emerge (Rosling, 2009). Sight is the fastest of our senses, with the same bandwidth as a computer network (McCandless, 2010). But of all the daily visuals and patterns pouring in, we're only consciously aware of about 0.7 percent of what we see. Rosling helped create a free software, Gapminder World, that offers and animates vast amounts of ready-made data. It's an engrossing "fact tank" that exemplifies well the potential of data visualization. Google, ever the early adopter, started using this software in 2007 (Gapminder World Offline, 2013).

- *Make them actionable.* Without some link to a future course of action, data overload is overwhelming and counterproductive. It's tempting to throw around best practices and measure everything we can get our hands on. But we cannot realistically embrace 20 improved practices at once without ranking them by importance. Google figured out they could improve their onboarding process by 25 percent (a full month faster) by sending a simple reminder email to the hiring manager the Sunday before the new hire starts (Sullivan, 2015). The email highlights five quick bullets: Have a role and responsibilities discussion, match your new hire with a peer buddy, help your new hire build a social network, set up onboarding check-ins, and encourage open dialogue. That's it. Their data show that employees work best under the assumption that they are smart and can figure things out. So, rather than dictating from on high, the company steers, reminds, and empowers the employees to take care of the rest.

Kenneth Cukier, Data Editor of *The Economist,* says, "Data doesn't just let us see more of the same thing we were looking at. More data allows us to see new. It allows us to see better. It allows us to see different" (Cukier, 2014). Some call it "the new oil" (Rotella, 2012), others "the new soil" (McCandless, 2010), but whatever it is, it's all around us, and it's a fertile, creative medium. Take these steps to properly refine your data and use it to your advantage.

Chapter

Set a Communication Cadence

(Or, Why Routine Is Anything but Routine)

O ne of the easiest improvements you can make to your employee engagement strategy, as we've mentioned before, is better communications. And we don't only mean better in terms of the content (though obviously that is critical). We also mean better in terms of timing and consistency. Todd believes so strongly in the importance of maintaining a communication drumbeat that he named his previous company Cadence Consulting.

Employees should be crystal clear on what to expect in your communications. They should know how they will be communicated to, how often it will happen, through what channels, by whom, at what time, and about what information. They should also know where to go with questions and feedback.

Will communications take the form of a weekly stand-up touch-base? Perhaps a daily executive email? Does it involve a quarterly all-company meeting? Maybe a Google hangout, phone call, or series of enthusiastic texts? That's entirely up to you and should be based on the channels your employees respond to best.

Employees whose managers hold regular meetings with them are almost three times as likely to be engaged as those whose managers do not. These do not have to be excessive meetings (preferably not), they just need to be expected (Adkins & Harter, 2015).

As humans in a volatile world, we function rather well in structure. Sometimes, when it seems like a lot of things in our lives are up in the air, it's really quite soothing to know we can rely on social structures like the train arriving, or the person standing in front of us at the grocery store to not instigate a mass food fight. We depend on countless structures, habits, and norms to tell us how to function in the world and to give us the ability to automate our lives to an extent, which sounds a little despondent but is actually quite freeing.

Think how much free mental space you get by being able to let your mind wander while you navigate routines like restaurant waiting lists, bus stops, and checkout lines. The fact that we can come to expect certain specified structures in our lives allows us to dedicate our time and energy to areas that need it.

Such is true with communication. By knowing exactly what, when, where, and with whom you need to routinely communicate in the workplace, you no longer have to worry about concerns such as if your manager has forgotten about you, what is expected from you during a time of transition, why no one acknowledged the work you did, or what another team member is doing.

There's quite a bit of conversation pushing for *less* routine in our lives, because it can help spark the creative juices. We get that. Sometimes we too appreciate walking a different route to the office, trying a new local hangout, traveling, or otherwise jostling our creative brains. However, in communication, we do not want ambiguity. We want an expected, reliable cadence that frees up our mental faculties, focus, and productivity for the tasks at hand.

Chapter 35

Allow for Autonomy
(Or, Why We All Need Some Space)

A s much as we like to flatter ourselves that every employee works for us because they're so fond of the company and the leadership, we obviously know that is not the case. As we mentioned in the Preface, employees work for your organization for a host of unique reasons. They show up for a paycheck, for benefits, for engagement with coworkers, for interactions with their manager, or for the work they do. They show up for myriad reasons we could never presume to list or fully realize, and as leaders, we never know precisely which reason is going to keep each employee in their sweet spot.

Happily, though, we don't have to know, and we certainly don't have to dictate from on high.

We strongly suggest encouraging affinity groups, subcultures, and grassroots initiatives. Name them what you will, but give individuals opportunities to spread their wings, plant their roots, and get involved in your organization through nonwork initiatives. Maybe it's a philanthropic involvement in the community, maybe it's a sustainability initiative in the organization, maybe it's intramural kickball. All that matters is that your employees have one more thing keeping them engaged on a bad day.

In a word, subculture is community. It's how people relate to each other. Top companies want employees to bring their complete selves to work, beyond a mere transactional, compensation-driven relationship. In return, workplaces need to *engage* employees' complete selves.

195

At ExactTarget, subcultures happened naturally and we applauded them. We nurtured them. It's the subcultures that truly bind employees to a company and give them the opportunity to make an impact. In less than a decade, we grew from a private, 200-person, single-site operation to a public company with 3,000+ employees across 15+ global offices. Through that rapid growth, our Orange culture remained steadfast, so much so that after our acquisition, a group of former employees created an "Orange Crush" Facebook group to keep in touch with current and former employees. Within *three days* it had amassed 1,200 members and 1,800 photos, all shared by people on their own time, because they love or loved working for the company. People love this brand and what being part of the Orange culture means. It's a legacy of relationships that lasts a lifetime (Lacy, 2015).

In a large company, you have to dig in and find your own interests, your own microcommunity. Thankfully, a good culture does not mean a homogenous one. From the finance department to minority groups, new parents to Tuesday night soccer games, bubbly to snarky and everything in between—they all can exemplify your culture. Even in their differences, there are always common threads: dedication to the customer, flexibility, no fear of failure. The goal of a strong culture is not to make everyone conform, but to pull them all together to work as a unified whole.

Next we share three things we learned about subcultures through our ExactTarget experience.

Subcultures Are Agile Incubators for Ideas

Early on at ExactTarget, a group of employees founded ExactImpact, a cross-functional team that owned community outreach and philanthropy. This amazing group of people volunteered their time and became an essential part of driving all of our community outreach, from blood drives to school supply collections, fundraiser runs to Christmas gifts for families. They used company resources but determined their own direction and grew our corporate philanthropy.

We would love to be the first to say that strong company culture has a powerful positive impact on the bottom line. But there is also a risk that strong culture imposes a level of stability on an organization that, after a few years, can sometimes even inhibit long-term performance by preventing innovation and adaption.

Subcultures, however, provide autonomy and agility within the overarching company. They can be containers of creativity to formulate ideas and accommodate market ups and downs. They're havens and think tanks that enable employees to network, build communities, and stretch across walls and disconnects throughout the mass of large organizations. Ideas are freed to bubble up from the grassroots level, managers can enable without dictating, and the larger organization can implement the sticky ideas. There's no upper limit to that growth, because the subculture model can scale. It all comes down to hiring people you trust and nurturing groups within the broader culture.

Subcultures Are Grassroots

At ExactTarget, Todd was a sponsor for several employee groups, which mostly means that once a year he checked in with them to see if they needed anything. Otherwise, it was completely up to them. This hands-off approach is key. Groups will naturally form, and people will find their places. Resist the urge to direct them top-down. Some of the most influential leaders aren't on official organizational charts, but the fluidity and effectiveness of day-to-day work depends on those informal networks.

Google also sets a great example of the grassroots approach. In 2007, they bought 100 Huffys for employees to more easily bop around the sprawling campus (A Look at Google's Massive Bicycle Subculture, 2013). These first bikes exploded into a vibrant cycling culture, largely free of top-down management. They now have seven mechanics on staff to keep up their 1,300 bikes. From this, more hardcore cyclists emerged to ride the 42-mile commute from San Francisco together, which then turned into longer routes all around the surrounding mountains. What started as a weird experiment stuck, so the company made sure the group had the resources to thrive—more bikes, a few bike mechanics—while allowing most of the growth, development, and recruitment to come from the people themselves.

We should mention that these groups oftentimes are not explicitly tied to company products at all, but still hugely tied to the mission, values, financials, and development of the organization, because communities of people are the cartilage of the company. Ensure they're aligned with the larger organizational culture, then set them free.

Subcultures Bind People to the Organization

The bottom line is, people motivate each other, and it is your job to nurture that camaraderie. We encourage subcultures because those connections encourage our people.

Our ExactFun group was another grassroots, cross-functional group all about promoting the culture and designing engaging events for everyone to get to know each other better. They provided incredible ways for people to interact with others from all areas and levels of the company. It was not uncommon to see executives playing basketball with all levels of employees at morning pick-up games or directors attending happy hours with summer interns. They even held annual talent shows where employees got to experience their coworkers' nonwork savvy. Through building relationships and making sure people could enjoy each other, they helped create the platform for us to work together most effectively.

Peers account for 70 percent of workplace fun, and camaraderie with others is the number one motivator for employees to go the extra mile at work (The 2014 Employee Engagement Organizational Culture Report, 2014). What's more, recent research suggests that peers have significant impact on our stress levels and long-term well-being. Typically, we view stress in a negative light. But as it turns out, changing how we think about stress actually changes how our bodies respond to it. Stress in and of itself is not actually so horrible. It's our natural, necessary response to challenges, our bodies rising to the occasion, ready to weasel our ways out of sticky situations. Counterintuitive though it is, stress is only bad for us if we believe it's bad for us.

Stanford health psychologist Kelly McGonigal found that stress also makes us more social, motivating us to both give and receive social support (McGonigal, 2013). In a longitudinal study of 1,000 U.S. adults, she found that for every major stressful life experience, such as financial difficulties or family crises, the risk of dying increased by 30 percent. But people who spent time caring for others showed absolutely zero stress-related increase in dying. Remarkably, caring created resilience.

That said, we cannot realistically feel connected to everyone. Cognitively, we're not built to maintain more than about 150 meaningful relationships. That's why employee groups are an effective way to root and involve people within the bigger organization (Bennett, 2013). Organizational subcultures have a far greater influence on employee motivation than does organizational culture itself (Egan, 2008).

It all comes back to our hunter-gatherer ancestors, or our Christmas card lists (one and the same, really). Evolutionary psychologist Robin Dunbar studied our natural groupings and found the magic number of 150, which "seems to represent the maximum number of individuals with whom we can have a genuinely social relationship, knowing who they are and how they relate to us. . . . It's the number of people you would not feel embarrassed about joining uninvited for a drink if you happened to bump into them in a bar." This Dunbar Number of 150 stays consistent throughout various cultures and time periods: parish registers, village populations, army companies, hunter-gatherer societies, and yes indeed, Christmas card lists (Bennett, 2013).

Case in Point: GORE-TEX

W. L. Gore & Associates co-founder Bill Gore realized his factories were becoming less efficient as they grew larger and employees no longer knew each other (Don't Believe Facebook, You Only Have 150 Friends, 2011). Intuitively he grasped that you have to still know the people you're working with and care about them enough that you want to work hard. So he capped the factories at 150 employees, even if it meant building another factory on the lot right next door. It has to do with transactive memory, or knowing what other people know. Though you may not know how to solve a problem, you know who does know how, and you know where to find that person in your building. CEO Terri Kelly credits this culture of autonomy and familiarity with her three-decade W. L. Gore & Associates career and rise to leadership:

> I was fortunate to join GORE-TEX more than thirty years ago, when our strong cultural foundation was first established by founders Bill and Vieve Gore. They understood the importance of creating an empowered organization where creativity and entrepreneurship would thrive and every associate would feel empowered to make a difference and impact our collective success. These foundational values are still in place today, and all associates feel an incredible level of personal ownership and are shareholders of the company. The culture shaped my thinking early on in my career regarding the importance of creating a healthy work environment to achieve extraordinary outcomes.

Case in Point: Yoido Full Gospel Church

Churches have tapped into this idea of growing larger by getting smaller for years. The most successful megachurches are the most intentional about helping people belong in small groups. The largest church in the world, Yoido Full Gospel Church in Seoul, South Korea, built its congregation of 830,000+ members on a massive web of "cells" (aka small groups) of 5 to 10 households each ("Yoido Full Gospel Church," 2013). Since the first cells in the 1960s, whenever one grows to more than about 10 households, it splits in half and grows again. Senior Pastor Lee says the cells are the lifeblood of the church and that the "church is built around the cells, not cells around the church."

You can't know everyone. But you can know your team, or your small group, and if you know them enough to care about them, that's what separates the best organizations from the rest of them.

Although the number 150 gets all the fame, Dunbar actually coined a series of numbers, decreasing from 150 to 50, our close friends; then to 15, our confidants; and finally to our closest support group of 5 (Discreet Hierarchical Organization of Social Group Sizes, 2005). On the flipside, our groups expand from 150 to 500, our acquaintances; and then to 1,500, our limit of people for whom we can put a name to a face. For GORE-TEX factories, groups of 150 is the magic number. For Yoido church's small groups, it's 15 to 25 people, somewhere between close friends and confidants. Whatever the precise number may be for your type of work, the key is to cultivate small teams that can become the driving energy of your organization.

Subcultures are a natural occurrence in any organization. If you learn to nurture them, they can become some of the most essential pieces of your success.

Make It Personal
(Or, Why Nobody Leaves Their Personal Life at Home)

O f all the chapters in this book, we guarantee this tidbit of practical counsel will be most controversial. What you are about to read will be counter to everything your high-priced employment law attorneys have taught you, namely, "Don't get personal when you're managing employees." It will also fly in the face of most of what you have learned in business school as part of a traditional curriculum.

But we cannot speak at length about the importance of culture building and engagement without saying . . . you must get personal. Engagement is not sterile. It is not mundane. It is not one size fits all.

The corporate world isn't the only place this principle comes into play. Quinn Buckner, NCAA champion, NBA champion, and Olympic gold medalist, says, "The hardest lesson I learned about motivating teams was the importance of understanding different motivations for different individuals" (Buckner, 2016).

It is high time we rethink our widespread aversion to getting personal. Long-term management success depends on caring for the whole employee, including his or her personal life. You will only unlock your full leadership potential, thoroughly engage employees, and achieve maximum business success if you get personal with your employees and care about both their professional and personal interests.

Strong and effective relationships with employees, customers, and vendors drive business success. We forge strong and effective relationships when we find ways to build rapport and relate to each other through shared experiences, challenges, and perspectives. Obvious, right? Now as managers, why would we think for a second that we could focus strictly on the professional aspects of our employees instead of on cultivating an overall positive relationship? Clearly we should know whether an employee has the technical skills to complete a task or is operating as effectively and efficiently as expected. However, focusing solely on the acute professional needs of an employee wholly discounts what fundamentally makes us all dynamic humans, namely, our unique lives beyond work. Building personal bonds is an often ignored part of the holistic manager-employee relationship.

"Ultimately, we all want to be part of something that matters," says Yext's Jeff Rohrs. "But we are more than simply the people we are at work. The best corporate cultures embrace both the professional and individual and make each stronger" (Rohrs, 2016).

Connect on a Deeper Level

We challenge you to identify instances where you truly connected with someone over a strictly professional work topic. Have you forged a meaningful relationship with someone over a case you worked on, a pitch for a client, or a joint sale you made? The shared experience of any of those items may have provided some form of bond, but would you really consider it a connection that would lead to a long-term relationship? Probably not.

Now, consider instances where you have connected with someone on a park bench while watching your kids play, or while celebrating a friend's birthday, or while attending a philanthropic event. The connections made in these instances create natural relationships based on shared personal experiences.

A truly effective manager must create relationships with employees based on professional and personal traits. Only when the manager relates to the whole person can the employee's full potential and loyalty be unlocked, ultimately enhancing overall business goals. Countless business books detail how to enhance employee productivity through a variety of managerial practices that focus on professional development. Although these pieces add immense value to the manager-employee relationship, they neglect the most important part of the relationship-building dynamic: the personal side of the equation. According to Nicole Bickett of Mainstreet, "You have to reach the most internal parts of people, you must reach them in their hearts. As a young leader, I thought it was more about what I knew and what I contributed.

Now I know that it is about how you connect with the core of people, find their true talents and skills and bring them out. You must find ways to create hope that the things we never dreamed would be possible are indeed within our reach when we work together. Train other leaders in your organization to do this and the results will follow" (Bickett, 2016).

Employment law attorneys will commonly tell you not to engage employees around personal issues. They will counsel you to avoid discussions around personal struggles, physical or mental challenges, family matters, and other similar topics. And then they'll top it off with a cheery admonition that the less you know or are engaged with an employee on a personal front, the less risk you run of triggering an employment law claim. For example, if your employee shares with you that he or she is suffering from a medical condition and you subsequently separate that employee, he or she could sue you by claiming disability discrimination. If you never knew about the medical condition, you would have a much stronger defense. For this reason, attorneys typically preach that ignorance is bliss, and managers should remain as disconnected from employees' personal matters as possible.

Among these personal matters, typical attorneys would tell you to steer clear of childhood experiences, family background and makeup, outside activities and interests, religious preferences, marital and parenting challenges and accomplishments, and health issues. We tell you instead to embrace these topics as necessary pieces of a blurry, blended personal/professional world.

Rhett Trees, Partner at Caddis Capital, is a prime example of caring for the whole person:

Every morning, before I leave for work, I find a few minutes of silence to meditate and sit with my personal mission statement, "to change someone's soul today."

It sounds nearly impossible to do, but this short phrase has taught me more about business, spirituality, friendship and, most important, the foundation for a successful life. When I speak to business leaders, college students and budding entrepreneurs the first question they ask is, "What is your secret sauce?" My consistent answer focuses on one overarching trait: be vulnerable.

In nearly every business meeting, regardless if it is our first or 400th, I'll reference either my spirituality or my mission statement with the only intention of digging deeper into the soul of a fellow passenger on this journey called life. Oftentimes, if not always, the unintended benefit is the fact that my soul is the one that "changes" based on the conversation that follows.

Recently, I was originally introduced to this investor through a mutual friend, and I shared my spiritual journey with him during our first meeting. I wasn't confident that he would engage based on his reputation. However, this vulnerability led to the fact that we were both "recovering a--holes," seeking the answer to "Why are we here?" and struggling to be "everything to everyone."

My gut tells me that we would have been mired in pleasantries if not for the fleeting introduction of vulnerability into our initial conversation. Fast-forward to a later breakfast meeting, and it was like reconnecting with a spiritual guru or old friend after many years. We quickly caught up on business, but were both eager to dive deep into topics like our respective wives, kids, integrity moments, family members who are preparing or have passed to the other side, how our passions fulfill our soul, and the fact that "thoughts become things."

I know deep in my heart that vulnerability is the only reason this conversation occurred. There is no other foundation for this type of transparency, especially between businesspeople. Like anything, this concept might be outside of most people's comfort zones and feel off-limits at first. But try it and you just might change someone's soul today (Trees, 2016).

Care for the Whole Employee

Enduring relationships form when we start caring for the whole employee. Sometimes this runs counter to our short-term business objectives and may even result in a short-term "loss." But in the long haul, we want a loyal and engaged workforce, and we need that workforce in order to achieve our long-term business objectives. Nothing elicits that kind of long-term engagement and loyalty more than rooting deep personal connections.

Blair West of Cummins Inc. promotes this holistic approach in her role as director of corporate communications and functional excellence.

"Companies must offer resources and ways to care for an employee's whole self in a way that sets him or her up for success both personally and professionally. This may include recognition that, in addition to meeting the employee's financial needs, the company drives personal well-being, dependent care options, support and flexibility to care for family members or maintain outside-of-work commitments, access to healthy meal options and other healthy lifestyle choices, concierge services, and anything else that allows an employee to focus on being productive and effective while at the workplace" (Blair West, 2016).

Ellen Humphrey of Appirio thinks of it this way: "Our lives and work are more connected than ever. I don't want my team members to check their personalities at the door, nor do I want to check mine" (Humphrey, 2016).

One caveat: Bear in mind that general business principles (e.g., cost-benefit analyses) still govern how much attention should be provided to any particular employee. We have all had the employee who perpetuates a constant swirl of non-value-added drama, or the employee who cannot and does not want to be helped, or the employee who requires so much help that you would have to neglect other people and responsibilities in order to invest in him or her. We're not saying the balance is obvious or easy; we're saying use your judgment and treat people like the full humans they are.

37

Earn Trust

(Or, Why Trust Is the Foundation of Everything Else)

We talk a lot about culture, which we can work to shape and involve everyone in. But at its core, much of culture comes down to how people interact. As a leader, what do you know about your employees, and what do they know about you? How well do you know them? How do your coworkers think? How do they communicate? What motivates them? Do they see you as warm and engaging? Do they see you as competent? Do they trust you? Ultimately, what kind of culture are you creating with your people?

Intuitions Come First; Reasoning Comes Second

Moral psychologist Jonathan Haidt (2012) has found that humans are far less rational than we are rationalizing. In other words, we are primarily intuitive creatures whose gut feelings drive our strategic reasoning. We have automatic, instant reactions to things, and then we reason to defend those reactions.

We are often led to believe that reason is the highest of our faculties, but in actuality our unconscious mind does most of our thinking. Remember those millions of pieces of information flying at us every minute, of which our human brains are consciously aware of a measly 60? Our unconscious processes—emotions, intuitions, sentiments, gut feelings—are at the center of our thinking, handling the millions-minus-60 things to think about (Martin, 2009). They are the foundation of our reason because they tell us what to value.

Before people decide what they think of your message, they decide what they think of you. Trust and cooperation are not instructions; they're feelings.

Just ask Clay Robinson of Sun King Brewing. He says, "Authenticity is the key. Be true to yourself and communicate openly and honestly with your team. They will respond in remarkable ways" (Robinson, 2016).

What Happens Between Two Brains When They Interact

When we interact with people, our brains make snap judgments about them. Harvard Business School psychologist Amy Cuddy has found that we primarily gauge two characteristics: how lovable they are (warmth, communion, trustworthiness) and how fearsome they are (competence, strength, agency). With these two dimensions of social judgment, we answer two critical questions: "What are this person's intentions toward me?" and "Is he or she capable of acting on those intentions?"

If someone is competent but not warm, that elicits respect and resentment—we want to cooperate or affiliate ourselves with that person, but we also feel vulnerable to them. If someone is warm but not competent, that elicits pity and lack of respect—we help people we pity, but when it becomes difficult or inconvenient, we ultimately neglect them.

In business, this means that, more than your background, your message, or your ideas, how you interact with people matters—a lot.

Are You Warm or Are You Competent?

Ideally, of course, the answer is both—but in moderation, like a well-balanced social judgment diet. Interestingly, though, our brains process warmth before competence. The first thing we look for in others is evidence of trustworthiness, based on their warmth. But when we present ourselves to others, we often mistakenly try to show our competence first, establishing strength before trust. We want to tackle challenges, work the longest hours, present innovative ideas in meetings. But it seems that warmth, at least right off the bat, matters much more than strength. In a study of 51,836 leaders, only 27 were rated in both the bottom quartile of likability and in the top quartile of overall leadership effectiveness. In other words, the chances that a manager who is strongly disliked will still be considered a good leader are about 1 in 2,000.

As a leader, you have to show warmth. Competence is assumed— warmth is what makes the difference. Strength, without a foundation of trust, elicits fear. Fear undermines cognitive potential, creativity, and problem solving and causes employees to disengage. In short, people will obey, but they will not follow, engage, take ownership, or help others. Warmth, on the other hand, facilitates trust and influence. Trust increases information sharing, collaboration, and creativity. When we trust people, we naturally combine talents and strengths and work tirelessly to seize opportunities. How can you show warmth? By knowing and caring about your employees.

So in sum, our unconscious intuition, rather than reason, drives most of our thinking, we judge people based on their warmth and competence, and for leaders, warmth is often more overlooked but also more critical than competence. All this to say, neurological evidence shows that knowing and caring about your employees makes a difference for the bottom line.

How Do We Get People to Trust and Collaborate with Us?

- *Listen.* In his book *How to Win Friends and Influence People,* Dale Carnegie writes, "You can make more friends in two months by being interested in other people than in two years by trying to get other people interested in you," (Carnegie, 2006). Listen to what people say, and seek to understand what they need. Know what makes your employees unique. Show interest in their lives and remember details about what they tell you.

- *Ask.* After listening, ask more questions. Maybe start with, "What would you like from me?" or "What can I do to improve your experience?" or "How is your life outside of work?" Be invested in your employees as people, too, beyond work responsibilities. Care for the whole person.

- *Engage.* Be warm. Level with people. Try lowering the pitch and volume of your voice, as if comforting a friend. Throw in the occasional personal story. Validate feelings and worldviews. Smile and mean it.

Smiling is evolutionarily contagious, because it triggers mirror neurons in others and suppresses the control we usually have on our facial muscles.

- *Communicate.* In many cases, the effectiveness of a group is not determined by the IQ of the group but by how well they communicate. Some form of daily communication is ideal—phone, email, face to face, or a combination of those forms. And if someone asks a question you can't answer? "Be truthful, even when the truth is 'I don't know,' says Ellen Humphrey of Appirio (Ellen Humphrey, 2016).

- *Support.* Make workers feel safe and comfortable talking about anything—safe to experiment, challenge, share information, fail, and help each other. Management consultant Margaret Heffernan advocates that organizations need to develop enough trust that employees can safely disagree. We need thinking partners who aren't echo chambers, and to get this kind of candid conflict, we need high levels of trust and support. She has found in surveys that 85 percent of European and American executives acknowledge they have issues or concerns at work that they are afraid to raise because of conflict (Heffernan, 2015). Which means these organizations are not thinking together effectively. Which means that the leaders who run these organizations, who go out of their way to find the very best people they can, mostly fail to get the very best out of them. Show your employees that you support them as people—this is the core of a culture of trust.

How you engage people, what you know about them, and what they know about you have a profound impact on your workplace. Not simply because being nice to people is what your mother taught you, but because our brains actually unconsciously pick up on things like kindness, warmth, care, and engagement, and they affect tangible outcomes like performance, retention, creativity, and collaboration. So the next time you go to interact with someone at work, make sure you think twice about what kind of culture you want to create. How you treat people matters and directly affects both culture and employee engagement.

Chapter 38

Expel Poor Culture Fits
(Or, Why One Bad Apple Spoils the Bunch)

You know the drill: Everyone on the team gets along swimmingly, and then one scoundrel comes in with manipulation, malice, harsh words, laziness, or otherwise divisive behaviors. Try as they valiantly might, the group just cannot seem to overrule that one person's insidiousness. It's exhausting, it's demoralizing, it's counterproductive, and frankly, it's the worst.

In their research paper "How, When, and Why Bad Apples Spoil the Barrel: Negative Group Members and Dysfunctional Groups," Felps, Mitchell, and Byington (182–183) classify "bad apples" into three categories:

- Withholders of effort, who "intentionally dodge their responsibilities to the group and freeride off the efforts of others"
- The affectively negative, who "continually express a negative mood, emotion, or attitude"
- Interpersonal deviants, who "detract from the group's contextual environment by violating interpersonal norms of respect"

All less than desirable coworkers, to be sure. These negative group members can impede everything from cooperation to motivated effort, coordination to creativity, learning and helpful conflicts and everything in between, "eventually resulting in poor group performance, lower well-being, and possibly team collapse." What's more, the researchers report that one single negative employee can cause a 30 to 40 percent drop in overall team performance (Felps, Mitchell, & Byington, 178).

And so, as remaining conscientious group members who seek to improve such an aversive experience, we generally react in one of three ways (Felps, Mitchell, & Byington, 185):

- *Motivational intervention.* We try to change the negative person's behavior.
- *Rejection.* We remove the negative person.
- *Defensiveness.* We protect our own selves.

Both the motivational intervention and rejection options are fairly constructive and typically prevent said bad apples from ever spoiling the whole barrel. Defensiveness, however, often gets a little more ugly, manifesting in episodes of "lashing out, revenge, unrealistic appraisals, distraction, various attempts at mood maintenance, and withdrawal."

The good news is, researchers report that the two key factors that promote defensiveness are lack of power and the basic psychological tendency to react strongly to negative behavior, both of which are fundamentally matters of culture, in the people you choose to hire and in how serious you are about letting the deviants go (Felps, Mitchell, & Byington, 188–189).

Hiring and leveraging the right people fuels your culture. At its core, a company is the sum of its people and personalities. In other words, if you hire a bunch of assholes, it is unlikely that lumping them all together will rectify anything. Au contraire, hiring even one asshole can wreak havoc—see the earlier statistic on the alarming 30 to 40 percent drop in team performance.

Likewise, expelling poor fits quickly ensures your culture does not go off the tracks. Too many organizations justify corrosive behavior with extraordinary talent. For employees who have experience, tenure, or power, they employ an unspoken standard of "the more you win, the more of an ass we'll let you be." With pressures like sales goals and product development on the line, this may seem to be a viable method in the short term (it's still not), but over the long haul it will erode any semblance of employee loyalty you hope to have. Team members need to be able to trust the consistency and judgement of their leadership.

Brad Morehead of LiveWatch Security says:

> Every hire affects the company's culture for better or worse. Good hires almost instantly have a positive impact on the culture. They have a multiplier effect on those around them and those whom they lead. Bad hires do the opposite. Culturally bad hires cause internal discord, erode trust, and create inefficiency. When someone is not working out because he or she lacks the proper knowledge, work ethic or ability, that's one thing. It's bad, but it usually only affects one team. When people aren't working because they aren't a culture fit, they quickly become caustic and create negative repercussions for everyone around them. You have to get rid of them immediately. In the end, it's better for those people too, as they may be good employees at a company with a different culture.

Hiring Tips

- Leverage a tool like the Predictive Index ("Predictive Index") to get a deeper view of a candidate or an employee.

- Take the time to better understand what makes people tick. Consider bringing candidates in for a full day or two, giving them small projects to accomplish alone and with a team, and observing them interacting with others.

- Hire slow, fire fast. Don't let cultural misfits taint others, and don't be afraid to cite cultural disconnects as the reason for a breakup.

- Use orientation not just as a way to describe your culture, but to help facilitate a discussion around specifics of how the new employee will enhance the culture.

- Draw attention to cultural fit as a contributing reason for promotions.

- Create multiple opportunities to highlight cultural accomplishments.

- Recognize cultural all-stars on a regular basis, such as with culture awards for those that go above and beyond.

Worth the Effort

Hire for culture with the same level of rigor that you hire for aptitude. Yes, pay attention to mental faculties, work experience, and so on, but similarly count interpersonal skills, presence, and cultural fit.

Mobi co-founder and CEO Scott Kraege thinks of it this way:

> When molding a company culture, corrosive employees are one of the most damaging factors. If a new employee does not fit the culture of the company, he or she will either become extremely unhappy or will try to mold her new environment to their own values. While these employees can fit and work, they will not fully contribute if they are not there for the right reasons. Corrosive employees should be seen as such, and an organization should not hesitate to part ways with someone who works against the company culture, even if he or she possesses a high level of skill.

Be specific in detailing what that means at your company, in order to help potential employees self-select. It's a little extra time, but it's not rocket science, and it's well worth it.

Chapter 39

Communicate with Employees

(Or, Why Mobile Apps Simplify Everything)

E mployees, more times than not, don't want to be communicated with via email anymore. Their inboxes are already bursting at the virtual seams. Employees, more times than not, would prefer clear, concise, and maybe even witty or aesthetically pleasing messages. They would prefer to be reached at an opportune moment and not besieged in the middle of their creative maker hours. They would prefer a clear path through which they can direct questions and find more information. Is this so much to ask? We sure hope not.

Simplification Is Key

Simplification is dire and overdue. We are moving from "doing more with less" to "doing less better." Employees today have not one iota of care for any technology that does not materially make their lives better. Whole industries have been rocked by innovations that simplify the way we live, and the workplace is next in line. Peter Drucker wrote that "much of what we call management consists of making it difficult for people to work,"

(Drucker, 2006). HR should aim instead to be a catalyst for the entire organization to declutter. Simplify communications, disentangle processes, and consolidate information. Treat time capital with the same gravity you allot financial capital, and start by simplifying complexity through integrated technology. Instead of working more, we need a better, faster, more effective way of working.

At Emplify, we saw these needs of employees wanting and needing to be communicated with differently, and we overcame these challenges by doing what we do best—mobile apps.

We stumbled into the solution almost by accident. We initially designed it simply to address our own internal needs. In the midst of rapid growth, we needed a one-stop source for all things company related. As mobile app makers, what better way than by creating our own internal app platform? So we built the app, threw a launch party, and within a few months it became a wild success. We saw a 100 percent download rate, increased participation in events, and a record number of submissions for our recognition program (Jaramillo, 2015). It works because it's a central, mobile place where employees can access useful information. It's a focused, purpose-built tool for our internal communications team. It's a way to gather feedback, promote recognition, boost productivity, increase alignment, and centralize resources. It's a beautiful product that fits seamlessly with the reality of users' lives who, in this case, are our own employees. Santiago was featured in Forbes, saying "Our purpose as a company is to help organizations thrive by helping them communicate and engage with their audiences. Our most important audience for us to reach is our own internal people" (Burg, 2015).

We believe this solution meets head-on the common pitfalls to culture and engagement. Here's why it works:

- *It meets people where they are.* The lines between professional and personal are already blurred, and between the rise of online platforms, freelance work, and an on-demand economy, mobile apps just make sense. The top two reasons consumers download mobile apps are convenience and speedy access to information (2014 Mobile Behavior Report, 23). The readiness is already there; we are meeting people where they are. People's phones are already an extension of their arms, and an app is a great way to reach them in the way they're already consuming information. Plus, unlike the ultimate democracy of email, an app affords employees the choice of when to access work information and when to not. It will become the hub that merges together all work-related channels of information, just one finger tap away.

- *Outdated HR system, meet smartphone.* We are seeing a radically disruptive shift in HR from "systems of record" to "systems of engagement." It's a repurposing of software, from back-office data automation to self-service platforms, and from static, one-way communications toward a real-time dialogue of engagement. HR is going mobile, and it's working. Employees are two to five times more likely (Bersin, 2014) to access HR applications on their smartphones than their PCs, and they find them 60 percent more engaging (Mobile Apps Infographic, 2014). It's the consumerization of corporate systems, which essentially means treating employees like we treat customers (Hodson et al., 2014). Mobile, with its one-click, one-swipe ease, will become HR's primary interface.

- *Separation → Integration.* As knowledge workers, we do not innately separate work and life in our minds. Our old social constructs did that for us, because industrial life was pretty distinct from family life. But now we think about all of it all the time. You're one person, with one brain, and if you're stressed about work you will probably be stressed at dinner too. Work and life are very much intermingled. It's not about keeping them separate; it's about keeping ourselves feeling like we're in control. Which comes down to good design, and there's an app for that.

- *Longer sessions → shorter, more frequent intervals: the snackification of life.* We seek real-time collaboration, immediate feedback, and quick turnarounds. We juggle multiple work items interspersed with a steady stream of checking our email. We work throughout the day—at home, in the office, and everywhere in between.

- *It's miles ahead of your current social chatter service.* Only 13 percent of employees participate in their company's social intranet daily, and 31 percent rarely or never do (How a Mobile First Strategy Can Increase Employment Engagement, 2014, 8). We're talking here about real engagement, material improvements intermingled in their daily work, enabling them to do their jobs better. HR is seeing a major shift from static, one-way communications toward a real-time, mobile dialogue of engagement.

- *It markets to employees how you market to customers.* ExactTarget wrote in their 2014 Mobile Behavior Report, "The brand with the easiest-to-access content wins. Eighty-three percent of consumers said that a seamless experience across all their devices is somewhat or very important. They want the content they want where and when they want it" (2014 Mobile Behavior Report). We so easily digest this as marketers. Why does it not come as intuitively that we should do the same for our employees? Employees expect the same technologies at work that they have as consumers. It's not just the content that matters; it's how you present it.

Bottom line: Communicate with your employees in the same manner and with the same level of intent that you would use to communicate to your customers. That does not mean you need to become paralyzed with complexity. Make the most of cutting-edge technology, and keep it simple.

Conclusion

Winning cultures and engaged employees do not just happen. As a business leader, you must tend to your workplace culture with the same endurance, attention to detail, and intentionality with which a farmer tends to his fields. Each day will be different, and you must respond to your ever-changing climate and conditions. Some days, you need to plant seeds. Other days, you must roll up your sleeves and pull weeds. The work is unrelenting and requires continuous attention, so much so that you may sometimes wonder if the effort is worth it. Trust us, it is.

Culture building and employee engagement, like farming, is a long game. The reward, however, is a bountiful harvest that will nourish you (and many others) for years to come. And the best crops? They are 100 percent organic, the result of tender love and care—not shortcuts.

We hope this book has convinced you to reinvest yourself in your organization's culture and employee engagement. From research to practical guidance, you now have the tools you need to plant and cultivate fields of abundant engagement (and all the business benefits that result).

We have discussed:

- **The Engagement Engine:** We defined workplace culture and employee engagement and showed how they impact your business success.
- **The Workplace of Now:** We explored tectonic shifts in the workplace and uncovered key drivers of employee engagement.
- **The Engagement Canvas:** We showed you how to use the Engagement Canvas and Emplify Score to drive overall culture strategy and measure your effectiveness over time.
- **The Practice of Engagement:** We offered practical advice that will immediately help boost your engagement and business results.

What happens next? That is ultimately up to you. By no means do we claim to have all the answers. We are lifelong learners, all of us, when it comes to driving engagement and building winning workplace cultures. That's what makes these topics so fascinating.

And, like most things, we discover even more when we learn from each other. Being able to share your thoughts and learnings on engagement helps all of us achieve our culture goals. That is why we encourage you to visit us online to complete your own Engagement Canvas, review others' canvases, and share personal learnings and best practices with the Engagement Canvas community. Join the conversation at www.AgileEngagementBook.com or share your thoughts and questions with us directly by emailing connect@engagementcanvas.com. Together we can raise the bar for employee engagement and change the way people work forever.

Acknowledgments

Like creating winning workplace cultures, writing a book is a team effort. We would like to thank the following individuals for their incredible support throughout this process.

Todd: Special thanks to my best friend and stunning wife, Debbie; parents, Sue and Charlie; sister Lee; dear friend Lynne; and beloved sons, Ben, Jake, Zeke, and Blake. You have always been by my side while I chased my dreams, faltered and restarted, and embarked on countless crazy adventures. Every good thing and success in my life is the direct result of your unconditional love and support.

Thank you to my amazing role models, namely Ron Hellems, Steve Lyman, John Ryan, Chuck Morgan, Dan Horner, Jay Collins, Tom Eggleston, Steve McFarland, Scott Dorsey, Traci Dolan, Les Gleaves, Bryan Brenner, and Jay Height. You not only modeled the way to personal and professional success, you also showed me how to enjoy the journey and develop relationships that last a lifetime.

This book is a kaleidoscope of experiences, insights, and advice from the best business leaders, researchers, and creatives we know. Special thanks to Kimberly Collins, Brian Deyo, Nicole Ross, Renée Ross, Erin Marlow, Brianna Susnak, the team from Wiley Publishing, and the Butler Business Consulting Group, as well as all of the inspirational contributors who helped bring this dream to fruition.

Santiago: Heartfelt thanks to my parents, Roberto and Olga, who sacrificed life in their homeland to give their sons the opportunity to grow up and thrive in the United States. They modeled the dedication, commitment, and discipline necessary to grow a successful business. Special thanks to my brother, Felipe, for his loyal friendship, and to Kate for being my life's persistent sunshine and joy.

This book would not have been possible without the partners and mentors who generously invested in me throughout the years and gave me examples worth following. I've shared (and survived) the trenches of startup life with Adam Weber and Mitch Shields, my relentlessly committed co-founders, and for that, I'll be forever thankful. To Sherry Styers,

Dr. Phil Millage, John Wechsler, Don and Sharon Cady, Tim Kopp, Ron Brumbarger, Ian Illig, Luke Dubert, Bill Godfrey, Mike Simmons, Don Aquilano, John True, Scott Dorsey, Andy Medley, Trevor Yager, Mayor Scott Fadness, and every Bluebridge and Emplify employee, thank you for teaching, inspiring, and believing in me. It has made all the difference.

Author Biographies

Todd Richardson is a labor and employment attorney by trade. He began his career in private practice before becoming general counsel and head of HR for one of the largest private residential real estate companies in the United States at the time.

Richardson went on to serve as executive vice president of administration at ExactTarget and then Salesforce, following Salesforce's $2.5 billion acquisition of ExactTarget in 2013. During his seven years with Exact-Target, he oversaw all HR, risk management/legal, and real estate/facilities functions and helped scale the business from a private, 200-person, single-site operation to a public company with 3,000+ employees located in 15+ global offices. Under his leadership, ExactTarget earned numerous workplace achievement awards, and its Orange culture became such a competitive advantage that it was recognized in the company's S-1 filing. It was the first time culture has been cited as a competitive differentiator in an initial public offering filing.

Currently, Richardson serves as co-founder and chief people officer at Emplify, a mobile-first employee engagement app platform. The role is his dream job and allows him to help companies drive deeper employee engagement using cutting-edge technology.

Richardson often speaks on the topics of employee engagement, culture, and human resources. From keynotes for the Young Presidents' Organization/World Presidents' Organization, Vistage, and multiple technology company user conferences, he bridges the gap between theory and practical counsel.

In addition to his work at Emplify and various speaking engagements, Richardson is an adjunct professor at Butler University in Indianapolis, Indiana. He also serves on the Board of Visitors for Butler University's Lacy School of Business, Christian Theological Seminary, Indiana Secondary Market for Education, and Nextech. He also serves as entrepreneur-in-residence at FirstPerson Advisors and is on the Board of Advisors for Hyde Park Venture Partners.

He holds a B.A. in political science from Indiana University Bloomington and a J.D. from the Indiana University School of Law. He currently resides in Westfield, Indiana, and enjoys spending weekends at Lake Wawasee, traveling, and going on adventures with his wife and four rowdy sons.

Santiago Jaramillo is a serial entrepreneur and the CEO and co-founder of Bluebridge and Emplify, a mobile-first employee engagement app software-as-a-service platform. Jaramillo has grown the businesses from their humble beginning in his college dorm room at Indiana Wesleyan, where he was a business administration and marketing double-major valedictorian, to the world's premier platform for companies to more deeply engage their employees through mobile.

At Emplify he leads a team of mobile engagement experts and oversees the vision, strategy, and roadmap of the company's product and brand. The platform has already helped hundreds of global organizations engage their workforces through more than 20 million user sessions and 10+ million push notifications across 700+ apps in multiple app stores.

Jaramillo is a nationally recognized expert and keynote speaker on digital, mobile, and employee engagement topics to tens of thousands of people at events like Vistage, Future of Work, and state governors' conferences. In 2013 he was named to *Inc.* magazine's 30 Under 30 "World's Coolest Entrepreneurs." He was also invited to the White House by the Obama administration and recognized for his entrepreneurial contributions through the Champions of Change program. He was named TechPoint's Young Professional of the Year in 2013 and named to *Indianapolis Business Journal's* "Forty Under 40" list as one of the youngest honorees in the award program's history.

He hails from Cali, Colombia, and during the country's rampant insecurity of the 1990s, his family narrowly escaped kidnapping and immigrated to Weston, Florida, when he was 10 years old. He currently resides in Indianapolis, Indiana, and enjoys the outdoors, soccer, SCUBA diving, lobstering, international travel, vegetable gardening, and playing drums and guitar.

References

"2014 Mobile Behavior Report," Salesforce, 2014, http://www.marketing cloud.com/sites/exacttarget/files/deliverables/etmc-2014mobilebehavior report.pdf, 6, 7, 9, 14, 17, 18, 23, 33.

"2014 Word of the Year: Culture," Merriam-Webster, 2014, http://www .merriam-webster.com/words-at-play/2014-word-of-the-year/culture.

"2016 Internet Trends Report." 2016 Internet Trends. June 1, 2016. Accessed October 03, 2016. http://www.kpcb.com/internet-trends.

"244 Million International Migrants Living Abroad Worldwide, New UN Statistics Reveal," United Nations, 2016, http://www.un.org/sustainable development/blog/2016/01/244-million-international-migrants-living-abroad-worldwide-new-un-statistics-reveal/.

"A Look at Google's Massive Bicycle Subculture," *Relevant* magazine, 2013, http://www.relevantmagazine.com/slices/look-google%E2%80%99s-massive-bicycle-subculture.

"Action Office System," Herman Miller, 2016, http://www.hermanmiller .com/products/workspaces/individual-workstations/action-office-system.html.

Aiim. "Systems of Engagement and the Future of Enterprise IT." Accessed October 04, 2016. http://info.aiim.org/systems-of-engagement-and-the-future-of-enterprise-it.

"Annual Business Excellence Awards In Carmel," *Carmel City Magazine*, 2015, http://www.carmelcitymagazine.com/Fall-2015/Annual-Business-Excellence-Awards-in-Carmel/.

"Apple Reinvents the Phone with the iPhone," Apple, 2007, http://www .apple.com/pr/library/2007/01/09Apple-Reinvents-the-Phone-with-iPhone.html.

"Apple's Mac App Store Downloads Top 100 Million," Apple, 2011, https:// www.apple.com/pr/library/2011/12/12Apples-Mac-App-Store-Downloads-Top-100-Million.html.

"Apps and Mobile Web: Understanding the Two Sides of the Mobile Coin," Interactive Advertising Bureau, 2014, http://www.iab.com/wp-content/uploads/2015/07/IAB_Apps_and_Mobile_Web_Final.pdf, 3.

Barnes, Peter. "Teach for America: A Nonprofit Workplace Keeping Pace with Its Corporate Counterparts." Great Place To Work United States. December 11, 2014. Accessed October 03, 2016. https://www.greatplacetowork.com/blog/241-teach-for-america-a-nonprofit-workplace-keeping-pace-with-its-corporate-counterparts.

"Best Companies of 2016," *Fortune*, 2016, http://fortune.com/best-companies/wegmans-food-markets-4/.

"Big Data Just Beginning to Explode," Computer Sciences Corporation, https://www.csc.com/big_data/flxwd/83638-big_data_just_beginning_to_explode_interactive_infographic.

"BRICS Reach 30 Percent of Global GDP," BRICS, 2015, http://en.brics2015.ru/news/20150707/277026.html.

"Bring Questions. Build Answers," Google, https://www.google.com/about/careers.

"Bringing Big Data to the Enterprise." IBM. Accessed August 19, 2016. https://www-01.ibm.com/software/data/bigdata/what-is-big-data.html.

"Building Radically Better Community Culture," *Inc.*, 2012, http://www.inc.com/neil-blumenthal/neil-blumenthal-warby-parker-better-company-culture.html.

"Businesses Must Fight the Relentless Battle against Bureaucracy Decluttering the Company," *The Economist*, 2014, http://www.economist.com/news/business/21610237-businesses-must-fight-relentless-battle-against-bureaucracy-decluttering-company.

"Buy a Pair, Give a Pair," Warby Parker, https://www.warbyparker.com/buy-a-pair-give-a-pair.

"BYOD Insights 2013," Cisco, 2013, https://iapp.org/media/pdf/knowledge_center/Cisco_BYOD_Insights_2013.pdf, 4.

"CEOs and CHROs: Crucial Allies and Potential Successors," Korn Ferry Institute, 2014, http://www.kornferry.com/institute/ceos-and-chros-crucial-allies-and-potential-successors.

"Challenges for Human Resource Management and Global Business Strategy," Future HR Trends, http://futurehrtrends.eiu.com/report-2014/challenges-human-resource-management/.

"Characteristics and Preference for Alternative Work Arrangements," *Monthly Labor Review*, 2001, http://www.bls.gov/opub/mlr/2001/03/art2full.pdf, 28.

"Costs and Benefits," Global Workplace Analytics, 2015, http://globalwork placeanalytics.com/resources/costs-benefits.

"Daniel Kish," TED, https://www.ted.com/speakers/daniel_kish.

"Demand for HR Analytics Roles Strong, but Slowing," Bersin, 2015, http://www.bersin.com/blog/post/Demand-for-HR-Analytics-Roles-Remains-Strong2c-but-Slowing.aspx.

"Discreet Hierarchical Organization of Social Group Sizes," Royal Society, 2005, http://rspb.royalsocietypublishing.org/content/272/1561/439.abstract.

"Don't Believe Facebook, You Only Have 150 Friends," National Public Radio, 2011, http://www.npr.org/2011/06/04/136723316/dont-believe-facebook-you-only-have-150-friends.

"Don't Buy This Jacket," Patagonia, http://www.patagonia.com/email/11/112811.html.

Drucker, Peter. Managing in the Next Society. New York: St. Martin's Press, 2002.

"Employment by Major Industry Sector," Bureau of Labor Statistics, 2015, http://www.bls.gov/emp/ep_table_201.htm.

"Engaging and Integration a Global Workforce," Society for Human Resource Management, 2015, https://www.shrm.org/about/foundation/documents/3-15%20eiu%20theme%202%20report-final.pdf, 8, 13.

"Evidence from a Collective Intelligence Factor in the Performance of Human Groups," Harvard Kennedy School, 2010, http://gap.hks.harvard.edu/evidence-collective-intelligence-factor-performance-human-groups.

"Exploding Digital Flows in a Deeply Connected World," McKinsey, 2016, http://www.mckinsey.com/global-themes/digital-disruption/exploding-digital-flows-in-a-deeply-connected-world.

"Factories," Everlane, https://www.everlane.com/factories.

"Freelancing in America: A National Survey of the New Workforce," Freelancers Union, http://fu-web-storage-prod.s3.amazonaws.com/content/filer_public/c2/06/c2065a8a-7f00-46db-915a-2122965df7d9/fu_free lancinginamericareport_v3-rgb.pdf, 3.

"Gapminder World Offline," Gapminder, 2013, https://www.gapminder .org/world-offline/.

"Global Human Capital Trends 2014," Deloitte, 2014, http://dupress .com/wp-content/uploads/2014/03/GlobalHumanCapitalTrends2014_ 030714.pdf, 15, 16, 100.

"Global Human Capital Trends 2015," Deloitte, 2015, http://www2.deloitte .com/content/dam/Deloitte/at/Documents/human-capital/hc-trends- 2015.pdf, 10, 25, 35, 87, 89, 90.

"Google Application Security," Google, https://www.google.com/about/ appsecurity/programs-home/.

Haidt, Jonathan. The Righteous Mind: Why Good People Are Divided by Politics and Religion. New York: Pantheon Books, 2012.

"History," Warby Parker, https://www.warbyparker.com/history.

Hodson, Tom, Jeff Schwartz, Ardie Van Berkel, and Ian Winstrom Otten. "The Overwhelmed Employee." *Deloitte University Press*, March 7, 2014. March 7, 2014. Accessed August 20, 2016. http://dupress.com/articles/ hc-trends-2014-overwhelmed-employee/.

"How a Mobile First Strategy Can Increase Employee Engagement." Ortec Communications. February 2014. Accessed August 20, 2016. https:// www.orteccommunications.com/wp-content/uploads/2014/03/White- paper-employee-engagement-imgZine.pdf.

"Human Resources Management in a Recession," Lipscomb, http://www .lipscomb.edu/uploads/40050.pdf, 3.

"Information," Facebook, 2016, https://www.facebook.com/whitehat.

"Is Your HR Department Friend or Foe? Depends on Who's Asking the Ques- tion," Wharton, 2005, http://knowledge.wharton.upenn.edu/article/is- your-hr-department-friend-or-foe-depends-on-whos-asking-the- question/.

Jaramillo, Santiago. "Forbes Features Bridgelife Employee Engagement App." Emplify Blog (blog), December 29, 2015. Accessed October 3, 2016. http://emplify.com/blog/forbes-features-engagement-app/.

"Leadership and Emotional Cognition," Intentional Workplace, 2011, https://intentionalworkplace.com/2011/02/03/leadership-and- emotional-contagion/.

"Leading a Multigenerational Workforce," AARP, http://assets.aarp.org/ www.aarp.org_/cs/misc/leading_a_multigenerational_workforce.pdf, 8–13.

"Let My People Go Surfing," Patagonia, 2006, http://www.patagonia.com/us/product/let-my-people-go-surfing-paperback-book?p=BK501-0&src=pkw&netid=2&ps%7CGoogle+-+K70%7Clet+my+people+go+surfing&gclid=CjwKEAiAhPCyBRCtwMDS5tzT03gSJADZ8VjR1yFnFNgSETK1zPBFxshiz6m0sLmRS1Tpju_5UGseSRoC-vjw_wcB.

"Meet the Leadership," Mainstreet, http://www.mainstreetinvestment.com/meet-the-leadership.

"Mobile Apps Infographic," ADP, 2014, http://www.adp.com/~/media/RI/pdf/MobileApps_Infographic.ashx.

"National Human Genome Research Institute," National Institutes of Health, 2016, https://www.genome.gov/19016904/.

"Netscape Announces 'Netscape Bugs Bounty,'" Netscape, 1997, http://web.archive.org/web/19970501041756/www101.netscape.com/newsref/pr/newsrelease48.html.

"Our History," Manchester Bidwell Corporation, 2016, http://manchesterbidwell.org/about/about-mbc/history/.

"Plugging Skills Gap Shortages Among Plenty," Economist Intelligence Unit, 2012, http://www.cfoinnovation.com/white-paper/4927/plugging-skills-gap-shortages-among-plenty.

"Predictive Index," Predictive Index, http://www.predictiveindex.com/the-predictive-index.

"Screen Time Part I." *TED Radio Hour* (audio blog), September 11, 2015. Accessed August 19, 2016. http://www.npr.org/programs/ted-radio-hour/438902974/screen-time-part-i?showDate=2015-09-11.

"Should Employees Be Allowed to Use Their Own Devices for Work?" *The Wall Street Journal*, 2011, http://www.wsj.com/articles/SB10001424052970203716204577013901949065394.

"Smart Phones Overtake Client PCs in 2011," Canalys, 2012, http://www.canalys.com/newsroom/smart-phones-overtake-client-pcs-2011.

"Snacking Opportunities: Building Better Snacks," International Dairy Deli Bakery Association, 2015, https://www.iddba.org/pdfs/Building-Better-Snacks-IDDBA.pdf, 5.

"Telecommuting Statistics," Global Workplace Analytics, 2016, http://globalworkplaceanalytics.com/telecommuting-statistics.

"The 2013 Deloitte Global Finance Talent Survey Report," Deloitte, 2013, http://deloitte.wsj.com/cfo/files/2013/07/Deloitte-global-finance-talent-survey-report-2013.pdf, 6.

"The 2014 Employee Engagement Organizational Culture Report," Tiny-pulse, 2014, https://www.tinypulse.com/2014-employee-engagement-organizational-culture-report.

"The 2015 Conference Board CEO Challenge," The Conference Board, 2015, https://www.conference-board.org/ceo-challenge2015/.

"The Changing Role of the CHRO," *Harvard Business Review*, 2015, https://hbr.org/resources/pdfs/comm/visier/Changing_Role_of_the_CHRO_April_2015.pdf, 1.

"The Changing Role of the CHRO," *Harvard Business Review*, http://www.visier.com/lp/changing-role-of-chro/.

"The Decade of HR," Human Capital Institute, 2014, http://www.hci.org/files/field_brochure/2014_The-Decade-of-HR.pdf, 2.

"The Effects of Employee Recognition and Appreciation," Tinypulse, https://www.tinypulse.com/resources/the-effects-of-employee-recognition-and-appreciation.

"The Future of Jobs," World Economic Forum, 2016, http://www3.weforum.org/docs/WEF_Future_of_Jobs.pdf.

"The Multi-Generational Workforce," Boston College Center for Work & Family, https://www.bc.edu/content/dam/files/centers/cwf/research/publications/pdf/MultiGen_EBS.pdf, 2–3.

"The Social Economy," McKinsey Global Institute, 2012, http://www.mckinsey.com/industries/high-tech/our-insights/the-social-economy.

"The Yin and Yang of Telecommuting," Premiere Global Services, 2013, http://img03.en25.com/Web/PremiereGlobalServices/%7B4f12e990-778e-4c6a-b735-d40a216fdbed%7D_Yin_Yang_of_Telecommuting_PGi.pdf, 5.

"Total Number of Websites," Internet Live Stats, 2016, http://www.internetlivestats.com/total-number-of-websites/.

"Union Members Summary," Bureau of Labor Statistics, 2016, http://www.bls.gov/news.release/union2.nr0.htm.

"Us," Patagonia, http://www.patagonia.com/us/patagonia.go?assetid=2047.

"We the Basecamp," Basecamp, https://basecamp.com/about.

"Wegmans Food Markets," *Fortune*, 2016, http://fortune.com/best-companies/wegmans-food-markets-4/.

"What Is Big Data?" IBM, http://www-01.ibm.com/software/data/bigdata/what-is-big-data.html.

"Working Beyond Borders," IBM, 2010, http://www-01.ibm.com/common/ssi/cgi-bin/ssialias?infotype=PM&subtype=XB&appname=GBSE_GB_TI_USEN&htmlfid=GBE03353USEN&attachment=GBE03353USEN.PDF.

"Yoido Full Gospel Church," Yoido Full Gospel Church, 2013, http://english.fgtv.com/.

"You've Got to Find What You Love, Jobs Says," Stanford, 2005, https://news.stanford.edu/2005/06/14/jobs-061505/.

Achor, Shawn, "Positive Intelligence," *Harvard Business Review*, 2012, https://hbr.org/2012/01/positive-intelligence/ar/1.

Adhikari, Richard, "Microsoft Pays First-Ever $100K Bounty for Windows Bug," *Ecommerce Times*, 2013, http://www.ecommercetimes.com/story/79147.html.

Adkins, Amy, and Harter, James, "What Great Managers Do To Engage Employees," *Harvard Business Review*, 2015, https://hbr.org/2015/04/what-great-managers-do-to-engage-employees.

Akst, Daniel, "The Snackification of Everything," *The Los Angeles Times*, 2014, http://www.latimes.com/opinion/op-ed/la-oe-akst-snacks-20141221-story.html.

Anderson, Chris. *The Long Tail: Why the Future of Business Is Selling Less of More*. New York: Hyperion, 2006. Print.

Angotti, Arthur, online survey response to author, April 27, 2016.

Ariely, Dan, "What Makes Us Feel Good About Our Work," TED, 2012, https://www.ted.com/talks/dan_ariely_what_makes_us_feel_good_about_our_work.

Barnes, Christopher, Lanaj, Klodiana, and Johnson, Russell, "Using a Smartphone After 9 pm Leaves Workers Disengaged," *Harvard Business Review*, 2014, https://hbr.org/2014/01/research-using-a-smartphone-after-9-pm-leaves-workers-disengaged/.

Benioff, Marc R., and Carlye Adler. *Behind the Cloud: The Untold Story of How Salesforce.com Went from Idea to Billion-dollar Company—and Revolutionized an Industry*. San Francisco, CA: Jossey-Bass, 2009.

Benko, Cathy, and Volini, Ericka, "What It Will Take to Fix HR," *Harvard Business Review*, 2014, https://hbr.org/2014/07/what-it-will-take-to-fix-hr.

Benko, Cathy, "Finding Your Way in the Shifting Ethos," *HR Times*, 2013, https://hrtimesblog.com/2013/04/24/today-at-impact-finding-your-way-in-the-shifting-ethos/.

Benko, Cathy, Gorman, Trish, Steinberg Alexa Rose, "Disrupting the CHRO: Following in the CFO's Footsteps," Deloitte, 2014, http://dupress.com/articles/dr14-disrupting-the-chro/.

Bennett, Drake, "The Dunbar Number from the Guru of Social Networks," Bloomberg, 2013, http://www.bloomberg.com/news/articles/2013-01-10/the-dunbar-number-from-the-guru-of-social-networks.

Bennett, Shea, "Mobile Marketing Statistics," *Social Times*, 2014, http://www.adweek.com/socialtimes/mobile-marketing-stats/495997?red=at.

Berners-Lee, Tim, "The Next Web," TED, 2009, https://www.ted.com/talks/tim_berners_lee_on_the_next_web/transcript?language=en.

Bersin, "The Top Ten Disruptions in HR," *Forbes*, 2014, http://www.forbes.com/sites/joshbersin/2014/10/15/the-top-ten-disruptions-in-hr-technology-ignore-them-at-your-peril/#3192f1ec524b.

Bersin, "The Top Ten Disruptive HR Technology Related Trends," Deloitte, 2014. http://3blmedia.com/News/Bersin-Deloitte-10-Top-Disruptive-HR-Technology-Related-Trends-Poised-Reshape-Workplace-and.

Bickett, Nicole, online survey response to author, April 27, 2016.

Birkinshaw, Julian, and Jordan Cohen. "Make Time for the Work That Matters." Harvard Business Review. 2013. Accessed August 19, 2016. https://hbr.org/2013/09/make-time-for-the-work-that-matters.

Blank, Steve, "Why the Lean Startup Changes Everything," *Harvard Business Review*, 2013, https://hbr.org/2013/05/why-the-lean-start-up-changes-everything.

Boren, Wil, online survey response to author, April 27, 2016.

Broder, Lindsay, "How to Protect Corporate Culture in a Telecommuting World," *Entrepreneur*, 2013, https://www.entrepreneur.com/article/229300.

Brown, Chheng, Melian, Parker, and Solow, "Culture and Engagement," Deloitte, 2015, http://dupress.com/articles/employee-engagement-culture-human-capital-trends-2015/.

Bruce, Stephen, "The Results of Our Best HR Metrics Best Practices Survey Are In," *HR Daily Adviser*, 2015, http://hrdailyadvisor.blr.com/2015/07/20/the-results-of-our-hr-metrics-best-practices-survey-are-in/.

Bryant, Adam, "Google's Quest to Build a Better Boss," *The New York Times*, 2011, http://www.nytimes.com/2011/03/13/business/13hire.html?pagewanted=all&_r=1.

Bryant, Adam, "Neil Blumenthal of Warby Parker on a Culture of Communication," *The New York Times*, 2013, http://www.nytimes.com/2013/10/25/business/neil-blumenthal-of-warby-parker-on-a-culture-of-communication.html?_r=2.

Buchanan, Leigh, "Jim Collins' Big Hairy Audacious Goals," *Inc.*, http://www.inc.com/leigh-buchanan/big-ideas/jim-collins-big-hairy-audacious-goals.html.

Buckner, Quinn, online survey response to author, April 27, 2016.

Burg, Natalie, "How A Mobile App Helped One Organization Boost Employee Engagement," *Forbes*, 2015, http://www.forbes.com/sites/adp/2015/12/25/how-a-mobile-app-helped-one-organization-boost-employee-engagement/#77517e1d3d97.

Burke, Katie, "Inside Warby Parker: How Vision, Mission, and Culture Helped Build a Billion Dollar Business," Hubspot, 2015, http://blog.hubspot.com/marketing/warby-parker-business-lessons.

Felps, Will, Mitchell, Terence, Byington, Eliza, "How, When, and Why Bad Apples Spoil the Barrel: Negative Group Members and Dysfunctional Groups," http://openwetware.org/images/a/a5/Final_BA_ROB.pdf, 178, 182–183, 185, 188–189.

Caldow, Janet, "Working Outside the Box," IBM, 2009, http://www-01.ibm.com/industries/government/ieg/pdf/working_outside_the_box.pdf, 5, 9.

Campbell, Deidre, "What Great Companies Know About Culture," *Harvard Business Review*, 2011, https://hbr.org/2011/12/what-great-companies-know-abou.

Cappelli, Peter, "Can HR Be Saved?" *Harvard Business Review*, 2015, https://hbr.org/ideacast/2015/07/can-hr-be-saved.html.

Carnegie, Dale. *How to Win Friends and Influence People*. London: Vermilion, 2006.

Chesky, Brian, "Don't Fuck Up the Culture," Medium, 2014, https://medium.com/@bchesky/dont-fuck-up-the-culture-597cde9ee9d4#.bxb7rrq80.

Chouinard, Yvon. *Let My People Go Surfing: The Education of a Reluctant Businessman*. New York, NY: Penguin Press, 2005.

Clemons, Eric, "Digital Transformation: Becoming a Forgetting Organization," Wharton, 2015, http://knowledge.wharton.upenn.edu/article/digital-transformation-becoming-a-forgetting-organization/.

Collins, Jim, "Aligning Action and Values," Collins, 2000, http://www.jimcollins.com/article_topics/articles/aligning-action.html.

Collins, James C., and Jerry I. Porras. *Built to Last: Successful Habits of Visionary Companies*. New York, NY: HarperCollins Publishers, 2002.

Colvin, Geoffrey, "The Anti-Control Freak," *Fortune*, 2001, http://www.semco.com.br/en/download/media-coverage/fortune-november-2001.pdf.

Crabtree, Steve, "Worldwide, 13% of Employees Are Engaged At Work," Gallup, 2013, http://www.gallup.com/poll/165269/worldwide-employees-engaged-work.aspx.

Crowley, Mark, "The Proof Is in the Profits: Why America's Happiest Companies Make More Money," *Fast Company*, 2013, http://www.fastcompany.com/3006150/proof-profits-americas-happiest-companies-also-fare-best-financially.

Crowley, Mark, "Why Being Engaged at Work Isn't as Simple as Being Happy," *Fast Company*, 2014, http://www.fastcompany.com/3036399/the-future-of-work/why-being-engaged-at-work-isnt-as-simple-as-being-happy.

Csikszentmihalyi, Mihaly. Flow: The Psychology of Optimal Experience. New York: Harper & Row, 1990.

Cukier, Kenneth, "Big Data Is Better," TED, 2014, https://www.ted.com/talks/kenneth_cukier_big_data_is_better_data/transcript?language=en.

Daisyme, Peter, "The Unique Cultures of 10 Hugely Successful Companies," *Entrepreneur*, 2015, https://www.entrepreneur.com/article/249293.

Deal, Jennifer, "Retiring the Generation Gap," Center for Creative Leadership, 2007, http://www.ccl.org/leadership/pdf/landing/GAP10122007.pdf.

Dews, Fred, "11 Facts About The Millennial Generation," Brookings, 2014, http://www.brookings.edu/blogs/brookings-now/posts/2014/06/11-facts-about-the-millennial-generation.

DiNatale, Marisa. "Characteristics of and Preference for Alternative Work Arrangements, 1999." *Monthly Labor Review*, March 2001, 28. Accessed August 20, 2016. http://www.bls.gov/opub/mlr/2001/03/art2full.pdf.

Dominus, Susan, "Rethinking the Work-Life Equation," *The New York Times*, 2016, http://www.nytimes.com/2016/02/28/magazine/rethinking-the-work-life-equation.html.

Dover, Sara, "Study: Number of Smartphone Users Tops One Billion," CBS News, 2012, http://www.cbsnews.com/news/study-number-of-smartphone-users-tops-1-billion/.

Drucker, Peter Ferdinand. *The Effective Executive*. New York, NY: HarperBusiness, 2006.

Dudley, Drew, "Everyday Leadership," TED, 2012, http://www.ted.com/talks/drew_dudley_everyday_leadership/transcript?language=en#t-46785.

Duggan, Tara, "The Evolution of HR," Chron, http://smallbusiness.chron.com/evolution-hr-61238.html.

Duhigg, Charles, "What Google Learned from its Quest to Build the Perfect Team," *The New York Times*, 2016, http://www.nytimes.com/2016/02/28/magazine/what-google-learned-from-its-quest-to-build-the-perfect-team.html.

Ecofiltro, 2016, http://www.ecofiltro.org/en.

Edwards, Rob, online survey response to author, April 27, 2016.

Egan, Toby Marshall, "The Relevance of Organization Subculture for Motivation to Transfer Learning," Wiley Online Library, 2008, http://onlinelibrary.wiley.com/doi/10.1002/hrdq.1243/abstract.

Eha, Brian Patrick. "H-P Is Asking Telecommuters to Work On-Site. What Do You Think?" *Entrepreneur*, October 08, 2013. Accessed August 19, 2016. https://www.entrepreneur.com/article/229300.

Eustace, Alan, "I Leapt from the Stratosphere. Here's How I Did It," TED, 2015, https://www.ted.com/talks/alan_eustace_i_leapt_from_the_stratosphere_here_s_how_i_did_it?language=en

Evans, Benedict, "Mobile Is Eating the World," Andreessen Horowitz, http://a16z.com/2014/10/28/mobile-is-eating-the-world/.

Fecheyr-Lippins, Bruce, Schaninger, Bill, and Tanner, Karen, "Power to the People Analytics," McKinsey, 2015, http://www.mckinsey.com/business-functions/organization/our-insights/power-to-the-new-people-analytics.

Ferrazzi, Keith, "Why Relationships Are Crucial to Success," Wharton, 2014, http://knowledge.wharton.upenn.edu/article/keith-ferrazzi-relationships-crucial-success/.

Finkel, Michael, "The Blind Man Who Taught Himself to See," *Men's Journal*, 2012, http://www.mensjournal.com/magazine/the-blind-man-who-taught-himself-to-see-20120504.

Fisher, Lawrence, "Ricardo Semler Won't Take Control," Strategy Business, 2005, http://www.strategy-business.com/article/05408?gko=3291c.

Forman, David, "The Decade of HR," Human Capital Institute, 2014, http://www.hci.org/files/field_brochure/2014_The-Decade-of-HR.pdf, 2.

Fox, Mirza, Moss, Rubis, and Shea, "10 Changes that Rocked HR," *HR Magazine*, 2005, https://www.shrm.org/publications/hrmagazine/editorialcontent/pages/0550th10changes.aspx.

Frankl, Victor, "Youth in Search of Meaning," TED, 1972, https://www.ted.com/talks/viktor_frankl_youth_in_search_of_meaning.

Fried, Ina, "Business Use of Mobile Apps Continues to Rise," Recode, 2014, http://www.recode.net/2014/2/12/11623378/business-use-of-mobile-apps-continues-to-rise-while-iphone-gains.

Fried, Jason, "Why Work Doesn't Happen At Work," TED, 2010, https://www.ted.com/talks/jason_fried_why_work_doesn_t_happen_at_work/transcript?language=en.

Froehle, Tom, online survey response to author, April 27, 2016.

Fry, Richard, "Millennials Surpass Gen-X as the Largest Generation in U.S. Labor Force," Pew Research Center, 2015, http://www.pewresearch.org/fact-tank/2015/05/11/millennials-surpass-gen-xers-as-the-largest-generation-in-u-s-labor-force/.

Goldberg, Joseph, and Moye, William, "The First Hundred Years of the Bureau of Labor Statistics," Bureau of Labor Statistics, 1985, http://www.bls.gov/opub/blsfirsthundredyears/100_years_of_bls.pdf, 8.

Gopnik, Alison, "What Do Babies Think?" National Public Radio, 2013, http://www.npr.org/templates/transcript/transcript.php?storyId=179818675.

Graham, Paul, "Maker's Schedule, Manager's Schedule," 2009, http://www.paulgraham.com/makersschedule.html.

Grant, Adam. "Putting a Face to a Name: The Art of Motivating Employees." *Knowledge @ Wharton*, February 17, 2010. Accessed August 19, 2016. http://knowledge.wharton.upenn.edu/article/putting-a-face-to-a-name-the-art-of-motivating-employees/.

Grant, Adam, and Massey, Cade, "Can People Analytics Help Firms Manage People Better?" Wharton, 2015, http://knowledge.wharton.upenn.edu/article/can-people-analytics-help-firms-manage-people-better-est-in-people-analytics/.

Guthrie, Doug, "Choosing Corporate Culture Over Worker Independence," *Forbes*, 2013, http://www.forbes.com/sites/dougguthrie/2013/03/08/marissa-mayer-choosing-corporate-culture-over-worker-independence/#495958733a04.

Halvorson, Heidi Grant, "Understand How People See You," *Harvard Business Review*, 2015, https://hbr.org/ideacast/2015/04/understand-how-people-see-you.html.

Hamm, Steve "A Passion for the Planet," Bloomberg, 2006, http://www.bloomberg.com/news/articles/2006-08-20/a-passion-for-the-planet.

Hastings, Reed, "Netflix Culture: Freedom & Responsibility," LinkedIn, 2009, http://www.slideshare.net/reed2001/culture-1798664

Heffernan, Margaret, "Dare to Disagree," TED, 2012, http://www.ted.com/talks/margaret_heffernan_dare_to_disagree.

Heffernan, Margaret, "What Does Everyday Courage Look Like?" National Public Radio, 2014, http://www.npr.org/templates/transcript/transcript.php?storyId=368759610.

Heffernan, Margaret, "It's Time to Forget the Pecking Order at Work." TED, 2015, https://www.ted.com/talks/margaret_heffernan_why_it_s_time_to_forget_the_pecking_order_at_work

Heffernan, Virginia, "Meet Is Murder," *The New York Times*, 2016, http://www.nytimes.com/2016/02/28/magazine/meet-is-murder.html.

Hsieh, Tony, *Delivering Happiness*, 2015, 47–48, https://www.amazon.com/Delivering-Happiness-Profits-Passion-Purpose/dp/0446576220

Hsieh, Tony. *Delivering Happiness: A Path to Profits, Passion, and Purpose.* New York: Business Plus, 2010. Print.

Hinde, Natasha. "These Period Pants Stop Leaks So Women Can Get On With Their Lives Whether It's That Time Of The Month Or Not." *HuffPost Lifestyle United Kingdom*. The Huffington Post, 03 June 2015. Web. 20 Aug 2016.

Humphrey, Ellen, online survey response to author, April 27, 2016.

Hunt, Steven, "The Role of Technology in the Evolution of HR," Eremedia, 2011, http://www.eremedia.com/tlnt/the-role-of-technology-in-the-evolution-of-hr/.

Indiana University Health, 2016, http://iuhealth.org/.

Jackson, Henry, "In The Decade of Human Capital, HR Must Lead," World Economic Forum, 2015, https://www.shrm.org/about/governanceleadership/executiveteam/pages/in-the-decade-of-human-capital,-hr-must-lead.aspx.

Kahn, Mattie. "Everlane Lets You Decide How Much That Sweater Costs," *Elle*, 2015, http://www.elle.com/culture/news/a32915/everlane-sale-pay-what-you-choose/.

Kawamura, Kristine Marin, "Cross Cultural Management: An International Journal," Emerald Insight, 2014, http://www.emeraldinsight.com/doi/full/10.1108/CCM-08-2014-0094.

Khalaf, Simon, "Mobile to Television: We Interrupt This Broadcast (Again)," Flurry Insights, 2014, http://flurrymobile.tumblr.com/post/115194107130/mobile-to-television-we-interrupt-this-broadcast.

Khalaf, Simon, "Seven Years Into The Mobile Revolution, Content Is King . . . Again," Flurry Insights, http://flurrymobile.tumblr.com/post/127638842745/seven-years-into-the-mobile-revolution-content-is.

Kish, Daniel, "How Can You See Without Seeing?" National Public Radio, 2015, http://www.npr.org/templates/transcript/transcript.php?storyId=455906507.

Kraege, Scott, online survey response to author, April 27, 2016.

Lacy, Kyle, "I Just Witnessed The Best Example of Building a Great Brand," Open View Partners, 2015, http://labs.openviewpartners.com/being-orange-building-exacttarget-brand/.

Lehrer, Jonah, "Groupthink: The Brainstorming Myth," *The New Yorker*, 2012, http://www.newyorker.com/magazine/2012/01/30/groupthink.

Libin, Phil, "Evernotes CEO On The New Ways We Work," Harvard Business Review, 2015, https://hbr.org/ideacast/2015/05/evernotes-ceo-on-the-new-ways-we-work.html.

Limb, Charles, "Your Brain on Improv," TED, 2011, https://www.ted.com/talks/charles_limb_your_brain_on_improv/transcript?language=en.

Llewellyn, Mike, "Can Imagination Be Measured?" TED, 2014, http://ideas.ted.com/can-a-test-measure-your-imagination/.

Lohr, Steve, "Cubicles Are Winning War Against Closed Offices," *The New York Times*, 1997, http://partners.nytimes.com/library/cyber/week/081197cube.html.

Lord Kelvin. *Electrical Units of Measurement*. Image. Popular Lectures and Addresses, 1883. https://archive.org/stream/popularlecturesa01kelvuoft#page/72/mode/2up

Love, Lorna, "15 Stats on Telecommunicating and the Cloud," Premiere Global Services, Inc., 2014, http://blog.pgi.com/2014/04/15-stats-telecommuting-cloud/.

Martin, Fermín Moscoso del Prado, "The Thermodynamics of Human Reaction Times," Cornell, 2009, http://arxiv.org/abs/0908.3170.

Maslow, Abraham "A Theory of Human Motivation." *Psychological Review* 50.4 (1943): 430–437. Print.

Mateo, San, "Clarizen Survey Workers Consider Status Meetings a Productivity-Killing Waste of Time," Clarizen, 2015, http://www.clarizen .com/project-software-resources/press-releases/item/clarizen-survey-workers-consider-status-meetings-a-productivity-killing-waste-of-time .html.

Maurya, Ash, "Why Lean Canvas vs Business Model Canvas?" Leanstack, https://leanstack.com/why-lean-canvas/.

Mayer, Gerald, "Union Membership Trends in the United States," Cornell, 2004, http://digitalcommons.ilr.cornell.edu/cgi/viewcontent.cgi? article=1176&context=key_workplace.

McCandless, David, "The Beauty of Data Visualization," TED, 2010, https:// www.ted.com/talks/hans_rosling_at_state/transcript?language=en.

McCord, Patty, "How Netflix Reinvented HR," *Harvard Business Review*, 2014, https://hbr.org/2014/01/how-netflix-reinvented-hr.

McGonigal, Kelly, "How to Make Stress Your Friend," TED, 2013, http:// www.ted.com/talks/kelly_mcgonigal_how_to_make_stress_your_ friend/transcript?language=en.

McGregor, Jena, "'Star Wars' Meets the C-Suite: This CEO's Hologram Is Beaming into Meetings," *The Washington Post*, 2016, https://www .washingtonpost.com/news/on-leadership/wp/2016/04/13/star-wars-meets-the-c-suite-why-this-ceos-hologram-is-getting-beamed-into-meetings/.

McMillan, Robert, "IBM Gives Birth To Amazing Email-less Man," Wired, 2012, http://www.wired.com/2012/01/luis-suarez.

Meeker, Mary, "Internet Trends," Kleiner, Perkins, Caufield, and Byers, 2016, http://www.kpcb.com/internet-trends.

Moen, Phyllis, Kelly, Erin, Fan, Wen, Lee, Shi-Rong, Almeida, David, Kossek, Ellen Ernst, Buxton, Orfeu, "Does a Flexibility/Support Organizational Initiative Improve High-Tech Employees' Well-Being? Evidence from the Work, Family, and Health Network," *American Sociological Review*, 2016, http://asr.sagepub.com/content/81/1/134.abstract.

Morehead, Brad, online survey response to author, April 27, 2016.

Morieux, Yves, "As Work Gets More Complex, Six Rules to Simplify," TED, 2014, https://www.ted.com/talks/yves_morieux_as_work_gets_more_ complex_6_rules_to_simplify/transcript?language=en.

Mucciolo, Christina, "Knock Knock. Who's There? An Elated Edward Jones Advisor," Wealth Management, 2009, http://wealthmanagement.com/ institutions/knock-knock-whos-there-elated-edward-jones-advisor.

Nanterme, Pierre, "Accentures CEO on Leading Change," *Harvard Business Review*, 2015, https://hbr.org/ideacast/2015/12/accentures-ceo-on-leading-change.html.

National Labor Union, "The history of labor unions and fight for fairness at work," Union Plus, 2016, https://www.unionplus.org/about/labor-unions/history-origin.

Okell, Georgie, "Facing the End of Time," Headspace, 2015, https://www.headspace.com/blog/2015/05/22/radio-headspace-22-facing-the-end-of-time/.

Okell, Georgie, "Introducing Headspace on Learning," Headspace, 2015a, https://www.headspace.com/blog/2015/09/04/3185/.

Okell, Georgie, "The Journey with Chris Hadfield and Diana Nyad," Headspace, 2015b, https://www.headspace.com/blog/2015/08/07/radio-headspace-32-the-journey-with-chris-hadfield-diana-nyad/.

Orme, Hank, online survey response to author, April 27, 2016.

PatternEx, 2016, https://www.patternex.com/.

Pease, Allan, and Pease, Barbara, "The Definitive Book of Body Language," *The New York Times*, 2006, http://www.nytimes.com/2006/09/24/books/chapters/0924-1st-peas.html?pagewanted=all&_r=1&.

Perlow, Leslie, "Are You Sleeping with Your Smartphone?" *Harvard Business Review*, 2012, https://hbr.org/2012/05/are-you-sleeping-with-your-sma/.

Perlow, Leslie, "Breaking the Smartphone Addiction," Harvard Business School, 2012, http://hbswk.hbs.edu/item/breaking-the-smartphone-addiction.

Pink, Dan, "Dan Pink on Motivation," TED, 2009, http://www.ted.com/talks/dan_pink_on_motivation/transcript?language=en.

Pink, Daniel H. "Free Agent Nation." *Fast Company*. N.p., 12 Dec. 1997. Web. 20 Aug. 2016.

Pink, Daniel H. *Free Agent Nation: How America's New Independent Workers Are Transforming the Way We Live*. New York: Warner, 2001.

Pink, Dan, "The Rise of the Supertemp," *Harvard Business Review*, 2012, https://hbr.org/2012/05/the-rise-of-the-supertemp.

Porter, Michael, "Strategy and Information Technology," Harvard Business School, 2014, http://www.isc.hbs.edu/strategy/related-topics/Pages/strategy-and-it.aspx.

Porter, Michael, "Why Do Good Managers Set Bad Strategies?" Wharton, 2006, http://knowledge.wharton.upenn.edu/article/michael-porter-asks-and-answers-why-do-good-managers-set-bad-strategies/.

Rangaswami, JP, "Information Is Food," TED, 2012, http://www.ted.com/talks/jp_rangaswami_information_is_food/transcript?language=en.

Ransom, Diana, "Everlane and its Radical Idea of Fashion," *Chicago Tribune*, 2014, http://www.chicagotribune.com/bluesky/hub/chi-inc-everlane-bsi-hub-story.html

"Result Filters." National Center for Biotechnology Information. April 16, 2016. Accessed August 19, 2016. http://www.ncbi.nlm.nih.gov/pubmed/27145696.

Reynolds, Gary, online survey response to author, April 27, 2016.

Ricard, Matthieu, "How To Let Altruism Be Your Guide," TED, 2015, http://www.ted.com/talks/matthieu_ricard_how_to_let_altruism_be_your_guide/transcript?language=en.

Robinson, Clay, online survey response to author, April 27, 2016.

Robinson, Ken, "How Do Schools Kill Creativity?" National Public Radio, 2014, http://www.npr.org/templates/transcript/transcript.php?storyId=351552772.

Rohrs, Jeff, online survey response to author, April 27, 2016.

Rosling, Hans, "Let My Dataset Change Your Mindset," TED, 2009, https://www.ted.com/talks/hans_rosling_at_state/transcript?language=en.

Rotella, Perry, "Is Data the New Oil?" *Forbes*, 2012, http://www.forbes.com/sites/perryrotella/2012/04/02/is-data-the-new-oil/#5cbd59e677a9.

Rubis, Leon, Mirza, Patrick, Fox, Adrienne, Shea, Terence F., and Moss, Desda. "50th Anniversary HR Magazine: 10 Changes That Rocked HR." SHRM. December 31, 2005. Accessed October 3, 2016. http://www.shrm.org/publications/hrmagazine/editorialcontent/pages/0550th10changes.aspx.

Salbi, Zainab, "How Do People Live and Cope in the Midst of Violent Conflict?" National Public Radio, 2016, http://www.npr.org/templates/transcript/transcript.php?storyId=466044738.

Saval, Nikil, "The Post Cubicle Office and its Discontents," *The New York Times*, 2016, http://www.nytimes.com/2016/02/28/magazine/the-post-cubicle-office-and-its-discontents.html?_r=0.

Schalch, Kathleen, "1981 Strike Leaves Legacy for American Workers," National Public Radio, 2006, http://www.npr.org/templates/story/story.php?storyId=5604656.

Schulte, Brigid, "A Company That Profits as it Pampers Workers," *The Washington Post*, 2014, https://www.washingtonpost.com/business/a-company-that-profits-as-it-pampers-workers/2014/10/22/d3321b34-4818-11e4-b72e-d60a9229cc10_story.html.

Search Inside Yourself Leadership Institute, 2016, https://siyli.org/.

Seligman, Martin, "The New Era of Positive Psychology," TED, 2008, https://www.ted.com/talks/martin_seligman_on_the_state_of_psychology/transcript?language=en,

Semler, Ricardo, "How to Run a Company With (Almost) No Rules," TED, 2014, https://www.ted.com/talks/ricardo_semler_radical_wisdom_for_a_company_a_school_a_life?language=en.

Semler, Ricardo, "Radical Wisdom for a Company," TED, 2015, http://www.ted.com/talks/ricardo_semler_radical_wisdom_for_a_company_a_school_a_life/transcript?language=en.

Semler, Ricardo, "We Went Digital without a Strategy," *Harvard Business Review*, http://www.semco.com.br/en/download/media-coverage/how-We-Went-Digital-Without-a-Strategy-Harvard-Business-Review.pdf.

Semler, Ricardo, "Why My Former Employees Still Work for Me," *Harvard Business Review*, http://www.semco.com.br/en/download/media-coverage/why-My-Former-Employees-Still-Work-for-Me-Harvard-Business-Review.pdf.

Shirky, Clay, "Institutions versus collaboration," TED, 2005, http://www.ted.com/talks/clay_shirky_on_institutions_versus_collaboration/transcript?language=en.

Shirley, Steve, "How Do You Break into an Industry While Breaking All the Rules?" National Public Radio, 2015, http://www.npr.org/templates/transcript/transcript.php?storyId=443437169.

Sinek, Simon, "How Great Leaders Inspire Action," TED, 2009, https://www.ted.com/talks/simon_sinek_how_great_leaders_inspire_action.

Smith, A, and Sugar, O, "Development of Above Normal Language and Intelligence 21 Years after Hemispherectomy," National Center for Biotechnology Information, http://www.ncbi.nlm.nih.gov/pubmed/1172204.

Smith, Aaron, "U.S. Smartphone Use in 2015," Pew Research Center, 2015, http://www.pewinternet.org/2015/04/01/us-smartphone-use-in-2015/.

Smith, Bruce, "Top Workplaces 2016: Mainstreet," *The Indianapolis Star*, 2016, http://www.indystar.com/story/money/2016/04/15/top-workplaces-mainstreet/83044538/.

Smith, W. Stanton, "Decoding Generational Differences," Deloitte, 2008, http://public.deloitte.com/media/0507/250608/us_DecodingGenerationalDifferences.pdf.

Smith, Scott S. "Grounds For Success." Entrepreneur. May 1, 1998. Accessed October 03, 2016. https://www.entrepreneur.com/article/15582.

Sorenson, Susan, "Don't Pamper Employees—Engage Them," Gallup, 2013, http://www.gallup.com/businessjournal/163316/don-pamper-employees-engage.aspx.

Strickland, Bill, "Bill Strickland Makes Change with a Slide Show," TED, 2008, http://www.ted.com/talks/bill_strickland_makes_change_with_a_slide_show/transcript?language=en.

Sullivan, John, "How Google Is Using People Analytics To Completely Reinvent HR," Eremedia, 2013, http://www.eremedia.com/tlnt/how-google-is-using-people-analytics-to-completely-reinvent-hr/.

Sullivan, John, "Wow, Google's Simple Just-In-Time Checklist Improves Onboarding Results by 25%," Eremedia, 2015, http://www.eremedia.com/ere/wow-googles-simple-just-in-time-checklist-improves-onboarding-results-by-25/.

Tan, Chade-Meng, "Everyday Compassion at Google," TED, 2011, http://www.ted.com/talks/chade_meng_tan_everyday_compassion_at_google/transcript?language=en.

Taylor, Frederick Winslow, "The Principles of Scientific Management," 1910, http://nationalhumanitiescenter.org/pds/gilded/progress/text3/taylor.pdf.

Taylor, Jill Bolke, "My Stroke of Insight," My Stroke of Insight, 2010, http://mystrokeofinsight.com/index.html.

The Changing Role of the CHRO | Visier Inc." Visier Inc. Accessed October 03, 2016. http://www.visier.com/lp/changing-role-of-chro/.

Thompson, Leigh, "The Truth about Creative Teams," *Harvard Business Review*, 2013, https://hbr.org/ideacast/2013/04/the-truth-about-creative-teams.html.

Trees, Rhett, online survey response to author, April 27, 2016.

Twenge, JM, Zhang, L, Im, C, "It's Beyond My Control: A Cross-temporal Meta-analysis of Increasing Externality in Locus of Control," *Personal and Social Psychology Review*, 2004, http://www.ncbi.nlm.nih.gov/pubmed/15454351.

Ulrich, Dave, "A New Mandate for Human Resources," *Harvard Business Review*, 1998, https://hbr.org/1998/01/a-new-mandate-for-human-resources.

Wachob, Colleen, "The Founder of THINX Underwear on Breaking Taboos," Mindbodygreen, http://www.mindbodygreen.com/0-24132/the-founder-of-thinx-underwear-on-breaking-taboos-rethinking-your-period.html.

Walter, Ekaterina, "Want to Find Brand Ambassadors? Start with Your Employees," *Forbes*, 2013, http://www.forbes.com/sites/ekaterinawalter/ 2013/10/15/want-to-find-brand-ambassadors-start-with-your-emp loyees-2/#7920caf61ff6.

Wang, Dora, "12 Need To Know Statistics on Employee Engagement," Tiny-pulse, 2015, https://www.tinypulse.com/blog/dw-12-need-to-know-statistics-on-employee-engagement.

West, Blair, online survey response to author, April 27, 2016.

Woolf, Nicky, "Ten-Year-Old Receives $10,000 Reward for Finding Instagram Bug," *The Guardian*, 2016, https://www.theguardian.com/ technology/2016/may/03/instagram-comment-bug-10-year-old-hacking-finland-reward.

Woolley, Anita, Malone, Thomas, and Chabris, Christopher, "Why Some Teams Are Smarter Than Others," *The New York Times*, 2015, http:// www.nytimes.com/2015/01/18/opinion/sunday/why-some-teams-are-smarter-than-others.html?_r=0.

Index

Page references followed by *fig* indicate an illustrated figure.